ALTON TOWERS

A GOTHIC WONDERLAND

MICHAEL FISHER

with Foreword
by
CLIVE WAINWRIGHT

To Sarah and Paul

First Published 1999
Revised edition 2004

Printed in Great Britain by Counter Print,
17 Browning Street, Stafford, ST16 3AX

Published by M.J. Fisher,
35 Newland Avenue, Stafford, ST16 1NL

British Library Cataloguing in Publication Data.
A Catalogue record for this book is available
from the British Library

ISBN 0 9526855 2 3

Cover Illustrations: Watercolour of Alton Towers and grounds by an unidentified artist, dated 1870; *Inset:* Portrait of John Talbot, sixteenth Earl of Shrewsbury, by John Julius Hamburger, 1832 (formerly at Alton Towers, now at Ingestre Hall, Staffordshire).

Title Page: View of the Towers and gardens from the Gothic Temple. (MJF 1999)

Frontispiece: Pencil drawing of east end of Alton Towers chapel by the author, from study of original sources, pre-1950s photographs, and the chapel altarpiece now at S. Peter's Church, Bromsgrove.

The lettering used for the title and chapter-headings is adapted from an alphabet designed by A.W.N. Pugin about 1851 for Abney Hall, Cheshire.

ALTON TOWERS

A Gothic Wonderland

'A scholarly piece of architectural and social history written with passion. It revives for us the Alton that Disraeli knew, "formed in a sylvan valley enclosed with gilded gates".'

-Rosemary Hill, *Times Literary Supplement.*

CONTENTS

Foreword - Professor Clive Wainwright   7

Preface & Acknowledgements   9

1. Alton Lodge   15

2. Alton Abbey   22

3. "The Towers"   50

4. Earl & Architect   80

5. Pugin at Alton   103

6. The Towers Chapel   143

7. Conclusion   157

Notes to Chapters   167

Bibliography   177

Index   179

LIST OF COLOUR PLATES

Between pages 102 and 103

I	King Henry VI presenting a sword to the first Earl of Shrewsbury.
II	John Talbot, sixteenth Earl of Shreswbury, from the Bromsgrove altarpiece.
III	Altar and reredos from Alton Towers Chapel, now at Bromsgrove.
IV	Maria Teresa, Countess of Shrewsbury, from the Bromsgrove altarpiece
V & VI	Views of Alton Abbey, 1819.
VII	The Octagon looking west towards the Talbot Gallery, 1870.
VIII	The interior of the House Conservatory.
IX	View into the Music Room from the North Library, 1870.
X	Interior of the Towers Chapel, 1854.
XI	The Music Room looking west, 1870.
XII	Maria Teresa, Countess of Shrewsbury, 1832.
XIII	Pugin/Hardman glass in the dining-hall window.
XIV	The painted timber roof of the dining-hall.

PLANS AND ELEVATIONS

(Inside front cover) Plan of Alton Towers, principal floor, as in 1852.

Page 19	Plan of Alveton Lodge, 1804.
Page 28	Basement Plans (a) 1811 (b) 1998.
Page 36	The Long Gallery and Drawing Room.
Page 39	Elevation of South Front.
Page 56	Comparative plans of Fonthill Abbey and Alton Galleries.
Page 66	The West Wing.
Page 71	Comparative plans of Alton Abbey/Alton Towers, c.1835.
Page 105	Elevations of north front, 1823 and 1850.
Page 109	Plan showing the axial system of linked rooms and galleries.
Page 118	Elevation of East Front.
Page 132	Plan of Kitchens and Family Rooms.

FOREWORD

Alton Towers is now more widely known both in this country and in Europe than it ever was at the high point of its architectural glory in the 1850s. Few of those who come to enjoy a visit to present day Alton will have any idea before they arrive of the existence of the remains of the once celebrated Gothic Revival house and the remarkable landscape gardens which surround it. Indeed the attractions which today tempt the visitor to deepest Staffordshire are as important a manifestation of late twentieth century technology and taste as once were those of the house and gardens which attracted their Victorian predecessors. Interestingly, as Michael Fisher describes, the house was for many years in the nineteenth century open to the public and it was a considerable attraction. As one guidebook described in 1851 just after the railway had been opened; "This railway branches off from the Derby and Birmingham ... thus opening the splendid domain of Alton Towers both to the South and North and making it easily accessible from all parts to the public".

An increasing number of the modern visitors alerted by this book and also by noticing the imaginative programme of restoration being undertaken by the present owners will wish to visit the house. Indeed the Gothic style itself is rather popular at the moment in fashion and interior decoration and the name of Pugin is now much better known following the exhibition devoted to him at the Victoria & Albert Museum in 1994 and that in New York in 1995.

Michael Fisher is a prominent local historian and the author of the pioneering book *A Vision of Splendour: Gothic Revival in Staffordshire 1840-1890* published in 1995 who has for many years taken a particular interest in the nineteenth century architecture of Staffordshire. As he explains here the documentation concerning the history of Alton Towers is fragmentary and widely scattered. He has however been able by simultaneously searching for archives and illustrations and closely examining the existing building to build up a remarkably clear picture of how it once looked. He has also recently discovered the splendid watercolours which are published for the first time and help to make this such an attractive book. Furthermore Michael Fisher is also the publisher of the book.

This research has not just been an academic exercise; it is in this book shared with a wider public and one which is increasingly fascinated by the buildings and gardens of the past. This book represents local history at its very best, being well written, well illustrated and packed with new and interesting information. Also Michael Fisher's discoveries are underpinning the sensitive restoration of the building which is now being carried out.

Professor Clive Wainwright

Research Department,
Victoria & Albert Museum

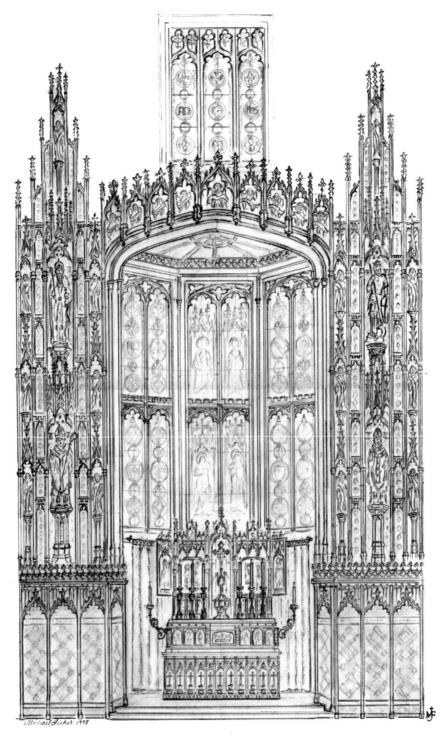

ALTON TOWERS CHAPEL
REREDOS and SCREEN by A. WELBY PUGIN c 1840

PREFACE AND ACKNOWLEDGEMENTS

Reputed to have been the largest privately-owned house in Europe, Alton Towers now serves as a picturesque backdrop to one of Europe's most popular tourist attractions; a significant slice of England's architectural and social history set in the midst of "white-knuckle" rides and a fantasy-world not entirely at variance with its nineteenth-century origins as a pleasure-park designed to challenge the imagination. The north facade of the house, which visitors see ahead of them on entering the park, has been incorporated into the company's logo. Thus featured on a wide range of giftware, printed material and television advertising, the silhouette of the Towers buildings has become familiar around the world.

Almost from the beginning Alton Towers drew praise and criticism from those who saw it in its heyday. Eulogised by Benjamin Disraeli as the "Muriel Towers" of his romantic novel, *Lothair* (1870), it was denounced by William Morris as a "gimcrack palace", and cited before a Parliamentary Committee as exemplifying what the interiors of the New Palace of Westminster might become if placed in the hands of the Gothic visionary, A.W.N. Pugin. Royal visitors included the future Queen Victoria and the dowager Queen Adelaide who saw the house in its unfinished state, and King Edward VII who considered the central feature of the famous north front - Pugin's great dining hall - to be the most magnificent room he had ever dined in.

Until the development of modern transport systems - the railway arrived in Alton in 1849 - the Towers was an isolated place. Set on the north-eastern edge of Staffordshire where the sandstones and gritstones of the rugged moorlands meet the gentler limestone hills of neighbouring Derbyshire, it was accessible only by means of rough and narrow country roads which plunged suddenly into deep river-valleys. Indeed it was the very remoteness of the place, and the precipitous and thickly-wooded valley of the River Churnet which fired the Romantic imagination of the fifteenth Earl of Shrewsbury to create a large summer residence out of what had been little more than a hunting-lodge. Yet even before the railway came, visitors were drawn to Alton by tales of a wondrous valley of delights created out of nothing by the earl who "made the desert smile", and of its crowning glory: a great Gothic mansion crammed with fine furniture and works of art. As early as 1839 members of the public were allowed into the gardens, and on occasion into the house itself, and it was not long before the splendours of Alton Towers and its gardens were reported in topographical books and travel-guides.

Guests invited to Alton Towers in the 1840s would normally have arrived by coach via the section of the Derby-Chester road which passes through the town of Ashbourne about eight miles to the north-east, i.e. the modern A523, then through country roads to the Quixhill Lodge, just outside the village of Denstone. From there onwards the glories of Alton would gradually unfold before the eye; first of all a two-mile drive through parkland bringing the carriage to the edge of the valley gardens, where passengers would catch their first glimpses of domed conservatories, a Gothic prospect tower, pagoda fountain, flower-filled terraces and parterres, cascades and pools. Finally the great house would come into view, the carriage passing through a barbican and along a fortified driveway to a tall entrance tower. Alighting from their carriage, visitors would ascend a broad flight of steps and pass between high doors into the tower where a blind Welsh harper played evocative music; thence into the Armoury filled with medieval weapons and suits of armour, dominated by the equestrian figure of the first Earl of Shrewsbury dressed as a Knight of the Garter. The next room, even longer than the first, was a Picture Gallery, its walls lined with paintings by celebrated artists of the Italian, French, Flemish and German schools. Beyond the Picture Gallery another change of scene awaited as guests entered a vaulted octagonal chamber reminiscent of the chapter-house of some great cathedral, with stained-glass windows and recumbent effigies of Talbot ancestors. Finally, having progressed through a Gothic conservatory filled with the colour and scent of exotic plants and the songs of birds in gilded cages, they would enter at last the great house itself; the journey through Entrance Tower, Armoury, Picture Gallery, Octagon and Conservatory - over 150 yards of it - having been no more than a prelude to the splendours of the State Apartments which lay beyond. The scale of these Romantic Interiors exceeded that of any of the castellated fantasies of other noblemen, but then Lord Shrewsbury was England's premier earl. The galleries at Alton were larger even than those created by the millionaire-commoner William Beckford at Fonthill, but, alas, they were equally short-lived.

The creation of Alton Towers and its unique gardens stemmed from the visions of two men: Charles Talbot who in 1787 became the fifteenth Earl of Shrewsbury, and his nephew John who succeeded to the title in 1827. The Alton estate was just one of many in England and Ireland owned by the Talbots, it was of no particular importance, and for a residence it had nothing more grand than a hunting-lodge. It was the expansion of "Alton Lodge" first of all into "Alton Abbey" and finally into "Alton Towers" which exercised the minds of its owners almost continuously over a period of fifty years. Several architects and designers were brought in: William Lees, Thomas Hopper, William and Peter Hollins, Thomas Allason, Joseph Ireland, John Buonarotti Papworth, Thomas Fradgley; and, for the gardens, John Claudius Loudon and Robert Abraham. Finally, in 1837, A.W.N. Pugin arrived. His contributions as a designer and decorator were considerable, his structural work was more extensive than has hitherto been supposed, and the relationship between the architect and his noble patron is one of the most fascinating aspects of the history of Alton Towers. It was at Alton that some of Pugin's most ambitious building and decorating schemes were discussed and tried out, while the Towers Chapel, newly-furnished and equipped by Pugin, provided many an object lesson in how Catholic worship ought properly to be conducted in the churches built according to his "True Principles" and financed to a greater or lesser degree by Lord Shrewsbury. Pugin's work at Alton also shows how his principles were sometimes compromised when he was obliged, against his better judgement, to carry out the wishes of a patron who knew what he wanted in his own home. Yet over some issues Pugin was able to push his ideas to the very limit, notably the building of the Great Dining Room over which he would brook no compromise. Alton Towers is therefore a key building in the assessment of Pugin's achievements and limitations as a domestic architect. It is a Georgian building in concept and plan - this being one of the constraints under which Pugin had to work. Various strands of the Gothic Revival are woven together: the Picturesque and Romantic as well as Pugin's own powerful blend of theatricality and historicism.

No longer do visitors to Alton Towers arrive by train and emerge from the station to pass under the arch of Pugin's Station Lodge across the road as thousands did until the Churnet Valley Line was closed in 1965. Instead they come by coach and car from motorways and major roads which siphon them into the same network of country roads which brought early-nineteenth-century visitors by carriage through the villages of Alton and Farley on the final stage of their journey. Having entered the park via the present public entrance, today's visitors may yet walk the carriage-drive along the edge of the still-splendid gardens, and arrive, as their Victorian predecessors would have done, at the steps of the Entrance Tower where two great stone dogs stand sentinel - the "Talbots" synonymous with the family which once dwelt within. There, however, the similarity ends. Recorded music from the theme-park attractions has replaced the soothing strains of the Welsh harp, and Towers employees in fancy dress have supplanted the liveried footmen of yesteryear. The Armoury still has its stained-glass windows depicting the twelfth-century origins of the Talbot family, but all the armour has gone. It was adapted for use as the Towers Gift Shop where visitors could purchase their souvenirs. The rest of the entrance was blocked off. The Picture Gallery became a workshop sheltering painters of garden furniture and theme-park scenery under a corrugated roof. Beyond it the great Octagon stood open to the sky, its central column toppled; while only weeds, brambles and wild birds inhabited the roofless and derelict conservatory. Yet the basic structures of these great galleries remained, and with them the possibility that some of the former splendour might one day be restored.

Between 1920 and 1955 over four hundred country houses of architectural and historic importance were destroyed: the consequence of economic and social changes which made it impossible for their owners to live in the style to which they had been accustomed before the First World War, and the failure to find alternative uses for great houses as they were vacated. Alton Towers was gutted in 1952 because its new owner saw it as a ready-made quarry for metals such as lead and copper which were in short supply just after the Second World War, and for thousands of cubic feet of the finest timber, door-frames, wall-panelling, fireplaces: in short anything that could be stripped out and sold.

Yet the stripping of Alton Towers began a century before the final indignity of 1952. It is one of those ironies of history that this great house and its fabulous contents barely survived the two men who had conceived and nurtured it all - the fifteenth and sixteenth Earls of Shrewsbury. The senior line of the Talbot family was notoriously bad at producing male heirs. The sixteenth earl was the fifteenth earl's nephew, and a sickly cousin waited in the wings to succeed to the estates in 1852. His death four years later marked the demise of the senior line. The ensuing legal battle over the succession, and the consequent emptying of the house in the Great Sale of 1857, represent the first stage in the decline of Alton Towers: the house was suddenly shorn of the art-treasures and furniture for which many of its rooms had been explicitly designed. The incoming family of Chetwynd-Talbots lacked the means to re-furnish it in similar style, Alton Towers was not in any case their principal residence, and they moved out in

1924 when there was another great sale of contents. Having been purchased by a group of local businessmen, the empty house and its gardens were developed as a tourist attraction, the State Apartments serving as a complex of refreshment rooms, where bentwood chairs and advertisements for Bass beers took the place of Louis-seize furniture and Florentine paintings. Commercial enterprise at least kept the roofs on, and the fine ceilings, architectural woodwork and stained-glass windows survived intact. Taken over by the Army during the Second World War for use by an Officer Cadet Training Unit, the Towers remained under requisition and locked-up until 1951 when it was finally returned to its owners. Leaking roofs, lack of proper maintenance during the war years, and alleged damage by army cadets were made the excuses for what happened next. In reality it was a thinly-disguised asset-stripping operation which took barely three months to complete. Shorn of most of its interior magnificence, the shell of the building has survived into an age more sympathetic than were the 1950s and '60s to Gothic Revival architecture, and it is to be hoped that the conservation and restoration work commenced in the mid-1970s will continue. Alton Towers is now protected by Grade II* Listed Building status.

Despite its fame and former magnificence, to say nothing of the great family who built it, Alton Towers has been neglected by historians. Though several contemporary accounts of the interior splendours of the house have survived, along with drawings and photographs dating from the 1840s through to the National Monuments Survey in 1951, no major study has been published until now. There have however been some significant landmarks along the way. Ross Williamson's article in the *Architectural Review* (May 1940) drew on some original material, including J.C Loudon's *Encyclopaedia of Gardening* (1834). Twenty years later Christopher Hussey wrote an excellent description of the house and gardens for *Country Life* (2nd & 9th June 1960), although no hard evidence has so far been found to support his conclusion that Robert Abraham (1774-1850) was a major contributor to the design of the house as well as the garden buildings. Documentary evidence for the involvement of James Wyatt (1746-1813) in the creation of "Alton Abbey" has also proved elusive, though his influence is discernible in the linked galleries built a decade and more after his death. Much as one might wish to establish a firmer link between Alton and the architect of Fonthill, there are no grounds upon which to proceed further than the cautious stylistic attribution made by Howard Colvin as long ago as 1954 and reiterated in the 1995 edition of *A Biographical Dictionary of British Architects*. One of Ross Williamson's comments -"There are many discoveries to be made in Staffordshire, but none more interesting than Alton Towers"- has proved to be correct, yet mysteries still remain.

My own interest in Alton Towers dates back to childhood days in Leek when steam trains still ran along the Churnet Valley Line, and Alton was a favourite destination for family outings. Even as a schoolboy I felt a sense of outrage at what people told me had been done to the Towers after the war, while I loved that Gothic paradise in Alton village - the castle and the hospital of S. John - which I still believe to be one of the most alluring places on earth. Having written a book on Gothic Revival in Staffordshire and produced a small visitors' guidebook for the Towers, I was invited to undertake a comprehensive historical and architectural survey of the Towers buildings in order to inform the owners of precisely what they had, how it came into being, and what needed to be done to conserve it. That work was completed in 1998 and forms the basis of this book. It draws on a wealth of original source-materials, some of which have never been examined in detail before. Chief amongst these is the very substantial collection of Shrewsbury family papers on deposit at the Staffordshire County Record Office, including the ledgers recording payments to the various contractors and craftsmen at the time the buildings were constructed. Correspondence between A.W.N. Pugin and the sixteenth Earl of Shrewsbury, the Pugin diaries, and a quantity of original drawings, designs, plans and prints, have been of considerable value in tracing the evolution of the house. Work in the buildings has brought to light the remains of Pugin's gilded and painted screenwork from the chapel and other significant artefacts, and in the autumn of 1998 a set of fourteen hitherto unknown watercolours of the Towers done in 1870 suddenly appeared. Many of these pictures are reproduced here; a unique set of "snapshot" views of the Towers and gardens painted by someone who clearly knew the family and who spent part of the summer of 1870 with them at Alton.

This work could not have been undertaken without the active help and support of staff at Alton Towers; in particular Damian Varley, the Estates Maintenance Manager, and Les Davies who has charge of the varied collection of photographs, archive material and memorabilia kept at the Towers, and who is making a valiant attempt to catalogue and organise it systematically. I am indebted to Divisional Director Ralph Armond for allowing me unlimited access to this material and for permission for items to be used in this publication. My thanks are due to Thea Randall, Head of Staffordshire Archive Services, and the staff of the County Record Office and William Salt Library; to Lucien Cooper of the Potteries Museum, Stoke-on-Trent, and Chris Copp of the Staffordshire County Museum at Shugborough Hall; to Pamela Taylor, the Archivist of Arundel Castle, to His Grace the Duke of Norfolk for permission to reproduce part of the 1811 plan of Alton Lodge kept in the Arundel archives, to the Earl of Shrewsbury and Talbot for allowing me access to his private collection of family papers, and to Michael Hadcroft, Librarian at Oscott College. The staff at the Birmingham Central Library and Mr Stanley Shepherd have kindly dealt with my queries about Hardman stained glass, the Derby Museum and Art Gallery have searched out important information about the Britannia Ironworks which supplied much of the ornamental cast-iron for the Towers. Local knowledge is invaluable, and I am particularly obliged to Alton residents Dorothy Brereton and Edward Bailey – a descendant of the Bailey family of stonemasons who worked at the Towers in the early nineteenth century – and to Mr & Mrs Jennings of Counslow Lodge for allowing me to visit their home. Acknowledgements to the owners of photographs and illustrations are included in the captions. I am however particularly grateful for the opportunities to look through the Lewis Family Collection of historic postcards, and Mr Basil Jeuda's collection. I thank the Head of Bilton Grange School for allowing me to visit and take photographs for use in this book, and Ms J. Blake for permission to photograph the Talbot portraits at Ingestre Hall. Lady Wedgwood has taken a keen interest in this project from its inception, and I am indebted to her for many helpful comments, suggestions and corrections. Paul Atterbury's help and advice, and the loan of photographs from his collection (colour plates II, III and IV), is much appreciated. I value Clive Wainwright's enthusiastic support, the fruitful discussions we have had as the work has progressed, and the new lines of enquiry which he opened up for me. I was delighted when he kindly agreed to write the Foreword. Self-publication was not my preferred method of producing this book, although it has several advantages, one of which is that the author is in full control of the project. The quality of the production depends however on the printer, and I approached Counter Print of Stafford in the knowledge that they would handle a major production of this kind in the same professional and sympathetic way in which they have undertaken work for me in the past. Finally I would like to thank my wife Isobel for the many hours she has spent with me at Alton, surveying, measuring and recording, and for her help with the selection and preparation of illustrative material. She too has known Alton Towers since childhood days.

MICHAEL J. FISHER

Candlemas 1999

The sudden death of Professor Clive Wainwright in July 1999 shocked and saddened all who had known him, and whom he had inspired by his scholarship, enthusiasm and geniality. As co-curator of the 1994 exhibition at the V&A: *Pugin: A Gothic Passion,* Clive played a crucial role in awakening the public to the breadth of Pugin's genius as an architect and designer. It was Clive who discovered the great chandelier from the Banqueting Hall at Alton Towers, lying in pieces in a second-hand dealer's shop, and arranged for its restoration and eventual relocation in the Palace of Westminster. The prospect of a book about Alton Towers excited him, amongst other things because of what it might reveal about the extent of Pugin's work there, and one of the last things he wrote was the Foreword to this book which owes a great deal to his encouragement and sound advice.

Clive also hoped that this book, and the survey of the Towers buildings which preceded it, might encourage the owners to initiate a systematic programme of conservation work, following the restoration of the chapel ceiling in 1993. These hopes have not been disappointed. In 1999-2000 the former Grand Entrance was re-opened as part of the public access to a new theme-park ride. The stained-glass windows in the Armoury were completely restored in the Hardman Studio; the Picture Gallery was re-roofed; the Octagon was cleared of accumulated rubble and undergrowth, the central column was rebuilt and the Pugin screenwork was restored. The current owners, Tussauds, have agreed a budget to enable a rolling programme of restoration to be implemented over the next ten years, and a Heritage Committee has been set up to make recommendations and to oversee this work. The same committee, advised by garden historian Peter Hayden, also holds a watching brief over the magnificent gardens and their listed buildings. The prospect for the historic buildings is thus far more encouraging and hopeful than it was four or five years ago. Much of the credit for this must be given to Damian Varley who was at that time Estates Maintenance Manager at the Towers, and who effectively commissioned the survey in the hope that it would stimulate some positive action, which indeed it has. Tribute should also be paid to Head Gardener John Salt and to Stonemason John Stubbs for their dedication and their clear love of the place which led them to give far more than duty required until they both left Alton in 2000. I am grateful also to all who have written to me since the publication of this book, offering additional information, or drawing my attention to errors or omissions which I have endeavoured to correct.

MICHAEL J. FISHER

Easter 2002

1
𝔄𝕷𝕍𝔈𝕿𝔒𝕹 𝕷𝔒𝔇𝔊𝔈

The history of Alton Towers is bound inextricably with that of the surrounding area of North Staffordshire and the Churnet valley. Bunbury (anciently Bumbury) Hill, upon which the house was built, was the site of an Iron Age hill-fort, traces of which may still be discerned near to the Flag Tower. Below the gardens is Slade Dale as it was known in the early nineteenth century, from an Old English word signifying a wooded hollow. Allegedly the scene of a battle in 716 A.D. between the Saxon Kings Coelred of Mercia and Ine of Wessex, it had, by the time of the 1881 Ordnance Survey, been corrupted to *Slain Hollow.* the result, one assumes, of Victorian romanticisation which may have begun with the discovery in 1834 of an Anglo-Saxon sword and a stone axe-head or "celt" in the vicinity of the hill-fort. In Alton village itself are the remains of the medieval castle built by Bertram de Verdun at the end of the twelfth century, and in a nearby valley are the ruins of the Cistercian abbey of Croxden, also founded and endowed by the Verduns. The fact that the area was steeped in the history of the Verdun and Furnival families, from whom the Talbot Earls of Shrewsbury were in part descended, is of significance in the development of the Towers buildings as an attempt by the fifteenth and sixteenth earls to recall their medieval ancestry. This also applies to the reconstruction of the castle and other work undertaken by Pugin and the sixteenth earl in Alton village. The Talbots were returning to their roots, and they were doing so at a time when, in the wake of the late eighteenth-century craze for Gothic archaeology and Sir Walter Scott's Waverley novels, medievalism was in fashion.

On the site of what is now Alton Towers was Alton Lodge, used as an occasional residence by the Earls of Shrewsbury who by the eighteenth century had established their principal residence at Heythrop in Oxfordshire. An engraving of Alton Castle by S. & N. Buck dated 1731 (**1**) shows in the background the top of Bunbury Hill, and on it a building labelled "Alveton Lodge" - Alveton being the ancient form of Alton. The house appears as a modest rectangular building with regular rows of square-headed windows and a square chimney; i.e. early eighteenth-century. Some outbuildings can be discerned at the rear. Alton Lodge is also mentioned by Dr Robert Plot in his *Natural History of Staffordshire,* which shows that it must have existed in 1686. Plot's reference to it as "the old Lodge" suggests an even earlier date, and within the Towers ruins there are features which would seem to pre-date the house as shown in Buck's engraving.

In the Staffordshire County Record Office there is a watercolour of Alton Lodge, undated but appearing to be of about 1800-1810 and inscribed, "East View of Alveton Lodge before Earl of Shrewsbury began building Alveton Abbey" (**2**). Drawn from a different angle from the Buck engraving, it confirms that the Lodge at this time was a rectangular building of two-and-a-half storeys, with a low-pitched roof concealed behind a parapet, and with an outbuilding to the south. Rising just above the roof is what appears to be the top of a circular tower with a

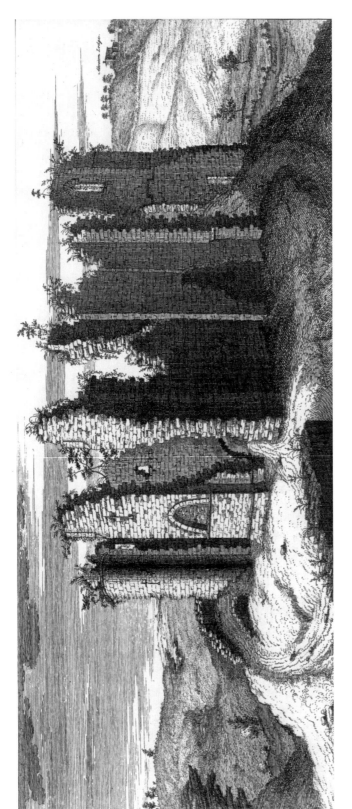

1a. Engraving of Alton Castle by S. & N. Buck, 1731, showing Alveton Lodge in the background

1b. Enlargement of Alveton Lodge from above view.

2a. View of Alveton Lodge *c.*1800, captioned "East View of Alveton Lodge before the Earl of Shrewsbury began building Alton Abbey". Note the top of the round tower appearing over the roof. (Staffs County Record Office, D554/187)

2b. East front of Alton Towers 1998 showing surviving wall of Alveton Lodge, and the old round tower. (MJF) small turret. A plan drawn in 1804 by Lord Shrewsbury's agent, George Padbury, shows what is evidently a tower with a spiral staircase. It is on the west side of the house, as indicated on the c1800 illustration, and at the junction of the Lodge proper with the steward's quarters **(3)**. The Alton Abbey accounts contain several references to work being carried out on the "old circular tower" in 1815-16[1] so it is clear that this tower was regarded even then as an important feature of the house, and of some antiquity. Though logic might have decreed that it needed to be demolished along with much else that was swept away at this time, considerable efforts were made to preserve and incorporate it into the new buildings along with other portions of the Lodge. The tower remains to this day, though much-altered, among the many towers which eventually gave the house a new name, and it is the only circular one. Preserved also is the east front of the old Lodge, with its regular rows of straight-headed windows. **(2b)**

From the plan of 1804 and surviving illustrations it seems that Alton Lodge was a small country residence built in the Classical style. On the ground floor two principal rooms known as the Great Parlour and the Little Parlour occupied the east front, the principal entrance and vestibule being on the north side. A rear entrance gave access to the kitchen and other offices. This part of the house appears to have been self-contained and run separately from the buildings to which it was linked on the west side, i.e. the rooms leased by John Burton and his family who seem to have been tenant farmers/stewards on the Alton estate. The Lodge therefore comprised two distinct halves: the Lodge proper which was used on occasion by the Talbot family, and an adjacent farm-house which may have been older, like the old round tower which stood at the juncture of the two premises giving access to the upper floors of the Lodge. It is of interest that the two parts of the house were constructed on divergent building lines with a difference of about ten degrees between them. The Burtons' part of the house had its own staircase and entrances. No contemporary plan or description of the rooms on the upper floors of either part has survived.

Until the beginning of the nineteenth century Alton Lodge appears to have been used by the family only for occasional summer visits. They were content to leave the administration of the estate in the hands of the resident steward. It was the fifteenth earl, Charles (1787-1827), who began to take a greater and more personal interest in the Alton estate. It is recorded[2] that Charles was so impressed with the location of Alton Lodge and the beauty of the surrounding area that he decided to extend the house and to lay out gardens with a view to spending more time there. From this modest improvement scheme there soon developed much more ambitious plans which, over the course of the next fifty years, saw the expansion of the house and gardens into one of the wonders of nineteenth-century England. There was scarcely a year between 1800 and 1852 when some major work was not in progress or in prospect. The Alton Lodge Cash Accounts record several improvements made to the Lodge in 1804-6, including the sinking of a cellar, the provision of new marble hearths and chimney-pieces, and masons' and carpenters' work. In October 1807 the sum of £207.5s.6d. was paid to masons, glaziers, slaters, carpenters and plasterers for the construction of a new drawing-room[3]. A hindrance to the development of the Lodge as an exclusive summer residence for the Shrewsbury family was that in 1773 the fourteenth earl had leased the house and 221 acres of adjacent land to Charles Bill of Sydenham[4]. Though certain rights in the property would have been reserved to the Earl, Charles Bill had, in 1793, sub-let it to Joseph and John Burton, and this lease was not due to expire until 1824. In October 1807 the fifteenth earl negotiated an agreement with Charles Bill

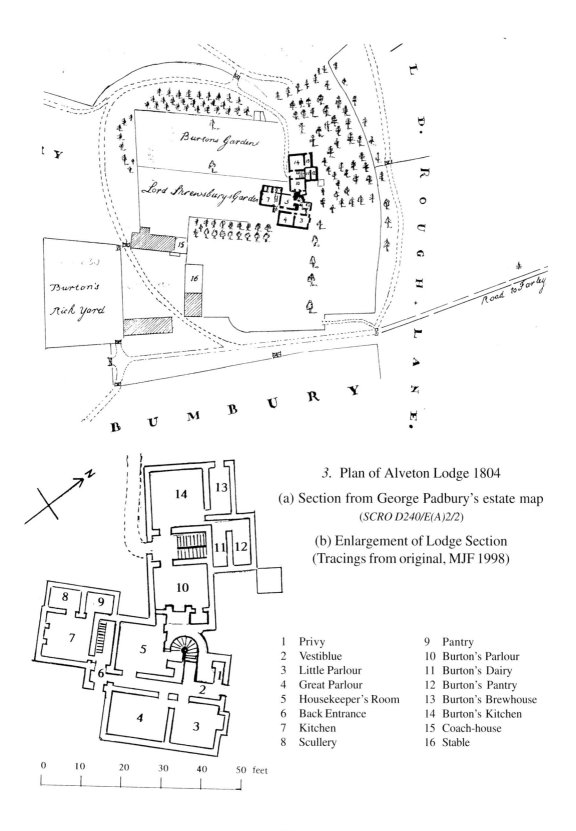

3. Plan of Alveton Lodge 1804

(a) Section from George Padbury's estate map
(SCRO D240/E(A)2/2)

(b) Enlargement of Lodge Section
(Tracings from original, MJF 1998)

1	Privy	9 Pantry
2	Vestiblue	10 Burton's Parlour
3	Little Parlour	11 Burton's Dairy
4	Great Parlour	12 Burton's Pantry
5	Housekeeper's Room	13 Burton's Brewhouse
6	Back Entrance	14 Burton's Kitchen
7	Kitchen	15 Coach-house
8	Scullery	16 Stable

and the Burtons whereby he bought out the Burtons and agreed to compensate Bill for loss of rent for the remaining seventeen years of the lease[5].

The way was now clear for the earl to develop Alton Lodge as he wished. By December payments totalling £306 were being made for work on a new dining-room, bedroom and passage[6]. The Lodge accounts also mention work in the grounds and "new gardens" including the construction of the fishponds and canal, while access to the estate was being improved by the building of a bridge (**4**) over the River Churnet at Quixhill[7]. A project of significance for the future was begun in 1810 with the laying of the foundation of "The Tower" - i.e. the Flag Tower west of the house - but it was to take many years to complete.

4. The Quixhill Bridge over the Churnet (MJF 1998)

As to the identity of the architect responsible for the first phase of extensions and additions to the Lodge, the accounts contain several references to "William Lees, Architect". In August 1804 he was paid £1.11s.6d. for drawing a sketch of the Lodge. In November 1806 he was paid two guineas for attendance over two days and making a plan and elevation of a new room, and in 1808 he received payment for five days' attendance[8]. There can be little doubt that this was the builder-architect William Lees who is known to have carried out alterations to two other country houses, Locko Park and Darley Abbey – both near Derby – in the early 1800s[9]. Lees had his practice in Derby, which in those days was the nearest large town to Alton, some eighteen miles away, and his was not the only Derby-based firm to be used by Lord Shrewsbury in work on the house.

East of the house lay a dry valley leading down to Slade Dale. Its only occupants at this time were the rabbits which had carved out a huge warren amongst the sandstone rocks, but the earl grasped its potential and until his death in 1827 he devoted much of his time and a good deal of his wealth to the transformation of this rocky wilderness into the gardens which have delighted successive generations of visitors. Essential to the entire scheme was the provision of running water, and this had to be brought in by conduits from a spring at Ramsor, two miles away in the Weaver Hills, to fill the lake which was excavated in front of the house, and other ponds on the north side of the valley. From there it could feed the various cascades, pools and fountains which were planned in the valley itself. Charles was personally involved with the design and layout of the gardens, but he also consulted the celebrated landscape architect and publicist, John Claudius Loudon, and employed two garden architects trained in the tradition which produced Stourhead, Stowe, and similar eighteenth-century gardens. These were Robert Abraham and Thomas Allason, the latter being also a major contributor to the extensions to the house.

The Alton Lodge estate had its commercial side; indeed it was revenues from the estate which helped finance the development of the house and gardens. There were rents from farms and cottages of course, but also an increasing amount of revenue from the direct management of the estate. As early as 1794 seventeen workers were employed in two nurseries at Alton and Farley. Their duties included the seeding and rearing of oaks, ashes and hawthorns, and the accounts of 1802 show that the Farley nursery supplied not only the estate, but also sold saplings and thornsets (for hedging) to local landowners and farmers. George Padbury's plan of 1804 shows large plantations to the west of the Lodge, and in 1806-7 huge quantities trees were planted and bedded out, including more than 5,000 conifers, and nearly 8,000 assorted broad-leaf trees[10]. This obviously represented a long-term investment, but it underlines the importance that the fifteenth earl now attached to Alton Lodge and its estate.

2
ALTON ABBEY

'In such a house something of an ecclesiastical exterior had been obtained at an enormous expense, and a casual passer-by might have supposed from some distance that the place really belonged to some religious community, but on a nearer approach the vision is soon dissipated, and the building, which had been raised somewhat in the guise of the solemn architecture of religion and antiquity, discovers itself to be a mere toy, built to suit the caprice of a wealthy individual, and devoted to Luxury' (A.W.N. Pugin, *True Principles*)

The classic view of Alton Towers is the one seen by all who enter the park through the main public entrance: the long irregular outline of the north facade, fronted by lawns sloping gently down to a lake.(5) Three main elements make up this view. First there is the "new" chapel with its ogee-capped turrets and ornate bell-tower; then the central block, the principal feature of which is the Great Dining Hall; finally the West Wing terminating with a diagonally-placed square tower - altogether a run of some 450 feet. It is the central block which comprises the oldest part of the house, the Chapel and the West Wing being additions of the later 1820s and 1830s. The central section has also undergone change, principally at the hands of Pugin who in the 1840s built the Dining Hall and added upper floors either side of it. All of this reflects a period of restless activity on the part of the fifteenth and sixteenth Earls of Shrewsbury spanning almost fifty years between the first alterations to Alton Lodge and the death of the sixteenth earl in 1852.

5. View of north front of Alton Towers, *c.*1930

The real starting-point was in 1811, when hitherto modest alterations gave way to more ambitious and carefully-planned schemes involving much demolition, rebuilding and extension. This was of course the period of the Napoleonic Wars, with economic and military campaigns now turning the tide against the French domination of Europe. The Earl of Shrewsbury, though a senior member of the English aristocracy, took no part in the wars. As a Catholic in the days before the Emancipation Act of 1829, he was more or less excluded from active participation in the affairs of State; unable even to take his seat in the House of Lords. It was the lot of the Catholic nobility and gentry to live quietly on their estates, to develop their properties in the way that Lord Shrewsbury was doing, and to practise their faith insofar as the limited concessions of the 1791 Toleration Act permitted. Staffordshire already had a number of landed Catholic families who had remained faithful through the darker years of persecution. They included the Giffards of Brewood, the Simeons of Aston-by-Stone, the Fitzherberts of Swynnerton, and the Draycotts of Painsley near Cheadle, all of whom maintained a Catholic tenantry, and provided facilities in their houses for Mass to be said by a domestic chaplain or an itinerant priest. Another such centre now came into being on the Shrewsbury estate at Alton, with a purpose-built chapel. The accounts for 1816 record payments to four chaplains maintained at Lord Shrewsbury's expense, and William Pitt's *History of Staffordshire* published in the following year observes that "a considerable number of Catholics are maintained in the family mansion"[1].

The expansion of Alton Lodge into a substantial country house was accompanied by a change of name. As early as June 1811 the estate accounts begin to refer to it as the Abbey House rather than the Lodge, and from July 1812 the accounts are consistently called the Abbey Accounts with the ledgers gold-blocked accordingly. The earl had evidently made his intentions clear before ever a stone was laid. The site itself held no medieval precedent for such a name: the ruins of the Cistercian abbey established by Lord Shrewsbury's Verdun ancestor lay in a valley to the south of Alton. The new name may have signified nothing more than the adoption of a Romantic architectural fashion of the Georgian period. Satirised by Jane Austen in her novel *Northanger Abbey,* the practice of applying the name "abbey" or "priory" indiscriminately to gentleman's houses of the period was part and parcel of the early phases of the Gothic Revival when medieval features such as tombs, niches and statues were copied and adapted - often in plaster - to adorn drawing rooms and picture galleries. The most celebrated example of this "abbey style" was Fonthill Abbey near Salisbury, built by James Wyatt for the millionaire antiquary William Beckford in 1796-1812. Fonthill had as its central feature a great octagonal saloon, the ceiling of which was a vault 120 feet high, surmounted by a lofty pinnacled tower.(6) It was a house of mystery and wonder, and although it fell down in 1825, it stood long enough to inspire and influence other architects and their patrons. Though there is no documentary evidence to suggest that James Wyatt had any direct hand in the buildings at Alton - and after all he died in 1813 - the influence of Fonthill is discernible in the original entrance hall built in 1813-18, in the (much later) enfilade of galleries linked by an octagonal saloon south of the main block, and in the fact that most of these great rooms were designed for display rather than habitation.

The transformation of Alton Lodge into Alton Abbey took about ten years to complete. Preparations for it included the demolition of those parts of the house formerly occupied by the Burtons, and the removal of dairying and related activities to a site north of the Abbey where

6. The north and west fronts of Fonthill Abbey: J. Rutter, *Delineations of Fonthill...,* 1823

new farm buildings were suitably hidden from view by an embattled screen-wall and towers.[3](7) The old Lodge was situated towards the summit of Bunbury hill, on an outcrop of red sandstone. A certain amount of levelling and clearing was necessary, but it was generally possible to build the footings directly on to bedrock. The accounts for March-August 1811 record payments for the removal of sand and stone, pulling down old buildings, underbuilding the ones to be retained, erecting cranes, making pulley-blocks and putting up scaffolding. At the same time new construction work was beginning north and west of the old Lodge, all in the Gothic style which contrasted with the surviving parts of the Lodge; but even these were

"gothicised" by the addition of battlements and the insertion of Gothic frames into the square-headed windows of the old east front. Care was taken to retain significant portions of the Lodge within the new buildings. The private apartments of the earl and countess remained in this old part of the building for the duration of the Shrewsburys' occupation of it. The sole surviving fragment of the Burtons' part of the house is a wall which runs westwards from the old tower and under the south wall of the present ban-

7. The castellated screen built to hide the farm buildings. (MJF 1999)

24

8. A wall of old Alveton Lodge cutting in at an odd angle under the south gable of the dining hall: a strange survival. (MJF 1998)

queting hall on a different line from the new buildings erected from 1811 onwards.**(8)**

The new buildings were constructed in what became known as the Romantic "abbey style", with a pronounced asymmetrical plan and skyline.**(9)** The main elements were an apsidal-ended chapel, a high-gabled entrance hall, and an embattled Long Gallery, all set transversely and separated by irregular blocks of domestic apartments with diverse windows. All of these are still in place, with the exception of the entrance hall which had a chequered history even before Pugin replaced it with his great Dining Hall

The east front of the house was formed by the east walls of the chapel and the old Lodge, with a square entrance tower leading into the private family apartments built at the junction of the two. Running from this point a terrace wall was built, incorporating a small gatehouse and terminating in an octagonal turret. The house was fronted at this time by a low embankment with a driveway along the top, and a flight of steps leading from the main entrance to the lawns below.

Starting at a slightly later date than the north front, building work on the south side of the Abbey comprised the south entrance and courtyard, and the Saloon or Great Drawing Room which was built at right-angles to the Long Gallery, extending the north front westwards as far as the octagonal stair-turret which was built at the angle. A Servants' Hall and associated rooms were constructed at basement level, and the house conservatory was built on the south side of the Drawing Room. Some of these develop-

9. Alton Abbey - view from the north-east, *c*. 1823 (Engraving by W. Radclyffe *after* J.P. Neale)

ments appear to have been haphazard, Lord Shrewsbury changing his mind as well as his architects as the work progressed. Consequently new rooms were no sooner complete than they were subjected to radical alterations and additions. There was however a certain logic to the way the buildings took shape. Behind the asymmetrical north front with its many additions and accretions a regular plan was developing: an axial system of linked rooms creating long enfilades and vistas taking in the length and breadth of the buildings.

Considerable quantities of building materials were needed for the new work. The principal material was sandstone, of which there were abundant quantities in the vicinity. "The earl's stone", as it was called, came principally from an excavation close to the house from which the Quarry Greenhouse takes its name, from other parts of the estate, and also from Alton Common. Some fine pink sandstone was brought in from the nearby Hollington quarries, and flooring stone from St. Helens.[4] Hopton Wood stone - a superb Derbyshire limestone quarried near Matlock - was specified by the fifteenth earl for the staircases in the entrance Hall,[5] and black marble for some of the chimneypieces and floors came from the Duke of Devonshire's quarries at Ashford, also in Derbyshire.[6] Much of the timber required was cut on the estate. In 1814 alone 135 oak trees were cut down for buildings at the abbey and for repairs to tenants' cottages.[7] A brick-kiln was set up on Star Green for brickmaker William Alsop to make bricks on the site, while lime for mortar was brought in from Caldon Lowe and plaster from Stoke-on-Trent from where large quantities of coal were also obtained.[8] The cutting of a branch of the Trent and Mersey canal from Froghall to Uttoxeter was completed in 1811, and a wharf was constructed at Alton. Known as Lord Shrewsbury's wharf, it was probably situated at the Wiremill, close to the "Jackson's Lodge" entrance to the estate.[9] This linked Alton with the country's main canal network, although references to stone being brought from London Bridge become less intriguing once it is known that there was a "London Bridge" with a stone-wharf on the Caldon canal not many miles distant.[10] Much of the structural cast iron used at the Abbey was supplied locally by Bassetts of the Winkhill foundry near Waterhouses, while lead for the roofs, gutters and pipes was supplied by Shaw & Co. of Wirksworth, Derbyshire.[11]

The building operations at Alton were carried out on a piece-work basis, the same artisans - "mechanics" as they were then generally called - being employed on the garden buildings, the Flag Tower and the Churnet bridge as well as on the house. It is clear however that in the years 1811-1820 the work on the house took priority. Names included in the wage-books included stonemasons Henry and Thomas Fower, Peter Ford, John Clewes, John Green, and Thomas Bailey - one of several generations of Baileys employed at Alton through to the 1850s. Fower was responsible for cutting hundreds of holes and grooves in the internal walls to receive plugs for fixing the battens, and following the stripping of the interiors in the 1952 his work is visible as it was never meant to be. Bricklayers John Evans and John Farnell were responsible for the (largely concealed) brickwork, Farnell being another employee of long-standing, still at work in the 1840s. Carpenter William Finney, lathcleaver John Askey, and plasterer John Dixon carried out the finishing of the rooms, plumbing was undertaken by William Mellor, while much of the glazing and painting was done by Thomas Kearns who was to become an interior decorator of some note.[12]

The architects employed between 1811 and 1820 were Thomas Hopper, William Hollins, and Thomas Allason. Hopper (1776-1856) built a Gothic conservatory at Carlton House for George, Prince of Wales, in 1807, and he was to go on to build Margam Castle (Glamorgan) for a junior branch of the Talbot family, and Penrhyn Castle (near Bangor) which he fitted out with a sumptuous array of carvings and furnishings, all in the Norman style (1820-1833). He also submitted Gothic designs for the new Palace of Westminster. Hopper's attendance at Alton between 1813 and 1815, along with his clerk, is recorded in the Abbey accounts, including the provision of a dozen bottles of port.[13] A drawing signed by Hopper showing a detail of the house conservatory exists in the Towers archive, dated July 1815.

Birmingham-based William Hollins (1763-1843) was responsible for alterations in the old part of the house in 1817, for the installation of heating in the entrance hall and lobby, and for sculptured details such as the pinnacles and cross for the hall gable.[14] As an architect Hollins was not well-known outside Birmingham where his buildings included the Union Street Library and the restoration of Handsworth parish church; he gained a wider reputation as a sculptor, though he was outshone by his son Peter (1800-1886) who for a time was an assistant to Francis Chantrey. Both William and Peter Hollins were in residence at Alton at various times in 1818 and were paid £142 for attendance, coach hire, and marble work. They were still being consulted in 1825. It would appear that their principal contribution to the abbey buildings consisted of statuary and other ornamental stonework rather than structural work.[15]

10. The Flag Tower *c.*1930

Thomas Allason (1790-1852) was surveyor to the Stock Exchange, and as an architect he was more conversant with the Greek style than with the Gothic. He was nevertheless commissioned by Lord Shrewsbury in 1818-19 to undertake extensive work on garden buildings at Alton, and also structural and decorative work at the Abbey. This included the completion of the entrance hall on the north front, likewise the chapel, the great Drawing Room, Long Gallery and dining room. Allason was personally supervising work at Alton in June and November 1818 and his principal assistants/surveyors appear to have been a Mr Mordant and a Mr Sinclair whose names occur in the accounts, sometimes with Allason's.[16] Two very fine aquatints by Allason dated 1st May 1819 show different views of the north front of the abbey as completed - or as intended to be completed. The full significance of these pictures will be considered later. Allason was still involved with the buildings at Alton in 1822, for his name appears in the notes on the drawings for the Quixhill Lodge (July 1822).[17] Local architects' names appearing in the accounts include Joseph Ireland and a Mr Trubshaw. Ireland was the architect of a number of Catholic churches in Staffordshire, and the Trubshaws - five generations of them - were also church architects. Precisely what Ireland and Trubshaw did at Alton is not recorded, although tradition has it that Joseph Ireland designed the Flag Tower which was built on the highest point of Bunbury Hill, west of the house. Rock-faced in contrast to the house itself, and standing five storeys tall, it gave commanding views over the surrounding countryside, while proclaiming to all corners that they were approaching an estate of some importance **(10)**.

In between visits by the architects and their clerks, building work would have been supervised by locally-based agents and surveyors, and by Lord Shrewsbury's own steward and clerk-of-works. George Padbury, who drew the estate-map of 1804, was the earl's estates surveyor, and he also kept the Alton Lodge accounts until 1812 when - probably because of the increased amount of activity at Alton - a separate accountant was employed, namely Matthew Leadbitter, followed by Michael Bick and Anthony Todd. Quantity surveyors and architects'

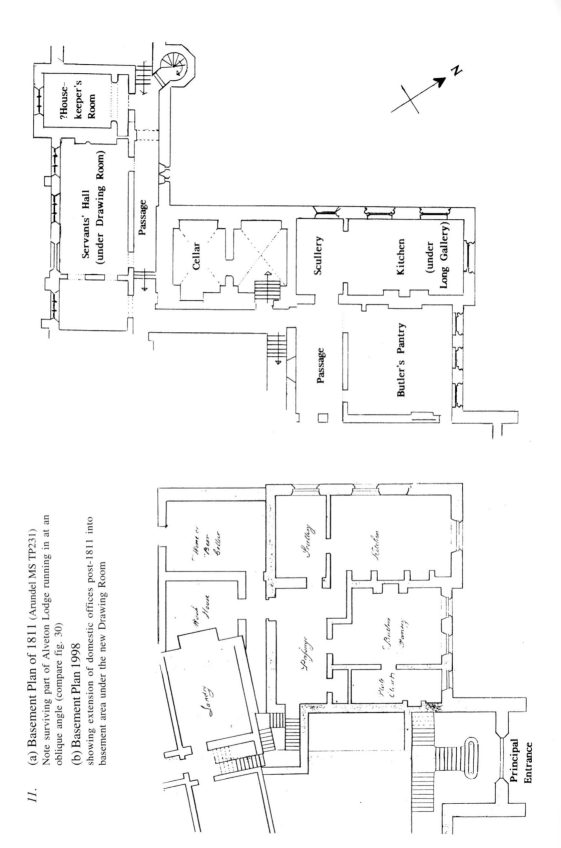

11. (a) Basement Plan of 1811 (Arundel MS TP231)
Note surviving part of Alveton Lodge running in at an oblique angle (compare fig. 30)

(b) Basement Plan 1998
showing extension of domestic offices post-1811 into basement area under the new Drawing Room

agents mentioned in these accounts include the names of Boden, Jephson, and Hawkins. Amongst the resident clerks-of-works were the ill-fated Mr Fone dismissed for incompetence - and Henry Hobden who was there in the early 1820s

The accelerating pace of building activity from 1811 onwards can be gauged from the payments made from the Abbey building accounts. From a modest £550 in 1811, the building expenses rose to £2,908 in 1812 and £3,503 in 1813. In 1816 masons' work alone accounted for over £2,000, and by this time the earl was making regular transfers into the Alton account of between £200 and £500 per month from his private account with the London banking firm of Wright & Co.[18]

A plan of the building dated 1811 and almost certainly by Hopper shows the new north front of the abbey, with details of the basement level at the west end (11). A new kitchen and associated offices were constructed, and although some of the internal walls and other features were subsequently altered, these rooms still exist in the level below the Long Gallery and the family dining-room; also the brick-vaulted wine/beer cellar. The line of the entrance hall and the apsidal chapel appear to the east, while the building labelled "laundry" cuts in at an odd angle following the line of the rooms formerly occupied by the Burtons. The plan also shows borders for flowers and shrubs running along the terrace, and a screen-wall running westwards from the kitchen block and terminating in a circular feature. There was at this time no fosse, or ditch, in front of the house, this being an addition of the 1840s.

THE ENTRANCE HALL

The most prominent feature of the north front was the new entrance hall, occupying the site of the present ban-queting hall which was developed out of it in the late 1840s. The main entrance to the Lodge had also been on the north side, but this was now obscured by the new buildings. Nevertheless the Classical portico of the old entrance was considered worthy of preservation, for in May 1813 stonemason Peter Ford was paid for removing a pair of columns from it and setting them up at the "Garden alcove".[19] It is almost certain therefore that the Tuscan columns and *antae* standing in front of the alcove known as *Le Refuge* down in the gardens are the ones in question, and it is possible that some of the fine masonry of the alcove itself may also have come from the Lodge (12).

12. "Le Refuge": columns from the old entrance to Alveton Lodge. (MJF 1998)

The 1811 plan indicates the new entrance as it was originally designed, projecting outwards from the north front. Inside, at basement level, there rose a flight of steps branching left and right to give access to the various rooms on the principal floor. An examination of the internal walls shows blocked arches in the projecting parts. These suggest that although it was not big enough for a *porte-cochère,* the lower part of the entrance as built in c1811 may have consisted of an open porch with arches at the front and sides supporting the superstructure. This arrangement was not to last for very long. The Abbey accounts show that extensive work was carried out on the entrance hall between 1813 and 1821. When completed it comprised a high-gabled building rising through all three levels, with a lead-covered pitched roof, as illustrated in a number of contemporary prints. In the north-facing gable~end was a large five-light Gothic window with elaborate tracery in the head, and below this were the main doors with buttresses either side. The gable was crowned with battlements, pinnacles, and a carved stone cross, and it had a distinctly ecclesiastical air about it (13). Similar in many respects to the one at Wyatt's Fonthill Abbey, the entrance hall may have been started by Thomas Hopper; William Hollins contributed to it - notably the cross and pinnacles for which he was paid £38 - but in its finished state it was substantially the work of Thomas Allason.[20]

Several problems were encountered during the building of the entrance hall. In 1813 one of the pinnacles fell off the gable and had to be replaced.[21] This was as nothing compared with the problems which arose in 1817. By this time the external structural work appears to have been completed, and work was in progress on the ceilings which were of Gothic form but executed in plaster. The architect's design was misinterpreted by Mr Fone, the clerk of works, and as a consequence the ceiling was wrongly constructed. It proved to be an expensive business. The plasterer, John Dixon, had to be paid both for time lost and for doing the work again. Mr Fone was held responsible for loss of materials, and was duly taken to court. The case was heard before magistrates in Ashbourne, and although the outcome is not recorded, Mr Fone's name

13. Detail of engraving by Hopwood *c.*1820 of the north front of Alton Abbey, showing the principal entrance and, on the right, the Long Gallery.

14. Alton Abbey - the entrance hall. This pencil drawing by Samuel Rayner, *c.*1842, shows the hall after it had been converted into the principal dining room, but the structural features remained unaltered until Pugin's complete reconstruction of the building in 1849-51.

(Photography by Guy Evans; courtesy of Potteries Museum & Art Gallery, Hanley, Stoke-on-Trent) does not appear again in the Abbey accounts.[22]

When completed the entrance hall was one of the most impressive rooms in the abbey, as no doubt it was intended to be. Though it was later turned into a dining room, it underwent very little alteration between its completion in about 1820 and Pugin's complete remodelling of it in 1849-51. The pencil drawing done c1842 by Samuel Rayner **(14)** therefore shows the hall looking very much as it had done twenty years earlier. Slender clustered columns and wall-brackets supported the rib-vaulted ceiling. One of the principal features was a geometrical spiral staircase at the southern end giving access to the Long Gallery and the other principal rooms which, it needs to be remembered, were on first-floor level. On the earl's instructions the staircase was constructed out of Hopton Wood limestone, and he specified brass for the balustrades which were made by Smith and Dearman of the Eagle Foundry in Birmingham.[23] Narrow galleries with gothic coving underneath ran down either side of the hall. These too had elaborate metal balustrades of Gothic form. Above the spiral staircase was a large gallery giving access to the rooms on second-floor level to the east and west. This - or perhaps another gallery on the north side - contained an organ, for there are references in the Abbey accounts to an organ-loft in the entrance hall, and also to the organ itself.[24] Niches for marble statues - almost certainly by Hollins - were cut into the walls just inside the doorway, and these still exist in what is now the lower level beneath the banqueting hall.[25]

In December 1817 Lord Shrewsbury issued instructions about the windows for the hall. A circular window was to be made high up in the south gable, and a larger one over the entrance door on the north side.[26] The drawings for the large window are preserved in the Towers

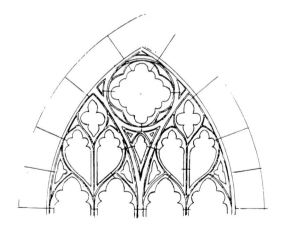

15. Ink/colourwash drawing for north window of entrance/dining room *c.*1815. On the back a working drawing giving details of the tracery. (Alton Towers Archive)

archive: a coloured one showing the form of the window, but without the details of the tracery, and on the back of this a working drawing in ink - made presumably for master mason Thomas Bailey - showing the tracery and the jointing of the stones (15), This was the only large window installed at the Abbey at this time with stone tracery; all of the others had tracery made of wood or cast iron. Both of the hall windows were to be filled with stained glass, and the artist chosen was Birmingham-based William Raphael Eginton, son of the more celebrated Francis Eginton (1737-1805) who had been largely responsible for the revival of glass-painting in the 1780s and for much of the glass for Fonthill Abbey. In September 1818 William Eginton received payment of £136 for the large window and in May of the following year part payment of £30 for what was known as the "star window" in the south gable.[27] Both windows were removed when the hall was rebuilt in 1849-51, and the fate of the glass from them is not known. The last structural addition to be made to the entrance consisted of the battlements added to the gable in 1821; another example, so it would seem, of an after-thought, and the Eginton window had to be covered over to protect it from possible damage when the scaffolding was erected.[28]

THE FAMILY ROOMS and CHAPEL

New rooms built east of the entrance hall at this time consisted of various private apartments for the earl and countess, the east entrance tower, and the chapel. Work also went on in the surviving portions of the old Lodge, incorporating them into the new house. The east terrace wall and towers date from 1813 and were the work of mason John Clowes who was paid £275 for his efforts.[29] Clowes and Bailey were also refurbishing the old circular tower which gave access to the upper floors. It was extended upwards and given a new parapet with battlements, and a flying buttress to prop it on the south side (16). New doorways had to be cut into it, and a new wooden staircase constructed.[30] At the bottom level north of the tower passageways were cut out of solid bedrock to link the basement areas of the old and new buildings (17).

16. View from roof showing round tower and buttress, and south gable of dining room. (MJF 1998)

The chapel formed one of the three transversely-placed elements of the north front, and although in the 1830s it ceased to be the chapel and was adapted for other purposes, it is still recognisable as the polygonal building with tall Gothic windows at the north-cast corner of the house (18). The Abbey accounts refer to work taking place on it in 1818 and 1819. Carpenter William Finney was responsible for putting in floors, doors, benches and kneeling-stools, and plasterer John Dixon made the ceiling which was no doubt Gothic in form like the one in the entrance hall. It appears that the chapel had a tribune, or

17. Passages cut in bedrock to link old and new parts of the house. (MJF 1998)

18. The north-east corner of the house, showing the former chapel with its pointed windows. To the left is the east entrance tower. The room over the chapel with its buttressed oriel window, was added by Pugin *c*.1843. (MJF 1998)

19. Cast-iron Gothic tracery in chapel window. (MJF 1998)

gallery, giving direct access for the family from their private apartments nearby, and an organ. In April 1819 Thomas Kearns was gilding the altarpiece, and crimson velvet was ordered for the lining of the Tabernacle.[31] The Gothic window-tracery in the apse was made, not of stone, nor of wood as in the windows of the Long Gallery, but of cast iron (19). The firm responsible for making this, and other intricate ornamental casting at Alton, was the Derby-based Britannia Ironworks owned at this time by Weatherhead, Glover & Co., and later by Messrs. Marshall, Barker and Wright.[32] It seems that, when completed, the chapel was not just for the private use of the family. The village of Alton had no Catholic church of its own until S. John's was opened in 1842, yet the Baptismal register at S. John's dates back to 1820, suggesting that the earl's chapel was used by the Catholic population of Alton and Farley in the 1820s and 1830s.

THE LONG GALLERY and GREAT DRAWING ROOM - THE EVOLUTION OF THE "T-ROOM"

The wing containing the Long Gallery is the largest single structure dating from this period. Built in courses of 1ft deep and 2ft thick ashlar, it runs a distance of seventy-two feet north-south, and is twenty feet in width. At its southern end the block containing the Great Drawing Room runs across at right-angles. This represents a later development. What was originally the end wall of the Long Gallery was then broken through at principal floor level to make a broad archway leading into the Drawing Room, thus creating a great T-shaped block. At principal floor level the Gallery and Drawing Room formed one vast open space known eventually as the "T-Room"

20. The recesses in the lower end of the Long Gallery. Designed originally to hold book-presses, they were boarded over when the Gallery was integrated with the Drawing Room. (Compare no. 28) (MJF 1999)

Work on the Gallery seems to have begun in 1811, and it consisted initially of a basement and principal floor, completed in 1813. The upper storey - almost certainly intended as servants' accommodation - was added in 1817 and given an embattled top.[33] The original cornice survives as a string-course running above the Gallery windows. Surprisingly for a Gothic structure of this size, the walls are unbuttressed, but to reinforce the building cast-iron beams were inserted at the cornice levels on the first and second floors, these now being visible on the inside. The building accounts for 1812 include payments to Thomas Bailey "cutting walls for ironwork", and "making holes for iron tyes etc.," and to Henry Fower "levelling the iron bond with brick".[34]

The Long Gallery was divided into two areas as indicated on the plan by the pilasters projecting from the east and west walls close to the doorway leading to the dining room. They indicate the position of an arch which marked off the Gallery proper (north) from the southern section which the fifteenth earl designated as a library, and there was also some kind of partition which was removed when the rooms were altered in 1819.[35] Tall pointed recesses

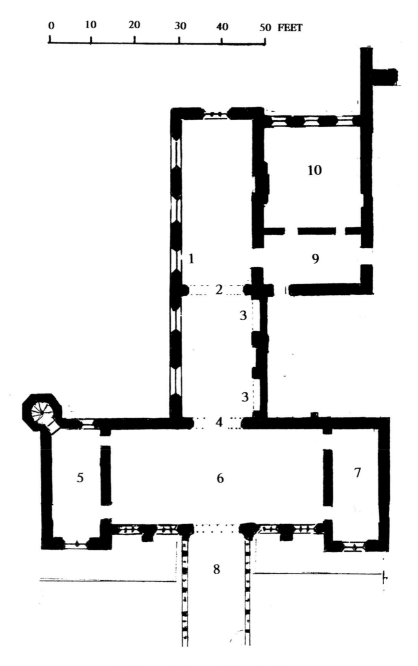

21. Long Gallery and Drawing Room
(The T-Room)

1   Black Prince Window
2   Archway dividing upper and lower sections
    of Gallery
3   Recesses for book-presses, later boarded-over
4   The Great Arch
5   Library

6   Drawing Room
7   Waxwork Room
8   House Conservatory
9   The Glass Corridor
10 Dining Room

either side of the chimney-piece in the southern section show where the book-presses stood (**20**). In the course of the later alterations they were obscured. The window-openings in the Gallery are large: sixteen feet tall by six feet wide. Though more pointed than the ones at basement level they were constructed in an identical manner, and with the same deep hollow-moulds in the jambs and arch. They are the only recognisably Gothic structural features; the remainder, such as the window-tracery, and the elaborate vaulted ceiling of c1820, with the columns and brackets which supported it, were made of timber and plaster. This was fairly typical of late-Georgian building practice; rough masonry overlaid with timber false-work supporting a lath-and-plaster interior. Thus the Long Gallery as photographed before 1952 appears a little narrower and certainly much lower than it does in its present gutted state (**22**).

It was characteristic of the fifteenth earl of Shrewsbury to change his mind frequently. No sooner were features in the gardens completed than they were altered or remodelled, and the same seems to have been true of the house. Extensions on the south side, begun in 1813, had a drastic effect on the appearance of existing rooms, notably the Long Gallery which was altered internally to harmonise with the new rooms to which it became linked.

The Steward's Cash Account for 1813 records payments to Messrs. Clay and Udale for excavating large quantities of stone and soil "for the foundation of new buildings south of Long Gallery".[36] Preparatory work also included the removal of the last vestiges of the former Steward's residence, namely the old wall of Burton's garden, and an old privy and shed on the south side of the abbey.[37] The rocky outcrop on which the Abbey was built inclined to the south, so that the basement level, which on the north front is above ground, had to be cut into bedrock as the buildings were extended southwards. Built at right-angles to the Long Gallery, the new block was symmetrical in plan and elevation, consisting of a tall central section with wings projecting southwards at either end (**23 & 30**). The central section was of two storeys (including basement) and the east and west wings were of three storeys and were referred to in the building accounts as the east and west towers.[38] The upper storeys with their corbelled-out bay-windows were added by Pugin in the 1840s.

The principal floor consisted of a large room set at right-angles to the Long Gallery, flanked by smaller rooms in the projecting wings east and west, all thoroughly symmetrical in contrast to the irregular north front of the house. The room on the west side was used as a Library, while that on the east eventually became the Waxwork Room, filled with figures modelled by the celebrated waxwork artist Samuel Percy. They were still in place at the time of the 1857 sale. Blocked windows in these rooms, east and west, indicate what were once the exterior walls prior to the subsequent phase of expansion. It would seem that the large central apartment was originally intended as a dining-room, and it is referred to as such in the Abbey accounts[39], but it was soon to become the principal Drawing Room.

The new room did not in any case retain its separate identity for very long. In 1817-20 it was integrated with the Long Gallery to form the great "T" Room - so called from its' overall shape - thus integrating what had originally been planned as three separate rooms. Preparations for this work included the packing up of books, pictures and statuary, and the removal of these items to the farm buildings where they were to be safely stored until the alterations were complete.[40] The alterations to the Long Gallery involved the removal of the central partition, and the breaking-through of the south wall to create the Great Arch giving access to the

22a. The Long Gallery *c.*1890 looking southwards towards the Drawing Room and House Conservatory. The door on the left led through the Glass Corridor to the Dining Room. (Staffordshire County Museum, Shugborough Hall)

22b. The same view in 1999 (MJF)

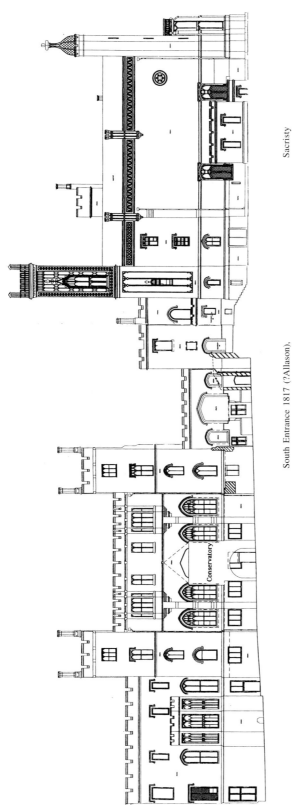

Music Room (Fradgley, c.1830)

Drawing Room Block
Basement (Servants' Hall and associated offices),
and principal floor by Hopper/Allason c.1811-20.
Upper storey over Drawing Room and top two floors
of towers by A.W.N. Pugin & E.W. Pugin, c.1849-56

South Entrance 1817 (?Allason),
blocked 1832

Chapel: Thomas Fradgley & Joseph Potter, 1832

Sacristy

23. Elevation of South Front
(On-Centre Surveys, Leamington Spa, 1992)

24. A sole survivor: an ornamental wooden column in the north-west corner of the Long Gallery (MJF 1998)

Drawing Room. The stonework of the walls either side of the Great Arch tells its own story of remodelling, demolition and reconstruction. Once the structural work was complete the Gallery and the Drawing Room were treated in identical fashion with the construction in wood and plaster of Gothic columns **(24)** and brackets to support vaulted ceilings. The Great Arch was given a wooden Gothic frame with carved leaf patterns in the spandrels, while to the north of it another tall archway served as a reminder that the Long Gallery had once consisted of two rooms under one roof. The accounts for May 1819 include payments to carpenter William Finney for "striking out ribs for groins of Long Gallery and large windows..... making brackets for the Long Gallery and putting up the same", while plasterer John Dixon was repairing lathing in the Gallery, and applying lathing to the wooden ribs prior to plastering.[41] It was at this time that the two tall recesses in the east wall of the southern end of the Gallery were boarded over. They do not appear in any known pictures of the gallery, and they came to light again only when the room was gutted in 1952.

In July 1819 Thomas Bailey was cutting the stone window-jambs in the Gallery to receive the frames.[42] This suggests that the large Gothic windows on the west and north sides were being altered, possibly to receive the wooden mullions and tracery, one complete example of which survives on the north side. The refurbishing of the Long Gallery carried on into the following year, with Finney building staging for the painters from London who were to carry out the gilding and painting of the ceiling and walls. Finney was also fixing the wooden columns at this time, which shows that they were purely ornamental, without any structural function.[43]

The windows in the south wall of the Drawing Room were of similar type and construction to those in the Gallery; three on either side of the doorway leading into the house conservatory. Again the inner frames, mullions and tracery were made of timber rather than stone. The heads of the windows in both rooms were filled with stained glass, the designer of which is not known for certain but he could well have been Francis Eginton. We do however have the name of the artist responsible for the stained-glass portrait of Edward the Black Prince which filled the gallery window opposite the corridor leading to the entrance hall. He was Charles Muss (1779-1824) which suggests that this window must have been in place by 1824, although some commis-

25. The Black Prince Window in the Long Gallery, by Charles Muss, c.1823 (1930s postcard in the Lewis Family Collection)

sions unfinished at his death were completed by John Martin (1789-1854).[44] The "Black Prince" window was put into its own frame and set into place at the back of the existing one. Still in place at the time of the NMR survey of 1951, it was removed a year later and, presumably, sold **(25)**. Traces of the fixings are still discernible in the jambs and arch.

Gothic fittings to the Long Gallery and Drawing Room included large pier-glasses in ogee-headed frames on the east and west walls, flanked by doors, set also in ogee surrounds, leading from the drawing-room into the rooms beyond. These doors had Gothic traceried panels made of cast-iron. *NMR* and other photographs show that the doors on the south side had glass in the panels. A large door which opened on to the east side of the Gallery is worthy of note since it was one of several glazed Gothic doors made to the same design for Alton **(26)**. All of them were still in place in 1951, but only one now survives, somewhat mutilated and no longer *in situ*. Standing 9' 6" tall and 3' 6" wide, it is made of timber, with vertical mullions dividing it into five glazed panels each with a crocketed finial at the top. On close examination, however, it turns out that the head of each panel, and the finials too, are made of cast iron, likewise all the Gothic elements above. The ingenious use of cast iron where one would expect to find wood or stone is a characteristic feature of Alton, and most if not all of the castings came from the Britannia Foundry in Derby which was well-known for its architectural ironwork. The alignment of doors so as to give uninterrupted vistas from one end of the house to the other was another important feature.

26. Glazed wooden door with cast-iron fitments rediscovered in 1998, similar to the one shown in plate 22a (MJF)

The result of these extensions and alterations was the creation of a vast "T"-shaped room which could be treated as an integrated whole, yet still allowing any of its three components to function separately if required **(27 & 28)**. It seems that the principal purpose of the "T" Room was the display of pictures, at least until the new galleries were built in the 1830s. Nineteenth-century drawings and photographs, and the reminiscences of those who saw the interiors before their destruction,[45] give the impression of a heaviness, even oppressiveness, about the groined ceilings with their ponderous chandeliers, and they contrast with the apparent lightness and airiness of the elegant entrance hall, and of Fradgley's Music Room and Libraries immediately to the west. Pugin could have taken little delight in the sham vaulting and plaster brackets, but there was little that he could do except to add colour and gilt, and to cover the walls with wallpaper printed with his own designs.

THE HOUSE CONSERVATORY

A prominent feature of the south side of the house was the conservatory running out from the Drawing Room and contemporary with it. The architect was almost certainly Thomas Hopper. Evidence for this attribution may seem slight: a drawing signed by Hopper and dated July 1815 shows only a detail of a window mullion, but it matches exactly the form of the

27a. The Great Drawing Room/"T"-Room looking east, *c*.1890. On the extreme left is the Great Arch connecting with the Long Gallery. Pugin-Crace wallpaper is recognisable. (Staffordshire County Museum, Shugborough Hall)

27b. The same view in 1999. (MJF)

28. The Long Gallery/"T"-Room looking north, *c*.1842. Pencil drawing by Samuel Rayner. Several items of furniture listed in the 1857 Sale Catalogue are identifiable including, on the right, a fine marqueterie cabinet, and half-way along on the left a large German musical clock by George Grunning. The Gothic table in the foreground could be a Pugin design. (Photography by Guy Evans; courtesy of Potteries Museum & Art Gallery, Hanley, Stoke-on-Trent)

mullions in the conservatory (29). The plan shows that they were originally intended to be made of a timber/iron laminate, but a note in Hopper's handwriting reads, "Agreed to be stone". Hopper had some considerable experience in conservatory design, having built a particularly grand one, in Gothic style, for the Prince Regent at Carlton House in 1807. It had glazed iron fan-vaulting inspired by the ceiling of Henry VII's Chapel in Westminster Abbey. Some writers have mistakenly attributed the house conservatory at Alton to Pugin.[46] He did indeed renew the roof, and he designed other conservatories for Alton Towers,[47] but it is clear that the one adjacent to the Drawing Room was in existence some twenty years before Pugin arrived on the scene, and that the architect was Hopper.

Preparations for the building of the house conservatory are recorded in the Abbey accounts. Since it was to be on the same level as the Drawing Room it had to be

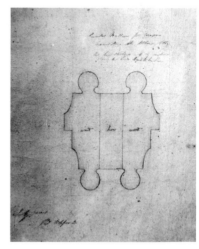

29. Signed drawing by Thomas Hopper showing section through mullion for conservatory; dated July 1815. (Alton Towers Archive)

carried on brick arches built over the area at the rear of the Servants' Hall, and then along a specially constructed embankment beyond. Under the embankment a brick service tunnel was constructed so that coal and other goods could be brought into the house unobserved from the state rooms **(30)**. Coal vaults and a heating chamber for the conservatory were constructed in the area either side of the tunnel exit. This preparatory work began towards the end of 1815 with the excavation of the tunnel and the construction of the brick arches. At the end of November bricklayer Richard Keates was pounding clay on to the arches to protect them from frost when work ceased for the winter.[48]

30. Drawing-room block and house conservatory 1999. The embankment conceals a service-tunnel and places the conservatory on the same level as the principal rooms. (MJF)

The Abbey accounts do not give precise details about the building of the conservatory itself. It is known however that the arch leading from the conservatory into the Drawing room was in place by November 1817.[49] There is some evidence for the involvement of Thomas Allason in the later stages, for example his instructions to stone-mason Thomas Bailey for the alteration of cills to fit the cast metal frames, and to the carpenter to proceed with the roof.[50] These instructions are dated November 1818 and suggest that the conservatory was nearing completion by then.

31. View of house conservatory from Her Ladyship's Garden, *c.*1890. (Staffordshire County Museum, Shugborough Hall

The conservatory was built of stone, with iron window-frames and a glazed wooden roof. Though now (2002) in a dilapidated condition, photographs taken between c1900 and 1951 show its completed form **(31)**. It was composed of three main elements: two long glasshouses linked by an octagon with Gothic windows. A fourth element, namely a vestibule at the southern end, was added in 1824 to connect the conservatory with the new Octagon Gallery. Opening into the "T" Room immediately to the north, the conservatory formed an important element in the developing axial plan of the house.

THE SOUTH ENTRANCE and EASTERN RANGE

The principal entrance to the Abbey was via the entrance hall on the north front. There were at least two other entrances, on the south and east sides. The southern entrance adjoined the eastern tower of the "T" block and consisted of a broad "Tudor" archway flanked by two smaller ones **(32)**. Though blocked in the 1830s, these arches remain a feature of the south front of the house. In front of them was built the screen-wall, battlemented and with octagonal turrets at the angles, and a gateway on the eastern side. This dates from 1817.[51] Inside the screen there would have been just enough room for a small carriage to turn. This area was later completely excavated to make the game larders at the lower level **(55)**. Inside the south entrance archway a flight of steps would have led up to a central courtyard from which there was access to the old and new parts of the house. Alterations in the old part of the house at this time included "pulling down old part of building"[52] sug-

32. The blocked arches of the former south entrance. (MJF 1998)

gesting that improvements may have been taking place in the vicinity of the old round tower. Though subsequently overbuilt by the new kitchens, this area retains some echoes of its former role as an open courtyard on an intermediate level between the entrance and the *piano nobile*.

Adjoining the south entrance on the east side was another tower-block of three storeys with a battlemented top. On the north side it was joined to the surviving part of the old Lodge, and was given square-headed windows to match the old work. Blocked-up windows here indicate former exterior walls: the south wall of the Lodge, and the east wall of the new work later built up to form the west wall of the (1833) chapel. No illustrations are known to exist of the interiors of this eastern wing of the Abbey which was clearly the "family end" of the house. The building accounts contain several references to an octagonal lobby situated somewhere between the east entrance tower and the hall.[53] It would appear that this lobby gave access to the various family rooms and to the staircase leading to the upper floor. Not a single trace of it survived the collapse/demolition of the interior walls in the 1950s.

In this area too would have been the billiard room which was being fitted-out and decorated in 1824.[54] Though the game of billiards dates back to the 1500s it was not until the nineteenth century that separate billiard rooms began to appear in country houses as the nucleus of the "male preserve" to which the gentlemen would retire after dinner. The provision of such a room at Alton is therefore something of a landmark which can be dated quite precisely, although in 1833 the building of the new chapel directly against the east front - with consequent blocking of windows - was undoubtedly a factor in the construction of a new billiard room elsewhere in the house.

As one might have expected, the extensive building operations at the Abbey attracted the curiosity of the local population. Not all of it was welcome. Expenses incurred by the steward include payments to one Joseph Jackson for "attending new buildings 3 Sundays to prevent damage being done by Boys etc." [55]

At the earl's instructions an elaborate system of bells was installed for the summoning of servants to the various parts of the house. Twenty-nine bell-pulls in all were to be fitted.[56] A few lengths of copper tubing which contained the wires, and a bell/indicator board in the old part of the house are the only visible survivals.[57] Apart from the many fireplaces, steam heating for the house was provided by "hot-air dispensers" situated in the entrance hall and lobby, and installed under the direction of William Hollins.[58] The cast-iron pipes now visible in the area under the banqueting hall could well be a relic of this. Large quantities of coal were brought in by canal from the Woodhead Colliery, and new coal vaults were being excavated at the Abbey in 1824.[59]

Five illustrations dating from the time of the completion of the new work show the north front of the Abbey from different angles: a pair of magnificent aquatints by Thomas Allason dated 1st May 1819 (**Col. Plates V & VI**), and a pair of engravings by Hopwood, undated but evidently of a slightly later date and probably based on Allason's drawings for they show the building from exactly the same viewpoints. An engraving of the north front in volume 3 of J.P. Neale's *Views of the Seats of Gentry and Nobility* (c.1823) shows the battlements which were added in 1821 (see above, plate 9). The pinnacles either side of the gable appear to have been removed, and then replaced at a later date.

All five illustrations show the asymmetrical form of the north front as it had developed by about 1820. There is the east screen wall, with an octagonal turret at the angle, a small gatehouse where the present drawbridge entrance stands, and another small gateway closer to the house. The north-east corner of the old Lodge, disguised now with battlements, lancets and the square tower at the angle, rises above the polygonal apse of the chapel in front. Behind it is the old round tower, newly-furnished with battlements and a turret, and adjoining it is the great entrance hall with its fine window and double doors. To the west is the Long Gallery and the new drawing-room wing terminating with the octagon stair turret at the north-west corner. Though additional storeys were subsequently built, and radical alterations were made to the hall, many of these features are clearly recognisable today.

Allason's aquatints show a battlemented terrace wall running the length of the north front, broken by a flight of steps leading from the entrance hall down to the lawns. Hopwood and Neale (**9 & 13**) show only a plain low wall and embankment, much as indicated on the basement plan of 1811. This suggests that although Allason intended there to be an embattled wall, it was never constructed. Allason's view from the north-west shows another curious feature.

33. The north front of Alton Towers, *c.*1930

34. The principal front of Snelston Hall, *c.*1911 (demolished 1952)

Running out from the south side of the drawing room is a battlemented building with large Gothic windows. It appears to have a polygonal element built on two levels. This cannot readily be identified with any existing feature at Alton, nor with anything referred to in the Building Accounts for this period. Given the angle from which the drawing was made, it does however correspond approximately with the line of the house conservatory as it would have been seen from this point before the addition of the west wing obscured the view, and the conservatory does indeed have a central octagonal section with pointed Gothic windows. Given that construction work on the conservatory may still have been in progress in May 1819 one is tempted to conclude that what Allason shows is a somewhat fanciful representation of the conservatory as he imagined it would be when finished. The structure does not appear on the Hopwood engraving taken a year or two later from a similar standpoint. No illustrations of the south front of the Abbey dating from this period are known to exist.

As completed in the early 1820s Alton Abbey could take pride of place amongst a number of Gothic residences being built in the vicinity at about the same time. Among these was Ilam Hall, about eight miles away on the Staffordshire/Derbyshire border, built in 1821-6 by John Shaw for Jesse Watts-Russell who was to become a prominent figure in the Gothic Revival and a patron of George Gilbert Scott. About the same distance from Alton, and on the Derbyshire side of the River Dove, stood Snelston Hall built in 1828 to designs by L.N. Cottingham whose studies of "correct" Gothic forms predate Pugin by a decade. It is not unlikely that the north front of Alton Abbey influenced Cottingham's design for Snelston, which included a walled terrace with lawns running down to a lake, a screen-wall with turrets left of the main block, a great hall with a big Gothic window and battlemented gable set transversely, and a polygonal chapel-like structure adjoining it **(33 & 34)**. At first glance it bore a striking similarity to the north facade Alton, but unlike Alton it was swept away in the 1950s and so survives only in prints, photographs, and in Cottingham's own drawings.[60] A similar fate befell Ilam Hall, of which only the gatehouse and hall have survived. As for Alton Abbey, it soon found its way into publications such as Neale's *Seats of the Gentry and Nobility* (1818-23), and West's *Picturesque Views...... in Staffordshire and Shropshire* (1830). Both of these publications speak of Alton as the favourite residence of the Earl of Shrewsbury, "to whom it is indebted for much of its splendour, and the classic taste evinced by its erection" (West). The family were certainly spending more of their time at Alton; for example they were in residence from July 1819 through to February 1820. It had obviously become more than just a summer retreat. The Cellar Book for 1819 reveals an extremely well-stocked wine cellar, suggesting that the Earl was entertaining guests regularly in his new Staffordshire home. To help them find their way, cast-iron milestone plates showing the distance to the Abbey were fixed in various locations in the vicinity of Alton. This was done in the Spring of 1824, and a few of these plates are still *in situ*.[61] The main approach to the Abbey at this

35. The Quixhill Gate. (MJF 1998)

time was via the Quixhill entrance which brought visitors by the shortest distance from the main London-Chester road (the present A523) which they would leave just outside Ashbourne. A new entrance was built at Quixhill in 1822-24. Surprisingly, perhaps, it is not in the Gothic style but consists of two small lodges flanking a free-standing arch with Tuscan columns **(35).** The architect was J.B. Papworth, although the arch may incorporate an existing garden feature.[62] Annotated drawings for the entrance are in the Alton Towers archive collection. From Quixhill visitors would proceed by a long carriage drive through acres of parkland to the edge of the valley gardens where a fine array of ornamental buildings, and finally the Abbey itself, would come into view. Splendid as the house and its surroundings had already become, the fifteenth earl's nephew and successor was to double its size and further enrich its interiors to become the repository of one of the most extensive collections of paintings and fine furniture ever assembled.

3
"𝕿𝕳𝔼 𝕿𝕺𝖂𝔼𝕽𝕾"

'When the reader recollects that the whole of this vista is filled with works of art of the noblest character, or the remains of antiquity of the most interesting kind, he may have some idea of the magnificent coup d'oeil which presents itself and of the difficulty we find in giving anything like an adequate description of it' - **William Adam**

Compared with the restless building activity of the previous decade, the early 1820s saw few major additions being made to the house. For a time the emphasis seems to have shifted to the gardens in the valley to the north-east, incurring considerable expenditures from the Abbey accounts. The principal carriage-drive ran along the edge of the valley so that those arriving by coach would catch sight of the gardens below, and the main garden buildings were sited accordingly. Among these was the Gothic Temple built on a rock - "Thompson's Rock" - on the northern side of the valley. Viewed from this carefully-chosen spot the house appeared, much in the Picturesque tradition, as the crowning glory of the valley with the gardens cascading below (see title page), and it is probable that the later additions of towers and turrets took into account the prospect from the Temple, the alternative name for which is the Gothic Prospect Tower. It was here, on a plinth just in front of the Temple, that a bust of the fifteenth earl who "made the desert smile" was first set up, for it was from here that in life he could view the combined splendours of house and gardens to best effect.[1]

Apart from the house itself the two largest structures were the Flag Tower and the Garden Conservatory (**36 & 37**). Begun in 1810 the Flag Tower took over a decade to complete, and it never in fact acquired the curtain-wall and turrets around the base as illustrated in J.C. Loudon's *Encyclopaedia of Cottage, Farm and Villa Architecture (1833)*. Likewise the Pagoda Fountain, envisaged by Loudon as having six storeys, managed only three; nor did it ever have the forty gas-lit Chinese lamps suspended from the angles of the roofs as shown in Loudon's drawings (**38**). Designed by Robert Abraham and cast by the Coalbrookdale Iron Company, the fountain was nonetheless impressive, though like the Flag Tower it was several years in the making. Modelled on the To-ho pagoda in Canton, it was started in 1826, but even in its truncated form was not completed until the 1830s.[2]

The building of the Garden Conservatory

36. The Flag Tower as envisaged by J.C. Loudon. (Compare no.10)

provides yet another story of progress impeded by changes in design, and, in this case, a change of architect. In the Towers archive there is a drawing of a conservatory bearing no resemblance to the one which was actually built in the garden. In 1818 the Earl directed that the new conservatory in the garden was "to be finished agreeably to Mr Allason's directions",[3] yet Loudon and other contemporaries have no hesitation in assigning it to Robert Abraham. The change in design and architect is reflected in the building accounts. In 1821 stonemason Thomas Bailey was paid £47 for a quantity of unused worked stone: "cornice and frieze for new Conservatory, now useless, the plan having been altered."[4] It was not in fact until 1824 that the models for the domes were ready to be taken to the Britannia Foundry in Derby for casting.[5] There are seven glazed domes with decorative cast-iron glazing bars and

37. The Garden Conservatory. (MJF 1998)

pineapple finials. The central dome is larger than the others and has an earl's coronet for its finial. West of the conservatory an Orangery, known also as the Quarry Greenhouse, was built. It too was given glazed domes.

The Gothic Temple (or Prospect Tower) on Thompson's Rock **(39)** was also completed at this time. Though sometimes incorrectly referred to as the "Chinese Temple" its three-tier

38. The Pagoda Fountain
(a) as envisaged by Loudon and (b) as built. (MJF 1999)

39. The Gothic Prospect Tower.
(MJF 1998)

pagoda-like structure does have a hint of *Chinoiserie* about it, but the forms are all Gothic: "Tudor" arches on slender composite columns on the first two levels, then cusped and crocketed ogee arches at the top, and an encrusted ogee cap. Gothic it therefore is, but the Picturesque Gothick of Batty Langley and Sanderson Miller, a style which by the end of the eighteenth century was dead and buried. Yet Robert Abraham and Charles Talbot saw fit to resurrect it, and they - and the Britannia Foundry - gave the Temple a body of stone and cast iron. Though it is now painted entirely in white, its decorative features and window-frames were originally picked out in gold leaf. It was obviously a favourite feature with the earl, for he commissioned Hollins to make a miniature version of it, with Derbyshire marble columns, to be set up in the entrance-hall of the house.[6] Other water-features constructed at this time included several smaller fountains, cascades, and a "canal" which in reality is a lake constructed to create the illusion of a waterway. Thomas Allason designed a Gothic stone footbridge for it, but this was never built.[7] Instead there is a charming cast-iron bridge with three arches and chains, although the chains are ornamental rather than structural. To feed these and other water features in the valley, conduits were constructed from the lake in front of the house and the pools on the north side of the valley. The dam at the east end of the lake was cleverly disguised to resemble a bridge when viewed across the water. It was given a raised walkway and a Gothic balustrade of pierced stone. Pevsner attributes it to J.B. Papworth who, as we know, designed the Quixhill Lodge. South of the dam-wall, and in line with it, a real bridge was built to carry the road leading from the house to the farm buildings over the driveway descending into the gardens. Known from its white-painted iron balustrade as the "White Bridge", it was built to the design of Thomas Allason.[8] The lake itself, intended originally as a fish-pond, was integrated into the landscaped "pleasure-grounds" at the front of the house. A boat-house was built, and boats were purchased for the lake and for the "canal" in the lower gardens.

Although the house itself contained few examples of elaborate Gothic stonework - most of the Gothic details such as window-tracery having been executed in timber or cast iron - the Gardens afforded ample opportunities for skilled masons such as the Baileys and the Fowers to exercise their talents. An example of this was the Gothic Colonnade which Thomas Bailey was working on between 1813 and 1817. It consisted of a row of eighteen arches on

40. The Loggia. (MJF 1999)

Gothic columns with moulded caps and bases. Standing at the entrance to the gardens, and separating them from the lawns and lake, this "lofty Gothic arcade" formed "a highly ornamental feature of the scenery when viewed from below".[9] Sadly this grand colonnade appears to have had but a brief existence and is not mentioned in any description of the gardens after about 1839. It may be that, being at the top of the valley, the arcade obscured views of the house which by this time had become such an important part of the landscape. Another arcade was built lower down in the garden, but an Italianate one: the *Loggia* consisting of nine round arches on square-sectioned piers **(40)**. On the balustrade above were placed statues of the Nine Muses - almost certainly the work of Peter Hollins - which, according to William Adam were originally in the House Conservatory.[10]

Among the more bizarre garden buildings and ornaments were the so-called "Stonehenge" which in fact bears slight resemblance to the real thing. There was a huge lizard's head carved out of solid rock below the Gothic Temple, complete with a spear-shaped iron tongue and glass eyes; and an imitation cottage roof carved out of rock and fitted with dormer windows and a chimney. These were only two such features which made use of the sandstone rock protruding from the sides of the valley. Grottoes, seats, and even an Indian temple were cut out of it.[11]

The careful planting of trees, shrubs and flowering plants among this curious collection of buildings and ornaments was an equally important aspect of the development of the valley gardens, and one in which the fifteenth earl played a leading role. For example a memorandum dated December 1817 includes orders for the planting of a wide variety of trees and shrubs, the laying of turf and the digging of borders.[12] Landscape gardening of the kind that took place at Alton demanded a high degree of forward vision. Given the slow growth rate of many trees and shrubs, those who laid out such gardens knew that they would not live long enough to see them reach maturity. As things stood in the 1830s there were only saplings and young trees. The buildings and fountains predominated, and this drew criticism from contemporaries including J.C. Loudon who visited in 1826 and 1831 before the architecture could be softened by greenery. He clearly thought that the valley was grossly overcrowded, for his account of it in his *Encyclopaedia* contains an almost dizzying verbal prospect of all that could be seen. He pronounced that "The scenery of the valley of Alton Towers is not here presented as a model for imitation. On the contrary we consider the greater part of it in excessively bad taste, or rather, perhaps as the work of a morbid imagination joined to the command of unlimited resources."

Loudon was, of course, somewhat embittered. He had been asked for advice about the arrangement of the gardens, but in the end Lord Shrewsbury ignored it and went his own way. "Though he consulted almost every artist, ourselves among the number," Loudon complained, "he seems only to have done so for the purpose of avoiding whatever an artist might recommend". Even the inscription on the earl's monument at the head of the valley, "He made the desert smile" - became a source of mirth to some who stood by and looked at the accumulation of buildings and terraces: "And a very polite desert it was not to laugh outright".[13] Benjamin Disraeli was more gentle. In his novel *Lothair* in which Alton Towers becomes Muriel Towers, Lady Corisande is taken to see the gardens, "formed in a sylvan valley enclosed with gilded gates". 'Perhaps too many temples', said Lothair, 'but this ancestor of mine had some imagination'." Gilded gates there were at the entrance to what even Loudon had to admit was an

41. The Choragic Monument.
(MJF 1999)

Enchanted Valley; others have found themselves transported into the dream-world of Coleridge's *Kubla Khan* with its "stately pleasure dome" set amid "gardens bright with sinuous rills".

The Earl who made the desert smile died in 1827 and was succeeded by his nephew John who completed the gardens. He it was who erected the monument to his late uncle: a replica of the monument to Lysicrates built in Athens in 344 B.C. and known as the Choragic Monument. The Alton version was made - almost predictably - of cast iron. It shelters a bust of the fifteenth earl sculpted by Peter Hollins **(41).** The bust carved earlier by Thomas Campbell was removed to the Octagon Sculpture Gallery.

It was the sixteenth earl - "Good Earl John" - who instigated the next phase of additions to the house, and who effected the change of name from "Abbey" to "Towers" in 1832. Work already in progress at the time of his uncle's death had to be completed of course, but John also had ideas of his own. During his time the house expanded in all directions: downwards through the excavation of great coal-vaults and new cellars, upwards through the addition of new rooms above existing ones, outwards with the construction of the new chapel, the west wing and gallery range, and inwards with the building of new kitchens in the courtyard behind the south entrance. All of this amounted to a doubling in size.

The reasons behind these developments are various. Unlike his uncle, Earl John had children, and provision had to be made for them within the house. He was also a collector of paintings, sculptures and fine furniture. There was thus a need for additional space in which to display these treasures. Disaster also played its part: in 1831 what had been the Shrewsburys' principal residence at Heythrop in Oxfordshire was burned down. Surviving furnishings and effects were transferred to Alton where the design and décor of the newer parts of the house emphasised the Talbots' medieval past and their descent from two great Staffordshire families, the Verduns and the Furnivals.

According to the ledgers and account-books the change of name came about in February 1832, from which time the building was referred to exclusively as "The Towers", an apt enough name given the assortment of towers and turrets which already adorned it, and to which more were yet to be added. The abandonment of the name "Abbey" is not too difficult to explain. First of all it was a misnomer: an abbey is by definition a residence for monks or nuns, not for members of the aristocracy, although at the Reformation some abbeys and priories had been converted into family homes while keeping their ancient names. In any event the so-called "abbey style" of Gothic Revival building was but a passing phase, and the collapse of Fonthill in 1825 served to hasten its demise. Though Alton was becoming increasingly castellated by the addition of turrets and bartizans, battlements and - eventually - a fosse and drawbridge, it could not be called "Castle" for fear of confusion with the medieval one in the village. "Hall" was no doubt considered insufficiently grand for such a stately pile, so "Towers" it duly became.[14]

Another factor to be considered in explaining the development of Alton Towers in the 1830s is religion. The Talbots, as already mentioned, were devout Catholics, and following the Catholic Emancipation Act of 1829 Lord Shrewsbury was able to take his seat in the House of Lords and play the kind of role in public life that had been denied to his predecessors. More importantly he became deeply involved with the "Second Spring" of English Catholicism, in particular with the building of new churches for the growing Catholic population in North Staffordshire and elsewhere. Alton became the meeting-ground for those involved in this movement, and, under the direction of A.W.N. Pugin, its internal decorations and furnishings began to reflect the "true" Gothic Revival as distinct from the dilettante and Romantic aspects of the earlier "abbey" style.

Pugin did not come to Alton until 1837, by which time considerable additions had been made to the house by the sixteenth earl. The principal architect and builder from about 1830 was Thomas Fradgley (1801-1883). Born in Middlesex, Fradgley moved to Staffordshire in the 1820s and was eventually responsible for the design and construction of a number of schools, churches, and other public buildings in the Uttoxeter area. It is not known precisely how he became involved with the buildings at Alton Towers. His name first appears in the building accounts in December 1819 when he was paid expenses of £1/2/- for unspecified work. In the following year he was paid a year's salary of £12 from Ladyday (March 25th) 1819 to Ladyday 1820, again for work which is unspecified, and expenses of £2/1/6d for travelling from London to Alton.[15] This latter entry suggests that Fradgley may have been doing work for Lord Shrewsbury before moving from Middlesex, and that it may have been this work which led to his coming to Staffordshire. The Towers accounts record a payment made in 1824 for "painting Mr. Fradgley's office",[16] indicating that he was actually based at the Towers by this time. White's *Directory of Staffordshire* (1834) lists Fradgley as resident at Alton Towers, and also notes that he was clerk of the workhouse, clearly a misprint for clerk of the works, which was his official position at the Towers. With the exception of Bramshall church (1835) all his major public buildings date from the late 1840s onwards, i.e. after he had finished at Alton.

The estate accounts reveal that revenues from the Alton estate alone were not sufficient to finance the huge building programme at the Towers in the 1830s. Between 1831 and 1837 large sums of money - about £1,500 per year - were drafted in from Lord Shrewsbury's private bank account, increasing to more than £3,000 in 1838,[17] and between 1831 and 1837 payments totalling nearly £6,000 were made to Thomas Fradgley. Mid and later nineteenth-century descriptions of Alton Towers[18] credit Thomas Fradgley with the exterior east end of the new (1833) chapel, the chapel ceiling and tower, the corridor linking the chapel with the state rooms, the music room, north and west libraries and poet's bay, the state bedroom and other apartments in the west wing, the black oak corridor running along the east side of the apartments of the west wing, and the clock tower at the south-east corner of the house.

THE GALLERY RANGE

Strangely, none of the nineteenth-century descriptions of the Towers attributes directly to Fradgley the entrance tower and associated galleries on the south side of the house. Although no documentary evidence has so far been found to show conclusively that Robert Abraham

(a)

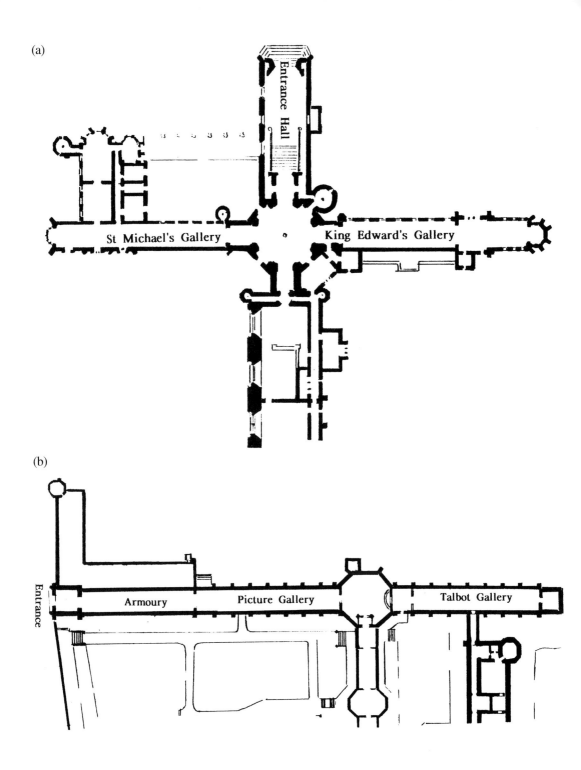

(b)

42. Comparative plans of (a) Fonthill Abbey and (b) Alton Towers, showing the axial system of galleries linked by a central octagon (not drawn to same scale). The combined length of the galleries and octagon at Fonthill was 280 feet; those at Alton 480 feet. (Fonthill plan after J. Rutter, Delineations of Fonthill, *1823*)

(1774-1850) was responsible for any of the extensions to the house, he could possibly have been involved with the building of the galleries which are roughly contemporary with his garden buildings at Alton, i.e. 1824-30. Employed by a number of Catholic families, Abraham carried out work at Arundel Castle for the Duke of Norfolk who was related to the Talbots. By the early 1820s he was already well-established as an architect working in the Gothic style, whereas Fradgley's career as a builder/architect was only beginning. The circumstances are therefore right, while the superb quality of some of the ornamental stonework, particularly the handsome screen at the entrance from the octagon to the conservatory (**45**), suggest an architect well-experienced in Gothic design – albeit "pre-archaeological" – and contrasts with the more prosaic and mechanical structural work done by Fradgley in the West Wing some years later.

The Gallery Range forms the longest of the *enfilades* at Alton Towers, a total of 480 feet, and it embraces five linked elements: the Entrance Tower, the Armoury, the Picture Gallery, the Octagon, and finally the Talbot Gallery at the western extremity. Linked to the house by the conservatory, they were built in stages between about 1824 and 1840 when Pugin added the Talbot Gallery west of the Octagon.

Two buildings already stood on part of the site, about fifty yards south-east of the house conservatory, namely a pair of coach-houses. It is said that the Picture Gallery and the Octagon were originally no more than covered carriage-drives leading from the coach-houses to the southern end of the house conservatory. Carriages would turn around in the Octagon and return to the coach-house via the covered way, leaving passengers to enter the house through the conservatory.[19] Even if this unlikely story is true, it is an arrangement which did not last for very long. What is certain however is that the coach-houses did in fact establish the line of this southern range of buildings, that in an altered form they were worked into the scheme of things, and that the completed galleries did eventually form a new principal route, though by foot, into the house.

The first element to appear was the Octagon, built in line with the coach-houses and just south of the house conservatory. A small extension was built out from the conservatory to join it to the Octagon. The Abbey accounts for 1824 record payments to stonemason Thomas Bailey for work on "additional part of conservatory" also referred to as the vestibule.[20] This is quite clearly the southernmost section of the conservatory which forms a distinctive element adjacent to the Octagon, slightly broader than the main conservatory, and at one time separately roofed. It is therefore probable that the Octagon was under construction as early as 1824.

The Octagon Gallery, and the developing axial system of linked rooms of which it formed a part, is of considerable historical importance. Fonthill Abbey had as its principal feature a great octagon hall inspired by the chapter-house at the Portuguese monastery of Batalha which had been visited and much-admired by both Wyatt who designed Fonthill and Beckford who commissioned it. The Fonthill Octagon stood at the centre of an axial system comprising linked galleries running *en enfilade* north and south, state rooms to the east, and a grand entrance hall to the west. There seems little doubt that Fonthill was the inspiration for the octagon and the linked galleries at Alton (**42**), and both Fonthill and Alton influenced the plan of the New Palace of Westminster with its octagonal Central Lobby. The Alton Octagon is therefore of much more than local significance. Nor was it the only octagonal structure to be built in the area at

43. Ilam Church: the octagonal Watts Russell memorial chapel. (MJF 1995)

this time. In 1819 John Shaw (1776-1832) built an octagonal chapel on the north side of the church at Ilam, barely eight miles away from Alton, for Jesse Watts Russell for whom he was also building Ilam Hall. It has buttresses terminating in crocketed triangular gablets, battlements, and a rib-vaulted stone roof, and its main function was to house a large marble sculpture by Francis Chantrey in memory of David Pike Watts who died in 1816.[21] This too may have influenced the design of the Alton Octagon (**43).**

Examination of the exterior stonework of the Alton Octagon (**44**) shows quite clearly that it was built in two stages, the first dating from c1824, and the upper stage along with the square tower on the south side belonging to Pugin's remodelling of it in 1841-42. The evidence for this is the projecting string-course which represents the original cornice, the different colour of the stonework above it, and the diminutive proportions of the buttresses which were obviously not intended to reinforce walls rising to their present height. In its original form, the Octagon would have risen not very much above the roof-level of the Picture Gallery immediately to the east of it.

Measuring 45 feet across, the Alton octagon - like the one at Fonthill - was modelled on a medieval chapter house, though Wells Cathedral rather than Batalha Abbey appears to have provided the model, notably for the central column which supported the roof. The column was built of fluted stone sections, the flutes being later filled with lengths of bead-moulding to give the appearance of a clustered column. The column supported an elaborate plaster ceiling, moulded to resemble Gothic rib-vaulting (**79**). The principal entrance - and probably the only one to begin with - was via a flight of steps leading down from the conservatory vestibule, the floor of the Octagon being on a lower level than that of the principal rooms to which the conservatory was connected at the north end. When the Grand Entrance via the Armoury and Picture Gallery was built, the exit from the Octagon to the conservatory was adorned with an elaborate triple-arched stone screen, with Gothic tracery, frieze, and cast-iron brattishing along the top. (**45, & Col. Plate VII**)

By the 1830s the Octagon was being used principally as a gallery for the display of sculptures, and

44. The Alton octagon - south-west face. The original roof-level is indicated by the lower cornice. (MJF 1998)

it is thus described in a Tourists' Guide of the mid-1830s[22] which states that the focal-point was a large marble statue by Ceccarini of the painter Raphael. It was done in 1833. Here is another parallel with the octagon at Ilam with its fine marble group, and one may even detect a little neighbourly rivalry. Other sculptures in the Alton octagon included a large bust of William Pitt the Younger (formerly in the gardens), the heads of Jupiter and Juno, and busts by Campbell of the sixteenth earl, and his countess, Maria Theresa. The same observer noted that illumination came from tall lancet windows, only four of which are still *in situ,* two having been replaced by the large five-light window in the south wall and the glazed wooden screen on the west side, as a part of the later remodelling by Pugin.

45. Entrance from octagon to house conservatory. (MJF 1998)

The Armoury was developed out of one of the coach-houses already referred to. The account-books for 1829-30 refer to the coach-houses being converted, one into the Armoury and the other into an adjacent billiard-room, and to the new Entrance Tower **(46)** leading into the Armoury from the eastern end.[23] The north wall of the coach-house, i.e. the one facing the Towers, was re-modelled accordingly, but the southern side remained largely unaltered. The tall archway connecting the two coach-houses, though now blocked, is still discernible. Immediately to the west of the Armoury the Picture Gallery was built to form the link with the Octagon, from which a ninety-degree turn led towards the existing house conservatory and thence to the "T" Room.

46. The Entrance Tower *c.*1930

An important function of the linked galleries was that when completed they constituted a new and impressive route into the house. A new entrance was in any case a matter of necessity. The imposing entrance-hall on the north front was being converted into the principal dining room, its front doors being blocked and replaced by a window. Meanwhile the south entrance was blocked to make the corridor connecting the state rooms with the new chapel. Having arrived by coach from the Quixhill Gate - just as they would have done a decade earlier - guests would now be taken via a new carriage-drive along the east side of the house to the new entrance tower, with its huge doors brightly painted with the Shrewsbury coat-of-arms and Talbot dogs. At Fonthill Abbey William Beckford had employed a liveried dwarf as doorkeeper to emphasise the loftiness of his grand entrance hall. At Alton the Shrewsburys kept a blind Welsh harper to play evocative music as visitors passed under the eighty-foot-high ceiling of the tower and into the Armoury, where the theme was

47. Related to the Talbots by marriage, the Verdun family commemorated in a window in the Armoury. Glass probably by William Warrington. (MJF 1998)

the Talbots' medieval origins. The walls were lined with figures clad in suits of armour standing on stone pedestals, and the lancet windows in the north wall were eventually filled with stained glass by William Warrington depicting members of the Verdun, Marshall and Comyn families, and King William I. Above was a fine panelled ceiling with carved and gilded bosses, only the framework of which is still extant. This no doubt formed a principal part of the carpenters' work carried out by Thomas Harris and Jonas Hartley during the transformation of old coach-house into new Armoury.[24] This concealed the existing coach-house roof, now exposed again following the removal of the ceiling-panels in the 1950s.

Once through the Armoury visitors would experience a change of atmosphere as they passed into the Picture Gallery where a significant part of the sixteenth earl's celebrated art collection was displayed. The gallery was top-lit by cast-iron skylights with ground-glass panels, and the roof was supported on wooden corbels in the shape of Talbot dogs holding shields between their fore-paws.[25] From the Picture Gallery the route into the house led through the Octagon Sculpture Gallery, and thence to the house conservatory which in addition to exotic plants had cut-glass chandeliers, marble statues, and song-birds in gilded cages: altogether four changes of scene along the 150-yard route from Entrance Tower to Drawing Room.

The new entrance-route made ingenious use of different levels in order to create an air of loftiness which was more apparent than real. The galleries themselves are not very tall - they had to nestle behind the domestic blocks without interrupting the skyline, and they were therefore always more impressive on the inside than externally. The carriage-drive was made to slope very gently upwards towards the entrance tower, but to join it well below the principal floor-level of the house itself, and lower also than the Armoury. A broad flight of steps leads up to the tower, and seen through the two sets of very tall doors the Armoury beyond appears much higher than it actually is. The Armoury, Picture Gallery and Octagon are all on the same level, but from the Octagon another flight of steps, more ornate than the first, leads up into the conservatory and the house beyond. Moving onwards through what was in effect a series of tableaux, visitors would also be progressing steadily upwards, wondering all the time no doubt what greater splendours could lie ahead, but as many a visitor was to testify, no amount of imagination could possibly match the reality of what lay beyond: the magnificent State Rooms of Alton Towers.

This gradual ascent from the lower end of the carriage-drive, up through the lofty entrance tower, then up again from the Octagon into the house itself, was all cleverly planned to impress, and it derives ultimately from Wyatt's Fonthill. Impress it certainly did. It may be no coincidence that when Charles Tennyson D'Eyncourt extended his Gothic manor house of Bayons (Lincolnshire) in 1839 he too abandoned his great hall-entrance in favour of a circuitous route by which visitors circled the house and passed through a succession of neo-baronial splendours before reaching the reception rooms.[26]

As part of the general re-ordering which took place in the 1830s the former grand entrance hall on the north front of Alton Towers was given a new lease of life as the principal dining room. Few structural alterations were necessary apart from the removal of the entrance doors and their replacement by a stained-glass window set below the existing one. The superb geometrical staircase was retained, guests now having to descend into the hall from the state rooms and boudoirs to take their places at table when the Shrewsburys entertained in style. Contemporaries were full of praise for this successful adaptation of a very fine feature of the house. The transformation appears to have taken place in about 1834. One subsequent visitor records that he was privileged to stand on the original narrow side galleries of the hall and view a splendid banquet in progress below.[27] Samuel Rayner's meticulous pencil drawing of c.1842 **(14)** shows the room as it was then. Clearly visible on the west wall is Lely's portrait of Charles II, and close to it a very large painting done in 1824 by J.P. Davis showing John Talbot - three years before he inherited the earldoms - and his family being blessed by Pope Pius VII. It earned the artist the nickname of "Pope" Davis. On the wall opposite, and not visible in Rayner's drawing, was a huge canvas by the brothers Ripenhausen depicting an incident which took place in Rome after the coronation of the Emperor Frederick Barbarossa. Said to be the largest picture ever framed in England, the Barbarossa measured 24 feet long and so occupied most of the available wall-space. Both pictures were later re-hung in the dining room after its remodelling by Pugin.

It was around the time of the conversion of the entrance hall that Thomas Willement first arrived at Alton as a supplier of stained glass and other decorative work. Noted principally as a stained-glass artist, Willement (1786-1871) was also a decorative painter, antiquary, and writer on heraldry whose publications included *Regal Heraldry: the Royal Insignia of the Kings and Queens of England* (1821). It was principally heraldic work that Willement was called upon to do at Alton, and he made significant contributions to the interiors of several rooms. These are documented in the Willement papers held at the British Library:[28] a valuable source of information for glass and other items which disappeared from Alton in later years. It was Willement who supplied the glass for the new lower window of the dining room which replaced the doors of the old entrance. The form of this window is known from a number of 1840s prints, but no details of the glass survive apart from Willement's own description which tells us that it was armorial and that it was done in 1834. The lower window, and the larger one above it, were removed by Pugin in 1849.

Running west from the gallery of the dining hall was a corridor leading past the small dining room to the Long Gallery. This was known as the "Glass Corridor", described in its day as one of the most minutely beautiful parts of the whole house. Constructed of oak, the sides of the corridor were panelled and gilt. Small clustered columns of similar pattern to those in the Long Gallery supported a groined ceiling which had ribs of painted and gilt oak. The spaces between the ribs, instead of being filled with lath-and-plaster, were fitted with panels of stained glass.

Willement supplied the glass in 1834, and a coloured drawing of one of the panels exists, confirming contemporary accounts of it as being of a minute geometrical pattern.[29] The drawing shows a lattice-work of blue, with yellow flowers and red circles at the intersections. The corridor was an internal one, illuminated from above by a skylight. The whole corridor would have been bathed in coloured light, while at the west end of it, framed by the doorway of the Long Gallery, the stained-glass portrait of the Black Prince could be seen in the wall opposite.

Willement's other work for Lord Shrewsbury at this time is described in his own words as "the whole of the painted decorations throughout the principal apartments", which must therefore be taken to include the heraldic work in the cornices of the small dining room, a fine heraldic painting on canvas over the arches of the Music Room, visible in pre-1950s photographs (120), and the decoration of the doors of the Entrance Tower and Armoury with huge - and still extant - representations of the Shrewsbury arms, complete with crest, and supporters in the form of Talbot hounds. Willement's work in the chapel, also of the 1830s, is described below, and he returned in 1840 to supply glass and heraldic painting for the remodelled Octagon and the new Talbot Gallery.

The buildings adjoining the Picture Gallery and Entrance Tower on the south side included, as already stated, the Billiard Room (adapted from the smaller of the two coach-houses), and adjoining it to the west was the Sussex Smoking Room - another feature of the "male domain". South of the Entrance Tower and built against the new screen-wall were the Chaplain's apartments consisting of a suite of seven rooms, those on the upper floor being reached by a circular staircase tower.[30] Running southwards from this tower the screen-wall includes an octagonal tower and clock tower. According to Redfern, Fradgley was responsible for the clock tower but not for the turret on its north-west corner.[31] The screen-wall and the south side of the Gallery range partially enclosed the extensive kitchen gardens that were being laid out at this time.

THE NEW CHAPEL

The existing chapel on the north front of the Towers had, from the beginning, been more than a private family chapel, and the Baptism Register[32] dating back to 1820 contains the names of children of Catholic villagers baptised there. The building of a new chapel several times larger than the old one was no doubt intended to make a bold statement about the newly-won freedoms enjoyed by Catholics as a result of the Catholic Emancipation Act of 1829. Lord Shrewsbury was after all the country's leading Catholic nobleman.

The building of the new chapel involved a considerable amount of excavation work east of the old part of the house. Part of the east wall of the house was built up to form the west wall of the chapel, with consequent blocking of windows and the conversion of others into doorways giving access to the chapel tribune which was built to the level of the principal floor of the house. The tribune was of course for the exclusive use of members of the family and their guests who would enter from the State Rooms via the new chapel corridor and through the door in the south-west corner of the tribune, or via the door in the north-west corner which connected with the private apartments and the east terrace entrance (121). Much of the soil and rock excavated from the chapel site was used to make the embankments and terraces to the north and east, and it was at this time that the openings in the north screen wall were blocked, with the exception of what later became the drawbridge entrance. Here a flight of steps was constructed to give access to the new terrace and thence to the chapel. It needs to be remembered that until 1842 the Towers Chapel continued to serve as a parish church for the local Catholic population. As with the old chapel on the north front, there was a need for entrances giving direct access for villagers and estate workers without their having to enter the house itself.

The old chapel with its polygonal apse was transformed into the "Plate Glass Drawing Room". The Gothic windows with their cast-iron tracery were retained, but the iron mullion and lattice-work in the lower half of each frame were removed and replaced with a single sheet of plate glass. On the inside the form of the windows was altered by the insertion of lintels which blocked off the traceried heads of the frames, although these were still visible on the outside **(48)**. On the inside, therefore, the "ecclesiastical" character of the old chapel was obscured.[33] The plate-glass windows, though commonplace by modern standards, were a novelty at the time, techniques for manufacturing glass in large sheets having been developed only in the 1820s and '30s. The name "Plate Glass Drawing-Room" was therefore a proud indication of an amenity that few other

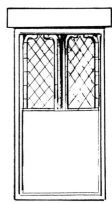

48. Exterior and interior elevations of windows in the Plate Glass Drawing Room showing how they were altered internally to conceal the Gothic heads. (MJF)

houses would have had at this time, and it merited special comment from those who visited Alton in the 1830s and 1840s.[34]

Two architects were involved in the creation of the new chapel. Thomas Fradgley was responsible for the exterior east end, the tower, and the sacristy on the south side. Other work was carried out by Joseph Potter who also worked on S. Mary's College at Oscott until he was replaced by Pugin in 1839. The Towers accounts record a payment of £1,000 to "Mr. Potter, Lichfield", in February 1832.[35] As completed in 1833 the Towers chapel was a capacious rectangular building with a polygonal apse containing the altar. Lined throughout with oak wainscot, it had a panelled but as yet undecorated ceiling borne on cross-beams resting on cast-iron corbels - coloured to resemble wood - in the shape of kneeling angels **(139)**. Apart from the windows in and above the apse, which had stained glass by Thomas Willement, the chapel would have been somewhat sombre and lacking in colour. All this was to change with the arrival of Pugin. Such is the significance of the Towers Chapel in the history of the Catholic Revival and in the career of A.W.N. Pugin that its detailed description and architectural history are reserved for a separate chapter.

The provision of access from the state rooms and family apartments directly on to the chapel tribune involved the construction of a new corridor running from the east end of the

49a. The West Wing (north-facing section) and corner tower. The small turret conceals a chimney. (MJF 1998)

49b. Pugin's satirical treatment of such features in *The True Principles...*, 1843

Drawing Room block. The "Chapel Corridor", as it was called, was the work of Fradgley. The provision of this new feature involved blocking up the arches of the (now superfluous) south entrance to form the southern wall of the corridor, and building a parallel wall on the north side. An internal corridor - the form of which is now lost in the ruins - connected this with the door to the chapel tribune, and doors from the private apartments also led into it. These corridors were used for the display of pictures, waxwork figures by Samuel Percy, and a large mineral collection which included a lump of rock from Napoleon's island prison of St. Helena.[36]

Thomas Fradgley's biggest addition to the Towers was the West Wing. This comprised an extension west of the octagon stair-turret on the north front, and an adjacent west-facing block, joined by a square tower placed diagonally at the north-west corner (49). Externally they are somewhat gaunt: rows of identical straight-headed windows relieved only by the diagonally-placed tower and an octagonal one at the south-west corner of this "L"-shaped block. Fradgley's rather mechanical style contrasts with the earlier and more Romantic work of Hopper and Allason immediately to the east, and with the Puginian additions of the 1840s. It is on the inside that this local architect is seen at his best: as an interior designer and decorator.

The new extensions contained - on the north front - the Music Room, North Library and Poet's Bay; and on the west-facing side the West Library, State Bedroom, Arragon and Chintz Rooms, the Grand Staircase and the south-west octagon tower (50). Unlike the older parts of the house which are built almost entirely of stone, the new extensions were built of brick with stone facings. The one exception was the south wall of the Music Room which was built entirely of stone. The treatment of the basement storey is of interest. The principal floor of the new extension needed to be on the same level as the Drawing Room so as to create a new east-west enfilade of rooms with doors aligned so as to give an uninterrupted vista from the chapel tribune to the new north library. Beyond the existing west end of the house the ground sloped downwards. The bottom level of the new extension was therefore set at 4′6″ lower than that of the old building. This allowed the basement area to be split horizontally, creating a mezzanine between the cellars and the state rooms. What therefore appears on the outside to be a three-storey building is in fact one of four storeys, the large windows on the lowest level of the west wall serving both basement and mezzanine. The mezzanine, it is thought, contained female servants' rooms. The carpenters' work (by Thomas Harris and Jonas Hartley) in the mezzanine, and elsewhere in the "west wing addition" is recorded in the accounts as having been measured off in May 1829 and paid for by the piece up to April 1834.[37] This effectively dates the actual building of the west wing, although its fitting and decoration continued for some years afterwards. Payments to Thomas Fradgley between 1831 and 1835 ran at an average of £1,200 per year which seems consistent with the amount of work being carried out at this time, both on the chapel and the west wing.[38]

ROMANTIC INTERIORS

The grandest of the new rooms was the Music Room, also referred to as the State Drawing Room. The treatment of the south wall included the building of a large polygonal bay window flanked by tall pointed ones. As in the older parts of the house, the glazing was set in wooden Gothic frames. Those in the bay window are somewhat curious in form, particularly at

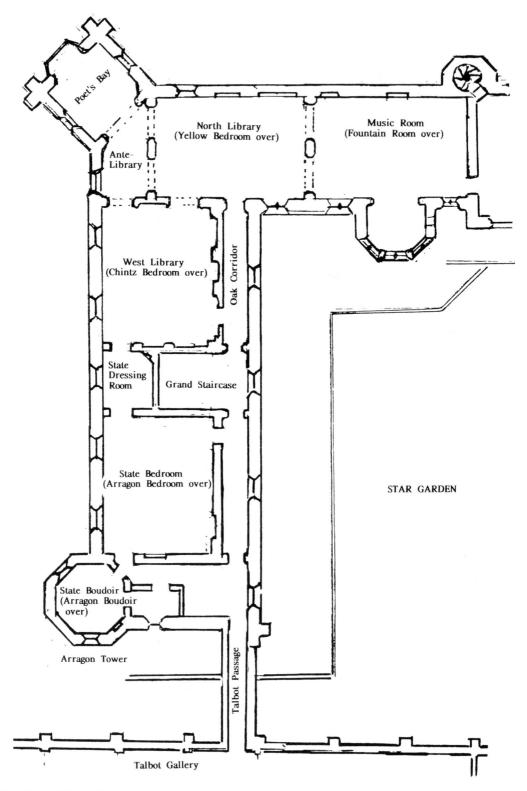

Poet's Bay

Ante-
Library

North Library
(Yellow Bedroom over)

Music Room
(Fountain Room over)

West Library
(Chintz Bedroom over)

Oak Corridor

State
Dressing
Room

Grand Staircase

State Bedroom
(Arragon Bedroom over)

STAR GARDEN

State Boudoir
(Arragon Boudoir
over)

Arragon Tower

Talbot Passage

Talbot Gallery

50. Plan of West Wing. (Survey by M.J. & I. Fisher 1998)

the top of each division which is set with stained glass depicting S. Cecilia (the patron saint of music) King David playing a harp, and angels with musical instruments: hence the designation of this room as the Music Room **(51)**. To the west a pair of open arches gave access to the North Library with the Poet's Bay in the tower at the northwest angle of the building. Another pair of arches, set in the south wall, opened into the West Library thus making it really a continuation of the north one. Music Room, Poet's Bay and the two Libraries were therefore built on an open plan, with no doors - not even glazed ones - to separate one room from the next.

51a&b. Awaiting restoration: the bay-window of the Music Room, with its panels of stained glass. (MJF 1998)

The decoration of these areas was likewise very different from that of the older parts of the house. Flattened "Tudor" arches constructed in plaster over the brickwork and painted white and gold, and ceilings enriched with deeply-moulded Gothic-style plasterwork in pale blue picked

52. Interior of Music Room looking west *c.*1842. The large bay window is on the left, note the richly-moulded ceiling and decorative plasterwork on the arches. (Pencil drawing by Samuel Rayner: Photography by Guy Evans; courtesy of Potteries Museum & Art Gallery, Hanley, Stoke-on-Trent)

out with gold, created an atmosphere of lightness and airiness in contrast with the more ponderous and intensely-decorated ceilings of the "T" Room **(52)**. Huge pier-glasses set strategically in these new rooms reflected the light flooding in from the south-facing windows. Those set in the specially-constructed recesses adjoining the bay-window of the Music Room would have been particularly effective, reflecting images of the Conservatory and the Star Garden as seen through the Gothic tracery of the great window. Artificial light came from two ormolu chandeliers decorated with Gothic motifs, and the furniture included a set of eight Louis XVI gilt chairs, covered with crimson and yellow satin damask.[39] Over the western arches leading to the Library there was a piece of rich heraldic painting by Willement executed on canvas and applied to the wall. It was still *in situ* in 1952 **(136)**. From the undersides of these arches hung crimson drapes with the Shrewsbury crest picked out in gold. They appear in the foreground of an 1870 watercolour which a gives a rare view eastwards from the Library through the Music-room arches towards the "T" Room and Chapel Corridor **(53b & col.pl. IX)**.

The Poet's Bay - an extension of the North Library - was separated from it by another pair of open arches with plaster mouldings, and included the square tower placed diagonally at the north-west corner of the block. A large oriel window in the tower was set with panels of plate glass giving superb views into the grounds. The ceiling, like those of the Libraries, was made of moulded and tinted plaster, while the walls were hung with "a beautiful paper, designed in the style of the illuminated borders of ancient manuscripts, and the windows with curtains of deep sea-green Indian silk: carved chairs of the sixteenth century, with cut velvet seats and backs, inlaid tables covered with ornaments, and a number of valuable paintings by Holbein, Mieris, and others, decorate this beautiful recess".[40]

If Thomas Fradgley was responsible for the treatment of these rooms - and near contemporary descriptions[41] leave little doubt that he was - then Fradgley was an interior designer of no mean talent. He had at his disposal of course a number of skilled carpenters, plasterers and painters who had been working at Alton for many years, gaining valuable experience in the process. The superb quality of their work may be judged from the *NMR* photographs taken as late as 1951, and from the surviving fragments which have stubbornly resisted erosion by wind and water in the years which followed **(53)**. It was all "wedding-cake Gothic", i.e. decorative rather than structural, and as such it had more in common with eighteenth-century antecedents such as Strawberry Hill - though minus the ubiquitous ogee - than with the more archaeologically correct Gothic of Cottingham and Pugin. Yet Cottingham used plaster mouldings at nearby Snelston Hall, and not even Pugin appears to have suggested to Lord Shrewsbury that he should destroy Fradgley's plasterwork and start all over again.

The western range - running from the square tower at the north-west corner to the south octagon tower - follows a very regular and functional plan, all the refinements having been in the (now destroyed) panelling, plasterwork and other decorations applied to the brick carcass. At all four levels a corridor runs along the east side. At the principal and upper levels this was lined with panelling of black oak. It was thus known as the Oak Corridor **(54),** and it is attributed to Thomas Fradgley.[42] On the west side of the block, doors leading from one room into the next were aligned to form another enfilade running from the North Library to the south octagon tower - a distance of about 100 feet. These rooms comprised the West Library, the State Dressing-Room, the State Bedroom, and the State Boudoir in the south octagon tower

53a. Contrasts: View from the North Library through the Music Room and Drawing Room towards the Chapel Corridor, 1999. Note the surviving plasterwork. (MJF)

53b. The same view in 1870 (Watercolour in private collection. See also Colour Plate IX)

54. Contrasts: (a) The Oak Corridor *c.*1930   (b) The same view in 1998. (MJF)

with adjacent ante-room and water-closet. The rooms on the top level were of identical dimensions and consisted of (running north-south) the Chintz Bedroom, Arragon Dressing-Room and Arragon Bedroom, with another Dressing-Room in the octagon tower. The dressing-room and water-closet for the Chintz suite were sited over the North Library and adjoining the square tower at the north-west corner of the block. The principal staircase was situated in the stairwell mid-way along the Oak Corridor. An early description of the new rooms comments on the treatment of the walls, which were "coated over with a composition to imitate richly variegated wood; and being covered with French polish, the figure or flower appears vividly beneath the varnish". This description, which dates from about 1835, makes the observation that the rooms were not then completely finished.[43] The finishing touches here, as in many other parts of the house, awaited the arrival at the Towers of A.W.N. Pugin.

Alton Towers as it stood in 1835 (**55**) comprised five main elements. First there was the new Grand Entrance and the linked galleries which were for display rather than habitation. Then there were the new State Apartments in the West Wing, which, allied to the older "T"-Room and dining-rooms were used on formal occasions when Lord and Lady Shrewsbury entertained on a grand scale, and for the accommodation of distinguished guests. Below these were the kitchens, sculleries and other offices which were the preserve of the domestic servants. The great new Chapel constituted another distinctive area which was both public and private: a family chapel and at the same time the parish church for the Catholic population of Alton and Farley. Finally there were the private apartments in the surviving parts of Alveton

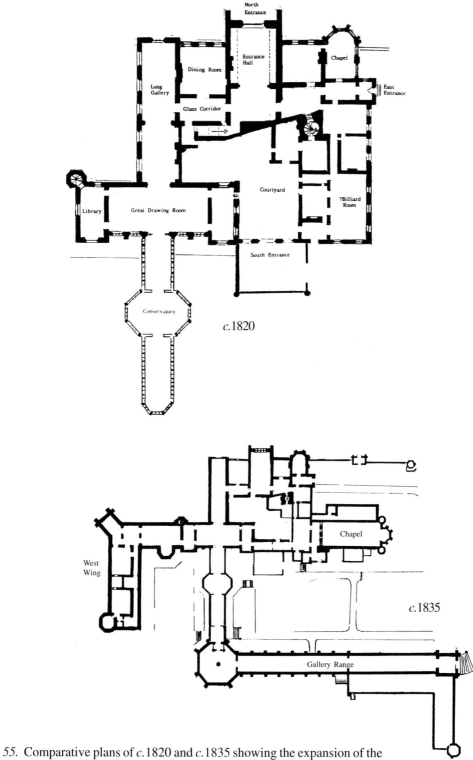

North
Entrance

Entrance
Hall

Chapel

Dining Room

Long
Gallery

East
Entrance

Glass Corridor

Courtyard

?Billiard
Room

Library

Great Drawing Room

South Entrance

Conservatory

*c.*1820

Chapel

West
Wing

*c.*1835

Gallery Range

55. Comparative plans of *c.*1820 and *c.*1835 showing the expansion of the house through the addition of the West Wing, Octagon and Gallery Range, and new Chapel.

Lodge and areas immediately adjacent to them east of the large dining room. In contrast to the Gothic state apartments and the galleries, the private apartments appear to have retained a Classical style of decor, and when the former chapel was converted into the Plate Glass Drawing Room it was significantly "de-gothicised". Notwithstanding the sixteenth earl's undoubted love of Gothic, it seems that when at home in their own rooms the family preferred a more Classical ambience. Such had been the style of their old family home at Heythrop, and a good deal of their time was spent in Rome and in southern Italy where Classical tastes prevailed.

Just as the galleries, octagon and house conservatory were carefully constructed and furnished to make a grand entrance-route into the house, so the State Rooms were linked together to form a majestic progress for guests to take on state occasions, and one that is not difficult even now to imagine or to describe. Descending the grand staircase of the West Wing, they might linger in the two Libraries and perhaps enjoy views of the park and surrounding countryside from the windows of the Poet's Bay until being summoned to dinner. Then, through the series of open arches and glazed doors, they would traverse the Music Room, Drawing Room and Long Gallery as far as the "Black Prince" window, radiant with colours in the light of the evening sun. Finally, via the jewel-like Glass Corridor, they would arrive at the splendid circular staircase leading down into the Hall, ready to dine beneath the plaster-vaulted ceiling and Eginton's stained-glass windows, at a table laden with silver-gilt and the finest china dinner-services. There were huge silver candelabra made by Thomason, a table-centre in the form of a temple made from cut-glass and ormolu, and several Derby dinner- and dessert-services, one of which included 178 plates in green and gold, adorned with the earl's coronet and lion crest.[44] After dinner the ladies might "withdraw" to one of the Drawing Rooms, or promenade the house conservatory illuminated by cut-glass chandeliers. Meanwhile the gentlemen might withdraw to the "male domain" the Billiard Room next to the Armoury, and the adjoining Sussex Smoking Rooms.

If a Ball was being given, it would have been an easy matter to transform the great hall into a ballroom, with musicians stationed on the organ gallery. Alternatively the Gallery/Drawing Room/Conservatory complex could be used. These inter-related rooms had the advantage of being able to be utilised equally well as one large space, or as distinct compartments, according to need, and were therefore readily adaptable to large or modest gatherings.

These vast interiors needed large quantities of furniture and *objets d'art* to fill them. The amazing growth of the house from the modest "Alveton Lodge" of 1810 into the sprawling mansion of c.1840 was accompanied by equally amazing feats of acquisition. It was the purchase of collections which rendered necessary some of the extensions, for example the Gallery Range. In other areas the buildings appear to have come first, for example the West Wing. When it came to emptying the Towers in the Great Sale of 1857 it took thirty days to clear almost 4,000 lots, excluding the contents of the Libraries which were auctioned separately in London. This is comment in itself on the scale of the collections built up by the fifteenth and sixteenth earls over a period of less than half a century.

The fifteenth earl was a Fellow of the Society of Antiquaries. It was he who began to investigate the medieval remains of Alton Castle, initiating the repair and conservation work which was continued by his successors. Though obviously attracted to Gothic styles of architecture, neither he nor his nephew introduced any great quantity of Gothic furniture into the

Towers, until, that is, the arrival of Pugin. Most of the furnishings were of seventeenth- or eighteenth-century date, including much of French and Italian origin. There were several pieces of Louis XIV furniture: a set of ten fauteuils in the Great Drawing Room; a settee, sofa, pier table and cheval screen in the state bedrooms, and other items "in the style of" Louis XIV. The later eighteenth century was reflected in the Louis XVI fauteuils in the Music Room, already referred to; another set of four in the principal State Bedroom, and a number of library tables.

The fifteenth earl is credited with laying the foundations of the huge collection of pictures at Alton. He appears to have taken expert advice in the selection of canvases, for it is recorded that "his choice and taste were directed by Mr Bryan, author of the *Dictionary of Painters*, whose selection of works were amongst the most valuable in the Towers".[46] It was however the sixteenth earl who acquired the bulk of the collection, some of his pictures representing the entire collections of other individuals. By the time of his death there were just over seven hundred pictures in the various galleries, state rooms and private apartments.

The early nineteenth century was a prime time for members of the English aristocracy and gentry to acquire furniture, paintings and collectables from the Continent in the wake of the French Revolutionary and Napoleonic Wars, and although it is not known for sure whether any of the French furniture at Alton Towers came by this route, the time was right. What is known for certain is that on a visit to Rome the sixteenth earl bought an entire collection of nearly two hundred paintings formerly belonging to Laetitia Bonaparte, mother of the deposed emperor. This collection doubtless included items procured by her son during his various military campaigns. The various Italian schools predominated: key works by Caraveggio, Guercino, Tintoretto and Raphael, for example. It also included a self-portrait by Van Eyck, Poussin's *Reposition of the Virgin,* and the Revolutionary artist J.L. David's celebrated *Belisarius.* The Picture Gallery west of the Armoury appears to have been purpose-built to accommodate the Bonaparte collection, which was catalogued and commented upon in 1838 by the noted German art historian Gustav Waagen.[47] It also housed collections of geological specimens such as fossils, crystals, ores and agates, and Italian marbles taken from famous buildings, all displayed in a series of specially-made glazed cabinets.

Some of the furnishings and *objets d'art* may well have been brought to Alton from Heythrop -survivals of the 1831 fire - as well as items brought in earlier. Since Heythrop had been built in the reign of Queen Anne, the tastes there would have been almost exclusively Classical and Baroque. Other items are known to have come from auction-sales. In 1817 Ball Haye Hall, a smallish Georgian house on the outskirts of Leek, was emptied prior to letting, and Lord Shrewsbury's agent attended the auction. What exactly was bought apart from gates and horses is not recorded, but this was an important period in the expansion of the house when Lord Shrewsbury is known to have been giving orders for the purchase of pictures, mirrors, bedsteads and other pieces of furniture.[48] A little later a set of ebony and ivory chairs brought from India by Warren Hastings was purchased by Lord Shrewsbury at a sale of private property belonging to Queen Charlotte, wife of George III, after her death in 1818. These were eventually put in the Arragon Rooms in the West Wing.

The Armoury at Alton Towers - 120 feet long - contained a vast collection of arms and armour put together in a very few years. This collection formed a significant part of the

Talbots' recreation of their medieval past, and although it is possible that some items may have come from other Shrewsbury properties such as Grafton Manor and Heythrop, much of the armour displayed at Alton would have been bought from brokers and dealers. As Clive Wainwright has pointed out, large quantities of armour were brought over to England from the Continent during and after the Napoleonic Wars via the London brokers, some of whom, like Samuel Pratt of New Bond Street, made it a speciality.[49] The 1857 Alton Sale Catalogue lists over three hundred items of armour and arms. There were twenty sets of full armour *(cap-à-pie)*, and two dozen three-quarter and demi-suits, some of them displayed on specially-made figures.

Replica armour may have been included in the Towers collection along with the real thing. It is known that Edward Hull, the Wardour Street broker from whom Lord Shrewsbury bought furniture, dealt with at least one French supplier of replica armour, and Pugin had recourse to him when it came to creating the *pièce de résistance* of the Armoury - the equestrian figure of the Grand Talbot. There were however some striking examples of genuine medieval/Renaissance sets, including a German suit of fluted armour dating from 1550 and a Spanish tilting suit of similar date described as "a magnificent specimen, of the highest quality". Another piece is described thus:

> "*A FIGURE, IN FINE CAP-À-PIE SUIT, consisting of helmet of salade form, with fluted visor and plume, gorget, pauldrons, arm pieces and gauntlets, a very fine breastplate, engraved with foliage and subjects of the Crucifixion and St. George and the Dragon, with rack for lance rest, backplate, tassets, engraved cuisses, jambs, and sollerets, with serrated edges*" (Lot 823)

As well as the full suits there were many separate helmets, breastplates, gorgets, gauntlets and other fragments, and an assortment of weapons. The ornamental gates at the west end of the armoury were covered with arms to the extent that they appeared to have been made from spears and halberds. Yet even in this most "medieval" of the Romantic Interiors of Alton there was room for eclecticism. Alongside the panoply of feudal arms there could be seen "the tomohawk of the North American Indian, the inlaid scimitar of the luxurious Asiatic, and the rude club of the South Sea Savage", while along the sides of the walls there were "a number of old carved chairs and seats of antique form, with a variety of fossils, and immense heads of the elephant, hippopotamus and rhinoceros".[50] Various banners and flags were displayed including the Banner of Ireland borne by the sixteenth earl at the funeral of William IV in right of his office as hereditary High Steward of Ireland: a reminder that the splendours all around, though newly-created and somewhat romanticised, were nonetheless inspired by the realities of the Talbots' medieval past.

The addition of the Talbot Gallery and the reconstruction of the Octagon by Pugin in 1839-41 afforded the opportunity of creating two more contrasting interiors designed to reflect the Shrewsburys' illustrious ancestry. In the meantime the area east of the Great Drawing Room became the location of a remarkable collection intended to catch the eye of visitors on their way to the Chapel, and also to stimulate their devotion. This area comprised the small room immediately adjacent to the Drawing Room, and the Chapel Corridors. The small room - known as the Waxwork Room - contained part of a collection of figures, medallions and tableaux modelled by the noted waxwork artist, Samuel Percy. Born in Dublin in 1750, Percy moved to London in 1777 and established a waxwork studio long before Marie Tussaud arrived in England in 1802. In the Waxwork Room at Alton there were six groups of rustic figures: a market scene, fishwives, a gypsy family, a prize fight, a race of chimney-sweeps on donkeys, and a soldier with a group of peasants. Each one measuring 31" x 21", they were set in carved gilt frames. Other work by Percy included busts of members of the Russian, Prussian and English Royal families, and medallion portraits of Nelson, Wellington, and others; these were located in the Dining Room and the Sussex Smoking Room.[51]

East of the Waxwork Room, two corridors - one leading into the other - gave access to the Chapel Tribune. Here the exhibits became progressively more religious in character. First there was a range of glass cases containing minerals, fossils and shells; then a display of curios such as the State Key of Croxden Abbey and rosaries of Pope Pius V and Mary Queen of Scots. Among a variety of crosses, seals and deeds once belonging to the Brigettine Convent of Sion - restored in 1557 by Queen Mary I in her efforts to reverse the damage done to the Religious Orders by Henry VIII - was a chased silver bell given to Sion by Queen Mary herself, and the Deed of Restoration. Pictures displayed in the chapel corridors included a series of two hundred miniature portraits of celebrated artists, Caracci's *Vision of S. Gregory,* and several other devotional works. A portrait of waxwork artist Samuel Percy himself, and a recent painting of an eruption of Mount Etna, added to the variety. "These corridors", wrote William Adam, "are filled with objects of the highest interest to the antiquary, naturalist, and lover of art, affording a never-failing resource, as well as a delightful lounge, for the family and visitors".[52]

No great house was complete without its Library, and Alton Towers, as we have seen, had three: the small library at the west end of the Great Drawing Room, and the North and West Libraries linked by the Poet's Bay. It is known from the catalogues of the book sales of 1857 and 1858 that Lord Shrewsbury had a collection of over 4,000 books.[53] Though there were some seventeenth- and eighteenth-century works - and a few even earlier ones - most of the books were of the early nineteenth century, and the earl continued to add new titles until about 1850. Compared with Sir Walter Scott's library of 20,000 books at Abbotsford, and a similar quantity collected by William Beckford at Fonthill, Lord Shrewsbury's collection was not massive. There is no knowing, of course, how much of the earl's library at Heythrop was destroyed in the 1831 fire. The Alton collection could well represent the steady building up of a virtually new library around the collection started there by the fifteenth earl, first in the Long Gallery, and then in the small library by the Drawing Room.

It was very much a scholars' library. Novels were in short supply, a notable exception being those of Sir Walter Scott, and the "Poet's Bay" was something of a misnomer for there was little poetry either. History, theology and topography predominated, both English and continental. Included in the topographical collection was the seventeen-volume *Voyages Pittoresques et Romantiques dans l'ancienne France*. Described in the 1858 sale catalogue as "the most extensively illustrated pictorial work ever issued from the press", this was a key text for French medievalists and gothic revivalists. There was also the dedication copy of Pistolesi's *Il Vaticano Decritto ed Illustrato,* in eight volumes (1829-38), dedicated by the author to the sixteenth earl of Shrewsbury. English topography and architectural history were represented by works such as Britton's *Architectural Antiquities,* published in five parts between 1807 and 1826, and fifteen English cathedrals volumes; Dugdale's *Monasticon,* and the four-volume *Remains of Ancient Monastic Architecture in England* (1844) by Joseph Potter, the Lichfield-based architect. As one might expect, there was a copy of almost everything published by A.C. and A.W.N. Pugin. Some of these were in special bindings. Conspicuous by its absence was the dedication copy of A.W.N. Pugin's *Apology for the Revival of Christian Architecture* (1843) which was inscribed with a glowing tribute to Earl John. It may be assumed that this, along with other items of special significance, was withheld from the sale.

Historical books included several relating to Sir Thomas More and Mary, Queen of Scots, and the eight-volume *Journal de la vie privé et des conversations de l'Empéreur Napoléon à Sainte Hélène* by Emmanuel de Las Casas. This is mentioned because it is known from another source that the fifteenth earl acquired the first volume of these memoirs via the architect Thomas Allason almost as it came off the press,[54] and also because it reflects the Shrewsburys' fascination with Napoleon Bonaparte. The writings of Las Casas were an important ingredient in the creation of the "Napoleonic Legend". As noted elsewhere, Lord Shrewsbury kept a piece of rock from the island of St Helena in the chapel corridor, where there was also some curtain-fabric from Napoleon's bed. There was a marble bust of the emperor in the House Conservatory and a bronze figure of him in the Armoury, while in the gardens there was a feature known as Napoleon's Arch.[55]

It comes as no surprise to find that the library of a Catholic nobleman contained volumes of Catholic theology and history, some of them quite old, for example Thomas Harding's *Catholic Answers to Bishop Jewel* (1564-8), a response to the Elizabethan Bishop of Salisbury's *Apology for the Church of England.* It is however intriguing to note that Lord Shrewsbury also had a copy of the 1644 *Directory of Public Worship* which Cromwell and the Puritans introduced following their suppression of the Book of Common Prayer. He also had the 1850 reprint of Richard Hooker's *Laws of Ecclesiastical Polity* - a theological defence by another Elizabethan bishop of the Anglican Settlement. Works by Newman and Pusey, and copies of *The Ecclesiologist,* show that Earl John was attempting to understand current trends in the Church of England, notably the Oxford Movement and the Anglo-Catholic revival.

The Towers libraries contained only a few books which by mid-nineteenth-century standards could be called antiquarian, but they are significant. There was a manuscript copy of the Sarum Missal and Antiphonal, complete with Calendar, dating from the fourteenth century, and a Book of Hours of 1532 printed on vellum with woodcuts coloured to resemble hand-illuminations. There was also a printed copy of a Sarum Missal of the time of Mary I, a rare survival for most had been destroyed during the reign of Elizabeth I. Another rarity was Cardinal Pole's address to Henry VIII *Pro Ecclesiasticae Unitatis Defensione.* Henry had forbidden its publication, and as a consequence of its appearing in print had offered a reward of 50,000 crowns for the author's head. Another formerly-banned book on the earl's shelves was an original (1594) edition of Doleman's *Conference about the Next Succession to the Crown of Ingland.* Doleman was a pseudonym for the English Jesuit priest Robert Parsons, and another co-author was Cardinal Allen of Douai. In the 16th and 17th centuries this book was considered so subversive that possession of it was counted as High Treason. Lord Shrewsbury's copy was inscribed, "This book was bought this 17 of June 1656 at the signe of the Hen and Chickens at a cost of ten shillings".

Although the 1857 Sale Catalogue lists the contents of the private apartments of the earl and countess, few visitors gained access to these areas. An exception was William Adam who was shown the countess's private Boudoir, otherwise known as the Plate Glass Drawing Room, and who left this description of it:

> "... *The BOUDOIR, or private Drawing-Room of the Countess, a delightful apartment, having its walls covered with cabinet paintings, miniatures in rich frames, and water colour drawings of the family: around are cabinets of ivory inlaid with silver, small china ornaments of every form and country, delicate bijouterie, and rich furniture, all arranged with consummate taste, and with that peculiar air of graceful negligence, aptly termed beau désordre, the exquisite elegance of which, feminine taste knows how perfectly to display. From the ceiling is suspended an exquisite chandelier of old Dresden china, valued at a thousand guineas"*[56]

In October 1832 the thirteen-year-old Princess Victoria visited Alton with her mother, the Duchess of Kent, and was entertained to luncheon by Lord Shrewsbury. The future queen was taken into the house via the new Grand Entrance, and she recorded her impressions in her diary:

> "*At one we arrived at Alton Towers, the seat of Lord Shrewsbury. This is an extraordinary house. On arriving one goes into a sort of gallery filled with armour, guns, swords, pistols, models, flags etc. etc. then into a conservatory with birds. We lunched there and the luncheon was served on splendid gold plate. At ½ past 2 we left*".

Princess Victoria did not record what she ate on this occasion, but we do know that the glasshouses at Alton Towers were producing some exotic fruits in the 1830s. There appears to have been a little friendly rivalry between Lord Shrewsbury and the Duke of Devonshire at Chatsworth who something of a horticulturalist. In 1834 bananas were being grown at Alton, and Lord Shrewsbury's chaplain, Dr. Rock, ventured to send one to the Duke, who had evidently never seen one before. He received the following response:

> "*My Dear Sir,*
>
> *A thousand thanks for the Banana, it arrived quite safe and I am delighted to have the opportunity of seeing that most beautiful and curious fruit. It is the admiration of everybody and has been feasted upon at dinner today according to the directions.*
>
> *Believe me,*
>
> *Very sincerely yours*
>
> *Devonshire*" [57]

In 1840 there was a visit by Queen Adelaide, widow of William IV. The Royal party was met at Quixhill Lodge by a mounted assembly of 300 local gentlemen who formed a procession along the drive, past the gardens, and up to the Entrance Tower. A feast was provided for the tenantry. By this time the State Rooms of the West Wing were complete, and it seems as though the earl made the royal visit an occasion on which to show off the interiors of the house. A hundred beds were made up for the accommodation of distinguished guests.[58]

By the 1840s it was possible for members of the public to visit the Towers by prior arrangement with Richard Orrell, tenant of the Shrewsbury Arms at Farley, who had sole charge of admissions by ticket. The grounds were open from Monday to Friday, and the House itself was shown on Tuesdays and Thursdays.[59] Thus the fame of Alton Towers and its fabulous collections gradually spread, so that by the time of the 1857 sale some individual items were well-known. Amongst a number of marble tables highlighted in the catalogue was one described as "The Celebrated Mosaic Roman Table". There was also a triptych painting by Holbein, with the Virgin and Child in the centre panel, and S. Catherine and S. Barbara on the doors. The outside was painted with the arms of Sir Thomas More, to whom it was said to have been presented by the artist (56). The "Thomas More Triptych" was kept in the Fleur-de-lis Room at Alton, along with a more celebrated one: a twelfth-century Limoges enamel triptych which became known generally as "The Alton Towers Triptych" (57). This latter item was among the few pieces of medieval art acquired by Lord Shrewsbury, probably at the instigation of Pugin who was himself a great collector of medieval artefacts some of which were used as study-pieces and models to instruct Oscott students and Hardman's craftsmen in "the real thing". Many of these items were brought from the Continent aboard Pugin's own boat. It is highly likely therefore that he would have encouraged Lord Shrewsbury to collect appropriate items both for the Towers and for the churches of the Pugin-Shrewsbury partnership. One such item was a fifteenth century Flemish altarpiece of carved wood which the earl thought might be suitable for S. John's, Alton. Unfortunately it did not fit in with the scheme of the east wall as already determined by Pugin. *"It would have blocked up the east window,"* he wrote. A home for it was found at the east end of the north aisle at S. Giles', Cheadle. *"It will fill up the blank wall against the sacristy most comfortably. It is just the place for it"*[60]

Lord Shrewsbury is also known to have done business with the Bond Street antiques dealer, Samuel Pratt, from whom he bought an altar-cross, almost certainly of medieval date, in 1840. Pugin congratulated him on obtaining such a fine thing:

> *"....The cross that you have secured at Pratts is so exquisitely beautiful that it may be considered dirt cheap at the price your Lordship gave. It is indeed a glorious acquisition"*[61]

Pugin thought it would be suitable for S. John's and promised to design a pair of candlesticks to match. To emphasise the stylistic continuity between the Middle Ages and his own revival of "the real thing", Pugin would often place his own designs in juxtaposition to medieval ones as if to challenge the observer to tell the difference. He also believed that an architect should be responsible not only for the structure but also for the sympathetic decoration and furnishing of a building. The application of such ideas, at Alton Towers and elsewhere, provoked more than one conflict of taste between the earl and his architect, but it also led to some of the finest achievements of the Gothic Revival.

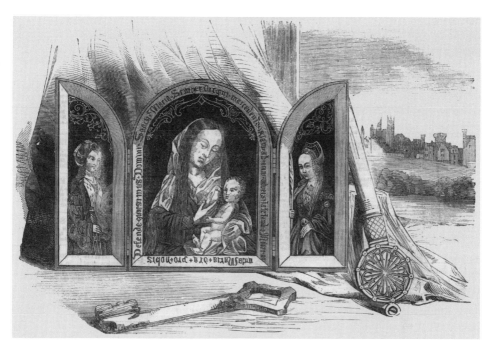

56. The Thomas More Triptych. (Illustrated London News, 5th September 1857)

57. The Alton Towers Triptych. (Trustees of the Victoria & Albert Museum)

4
EARL AND
ARCHITECT

"Pugin is decidedly <u>the</u> Catholic Architect of the day, with more zeal, talent, judgement and experience than perhaps any man so young has hitherto acquired in any profession whatever"
- Lord Shrewsbury [1]

In 1835 few people had even heard of Augustus Welby Northmore Pugin (1812-1852). A decade later he was accounted the country's foremost exponent of the Gothic Revival **(58)**. Author of several influential books, designer of cathedrals, parish churches, country houses; furniture, wallpaper, textiles, ceramics, jewellery and much else, Pugin was both innovative and controversial in his "passion for Gothic". A convert to Catholicism, he had become convinced that Gothic was the only true Christian style of architecture, that its basic principles needed to be rediscovered and applied, and that Gothic architecture could also be a powerful tool in the re-conversion of the English to the Catholic Faith of their forefathers. Thus Pugin gave to Gothic architecture the high moral and theological dimensions that were largely absent from the work of earlier architects of the Gothic Revival.

Pugin was also driven by technology. He demanded the highest standards of craftsmanship, yet saw no reason why, once a design had been worked out, the actual production of an item of brassware or woodwork should not be carried out with the aid of machinery. In this way he differed from many who followed him, such as the pioneers of the Arts and Crafts Movement who reacted against machine-industry. Pugin believed that modern technologies could come to the aid of the Gothic designer, making his work more generally available, and less costly. This was at least a part of the message of the "Medieval Court" at the Great Exhibition of 1851 where Pugin the designer joined forces with manufacturers such as Minton, Hardman and Crace. The pointed arch was not incompatible with the Railway Age which Pugin embraced enthusiastically.

In spite of his creative genius and legendary capacity for hard work, it is unlikely that Pugin would have come to occupy centre-stage in the world of architecture and design had it not been for the patronage of the sixteenth Earl of Shrewsbury for whom he carried out a number of projects which helped to establish his reputation and bring him into contact with other prospective clients. Among the most important of these were his improvements at Alton Towers, and the churches and other buildings of the Shrewsbury-Pugin partnership in Alton village and the nearby towns of Cheadle and Uttoxeter.

"If a cheese is sold for twopence-halfpenny a pound, how much will a rood-screen cost?" demanded Pugin when in the interests of economy Lord Shrewsbury proposed to let a local carpenter loose on the magnificent screen at S. Giles', Cheadle, rather than replace the expert woodcarver who had left it half-finished. To hammer home the view that the earl was "cheese-paring" Pugin illustrated his letter with cartoons of a rood-screen and a cheese.[2] He

58. Augustus Welby Northmore Pugin, 1812-1852. Portrait by John Rogers Herbert (1810-1890) in the Palace of Westminster.

also asked the question, *"What is the relative value between the price of cheese at Cheadle and Elizabethan grates?"* - a reference no doubt to the Elizabethan-style chimneypiece which the earl had recently installed in the small dining room at Alton Towers **(59)**, and upon which no expense had apparently been spared. Pugin clearly disapproved of the introduction into the Gothic palace of any reminder of "that female demon, Elizabeth,"[3] especially if it meant cutting back on his beloved S. Giles'.

59. Contrasts: (a) The small dining room in the 1930s, with the Elizabethan-style chimneypiece. (The Lewis Family Collection)   (b) The same room in 1998 (MJF)

That a young architect should have been able to address England's premier earl in such an abrupt manner, and get away with it, suggests a relationship somewhat deeper than the purely professional one of architect and patron, and so it was. Their correspondence ranged over many subjects such as the Irish Question, Chartism, the restoration of the Catholic hierarchy, and family matters too. They consoled each other in bereavement as for example when the earl and countess lost their younger daughter Gwendalyn aged only 23, and after Pugin's second wife, Louisa, died in 1844. When Pugin plunged himself into a fit of black despair following the frustration of his intention to marry Mary Amherst - whose mother had put her in a nunnery to thwart the plan - it was to Lord Shrewsbury that he poured out his heart. "I cannot eat, I cannot work," he wrote in April 1846. "I propose quitting England and giving up my profession .... I am a broken man, and it is no use trying to go on."[4] It was in fact his work that came to the rescue. A few days later he wrote to the earl, "I was at Alton and Cheadle Thursday and Friday; the sight of that glorious spire somewhat revives me."[5] Elsewhere he speaks of Cheadle as "my consolation in all my afflictions", and it is not difficult to understand why. Such pendulum-swings of mood were not untypical of Pugin, and they run through his correspondence and his writings. Violent outbursts of passion - whether on the subject of architecture and design, church furnishings, music or the conduct of worship - brought him frequently into conflict with patrons, clients, contractors and churchmen. Impatient with those who did not understand or agree with his principles, Pugin would sometimes push his ideas to the very limit, and in this way he even jeopardised the goodwill and friendship of his most ardent admirer - the sixteenth Earl of Shrewsbury.

Pugin's French father, Augustus Charles Pugin - had come to England in about 1792 as a refugee from the Revolution. He believed that the Pugins were related to a noble Swiss family,

60. John Talbot (1791-1852), Sixteenth Earl of Shrewsbury Posthumous engraving by Joseph Lynch after a painting by Carl Blaas, and dedicated to Bertram, seventeenth Earl of Shrewsbury. (Alton Towers Archive)

the Corbières of Fribourg. This appears to have been the origin of the *corbeau* or crow used by the Pugins as an heraldic device and adapted by the younger Augustus into the "temple-haunting martlet", a bird which because it lacks feet is never still. Combined with the motto *en avant* - "Forward!" - it was a fitting emblem for one whose life was characterised by ceaseless activity. A.C. Pugin was a skilled artist and illustrator, and it was from him rather than through much formal schooling that his son developed the acute powers of observation and the ability to draw accurately and quickly which were to be the foundation-stones of his career as a designer and architect. At the age of 15 he was designing furniture for Windsor Castle, while his interest in the theatre led him to design stage-sets and also to work as flyman at the Covent Garden Opera House. In his subsequent career as a designer of ecclesiastical and secular interiors, Pugin never lost his sense of the dramatic.

There is not a shadow of suspicion about the noble pedigree of John Talbot **(60)** who in 1827 inherited the earldoms of Shrewsbury, Waterford and Wexford from his uncle Charles. Born at Grafton Manor in Worcestershire on March 18th 1791, Earl John could trace his ancestry back to the first Earl John, "The Great Talbot" who had won fame - and his earldom - on the battlefields of France during the reign of Henry VI *(Col. plate I)*. The Talbots also acquired, by marriage, the lands and titles of the Verduns and Furnivals which included the Alton estate. There was a Welsh connection too. In the thirteenth century Gilbert Talbot, grandfather of the first Baron Talbot, married Gwenllian, daughter of Rhys ap Gruffydd, Prince of South Wales. One consequence was that the Talbots assumed the arms of the Princes of South Wales: *gules, a lion rampant or, within an engrailed bordure of the last,* to which they attached the motto *Prest d'Accomplir* ("Ready to accomplish"), and supporters in the form of Talbot dogs **(61)**. Gwenllian, in its anglicised form of Gwendalyn, became a favourite name for Talbot daughters.

61. The Talbot coat-of-arms on the Entrance Tower. (Alton Towers Archive)

The sixteenth earl was educated at Stonyhurst and St. Edmund's College, London. While at St. Edmund's he headed a rebellion amongst the boys, as a consequence of which he was asked to leave. His education continued at the hands of private tutors, and in 1812 he made a prolonged overseas tour, taking in Spain, Portugal and the Mediterranean. In 1814 he married a cousin, Maria Theresa, eldest daughter of William Talbot of County Wexford *(Col. Plate XII)*. By the time he succeeded to the titles two children had been born: Mary (1815) and Gwendalyn (1817).

Though prior to 1827 he had been plain "Mr. John Talbot", the sixteenth earl slipped easily into the role of *grand seigneur.* What is known of his life presents us with a jumble of apparent contradictions. He spent a fortune extending and completing Alton Towers, yet chose to live abroad for months on end. He filled state rooms and boudoirs with the most exquisite furniture and paintings, yet his own private room at Alton was as austere as a monastic cell.[6] Huge sums were expended on works of art, yet he considered envelopes an extravagant innovation, continuing simply to fold his letters and seal them with wax.[7] His concern for the poor was demonstrated by his support of schools and charities, and in the fact that he chose to build a hospital and a school for poor children rather than found a monastery. Work was created for the unemployed in the "hungry forties", including the laying of sixty-six miles of drives and gravelled paths in the grounds of the Towers; but an estate-worker who dared to dig his garden on a Sunday was turned out of his cottage. When the earl entertained on a lavish scale, and the Armoury and Galleries were banked high with flowers and plants, the gardeners had to be up in the early hours of the morning to begin tidying-up as soon as the last carriage had departed: not a trace must be left by breakfast time.[8]

Yet the sixteenth earl was remembered by succeeding generations as "the Good Earl", whose private affairs were governed by a near-ascetic rule of life, and whose public actions were directed increasingly towards the advancement of Catholicism. This accounts for yet another apparent contradiction. Though many influential Catholic families belonged to the landlord class, the stronghold of the Tory Party, Lord Shrewsbury declared, "I always was, and hope I always shall be a Whig; by which I mean an advocate for the greatest possible degree of civil liberty, and the greatest possible amount of religious toleration consistent with the institutions and condition of the country".[9] Like many of his co-religionists he could hardly forget that the Tories were the party of the Established Church and therefore generally opposed to Catholic Emancipation.

The circumstances under which Lord Shrewsbury first met Pugin are in themselves controversial. According to Pugin's principal biographer, Benjamin Ferrey, the earl first became aware of Pugin's genius as a designer as early as 1832. When looking for furniture for the new rooms at Alton Towers he visited Edward Hull, a leading London dealer, and noticed some drawings lying on a table in his shop in Wardour Street. On being told that the drawings were by A. Welby Pugin the earl asked if an introduction could be arranged. Having met Pugin for the first time, Lord Shrewsbury engaged him to carry out additions and alterations at Alton Towers.[10] Pugin certainly designed furniture for Hull, and bought items from him, but Hull did not move into Wardour Street until 1834, so Ferrey may have the date wrong. Alternatively, given that he was writing in 1861, he could have assumed that Hull had always been based in Wardour Street.

If indeed the initial encounter between the earl and the architect took place in 1832 it is all the more remarkable because Pugin was then only 20 years old and by that date he had neither embraced the Catholic Faith nor discovered the "true principles" of Gothic architecture. It does, however, seem unlikely. The first reference to Lord Shrewsbury in Pugin's diaries is under 3rd October 1836: "Sent answer to Lord Shrewsbury", indicating that some contact had already been established, but probably quite recently. It is possible that the earl's domestic chaplain, Dr Daniel Rock, had a hand in this. Like Pugin, Rock was a student of Gothic architecture and the pre-Reformation English Church, and in 1836 he wrote to congratulate Pugin on his newly-published book, *Designs for Gold and Silversmiths.*

Pugin visited Alton for the first time in September 1837, and stayed for four days. A month later he wrote in his diary, "Began Lord Shrewsbury". Thus began a working relationship between Pugin and Lord Shrewsbury that was to last for the rest of their lives, and which influenced architectural tastes and religious affairs long after their deaths. Although the Alton building accounts and related papers are by no means as detailed for the 1840s as they are for the earlier periods of building, this is more than adequately compensated by Pugin's diaries and the surviving correspondence between Pugin, Lord Shrewsbury and others relating to building, furnishing and decorating work at the Towers during this period. Consequently far more is known about Pugin's work at Alton than about that of any of those who preceded him as architects to the earl.

There was much at Alton Towers that would have irritated Pugin: a veritable catalogue of transgressions committed by his unenlightened predecessors who were ignorant of the "true principles" of Gothic architecture which he was beginning to rediscover and apply. These principles included honesty with regard to materials, so wooden pillars painted to look like stone, cast-iron roof-trusses painted to look like wood, and plaster vaulting - of which there was an abundance at Alton - were an abhorrence. Yet Pugin never seems to have suggested to Lord Shrewsbury that he should pull down what was already there at Alton and re-build in the correct manner, with the one exception of the great Dining Hall which to Pugin became a non-negotiable matter of principle and which was the subject of considerable disagreement between architect and patron. Elsewhere in the house the author of *The True Principles* had to tolerate existing plaster shams and cast-iron roof structures, and even acquiesce in the creation of new ones. Meanwhile Pugin's structural additions and alterations on the exterior of the buildings, with their correctly-formed weatherings, strings, windows and buttresses, challenge the earlier work of Hopper, Allason and Fradgley as effectively as a page from his influential book, *Contrasts* (1836), in which the "true" Gothic structures of medieval times are set side-by-side with some of the worst examples of the "debased" architecture of the modern age.

This kind of satire was continued in *The True Principles of Pointed or Christian Architecture* published in 1841. Here Pugin ridiculed the so-called "Abbey" style of country house with its mock-ecclesiastical exteriors. As for the so-called "castellated" style of mansion, Pugin was quick to point out the absurdities of "portcullises which will not lower down, and drawbridges that will not draw up". It is difficult to avoid the conclusion that he was poking gentle fun at Alton Towers when he wrote of the pointless multiplication of turrets:

> *"In buildings of this sort, so far from the turrets being erected for any particular purpose, it is difficult to assign any destination to them after they are erected, and those that are not made into chimneys seldom get other occupants than the rooks"* [12]

Pugin's most penetrating remarks about castellated houses read uncannily like a description of the Grand Entrance at Alton with its heavily-studded doors, and the Armoury bristling with weaponry yet leading to the state apartments via a Conservatory where all pretence of fortification was abandoned:

> *"..,On one side of the house machicolated parapets, embrasures, bastions, and all the show of strong defence, and round the corner of the building a conservatory leading to the principal rooms, through which a whole company of horsemen might penetrate at one smash into the very heart of the mansion! - for who would hammer against nailed portals when he could kick his way through the greenhouse?"* [13]

Yet in spite of such idiosyncrasies which he learned to live with - and some of which he managed to correct - there is no doubt that Pugin was thoroughly at home at the Towers. The diaries record frequent visits between 1838 and 1851, some of them spread over several days. In November 1845 he wrote to Lord Shrewsbury, *"I expect to be at Alton next week .... I am sure I do not need much inducement to stay, for I am nowhere so happy"*. [14]

Pugin's opinion of Thomas Fradgley, his predecessor as architect to Lord Shrewsbury, is not recorded, although in another context he had some unflattering things to say about Joseph Potter, the architect who collaborated with Fradgley in the design of the Towers chapel. Potter had been a pupil of James Wyatt whom he succeeded as architect at Lichfield Cathedral. To Pugin's mind, Wyatt was "a monster of architectural depravity", and after a visit to Lichfield in 1834 he wrote of Potter, *"... The man, I am sorry to say, who executed the repairs of the (cathedral) building was a pupil of the wretch himself, and has imbibed all the vicious propensities of his accursed tutor without one spark of even practical ability to atone for his misdeeds."* [15]

Fradgley seems to have escaped such censures; at the same time Phoebe Stanton's statement that his displacement by Pugin caused him much annoyance appears to be unsubstantiated. Fradgley was in any case still undertaking work at the Towers in 1840 although, newly-married to Clara Warner of Bramshall Manor, he had by this time set up his own home and was establishing his own architectural practice in the Uttoxeter area.

A key figure at Alton during the Pugin years was John Bunn Denny (1810-1892) who was clerk-of-works from 1839 to 1856. He was also directly involved in Pugin's building works in Alton village and at S. Giles', Cheadle. After the death of the seventeenth earl in 1856 Denny emigrated to Australia where he assisted the architect William Wardell as well as building several churches in his own right, some of them reflecting the strong influence of Pugin. During his years at Alton it was Denny's responsibility to carry out Pugin's instructions regarding the building and decorating, to report progress to the earl, and to handle payments to the various workmen.[16] Among the familiar names still on the payroll at this time were masons Peter and John Bailey, painter and glazier Thomas Kearns, and Thomas Harris the carpenter. A new generation of Finneys was following in the footsteps of William Finney who had executed most of the joinery in the Long Gallery in the first phase of extensions under the fifteenth earl, while plasterer John Dixon had been joined by Samuel Firth whose skills were to prove particularly useful to Pugin. Brickmaker William Alsop - another veteran of the pre-1820 years - was still turning out huge quantities of bricks for the Towers and other buildings of the Pugin-Shrewsbury partnership: 59,000 of them in 1840 alone. [17]

Pugin came to know some of these men personally. Kearns was to prove especially skilful in applying Pugin's coloured stencilling-designs to walls and other surfaces. Though Harris was considered not good enough to finish the rood-screen at Cheadle, Pugin was quite happy to use him for less demanding projects: "he is a capital mechanic in tracery and he is excellent but he has not the least idea of cutting foliage".[18] In December 1841 Pugin arrived at Alton to hear the church bell tolling for the funeral of Peter Bailey who had done so much of the fine masonry at Alton. "He died very penitent and received all the Sacraments", Pugin wrote to Lord Shrewsbury. "I designed a stone cross to be placed over his grave. He is buried under the yew tree near the hospital with a simple inscription cut on the cross".[19] Sadly the memorial no longer

62. S. John's Churchyard, Alton; burial place of Peter Bailey and many others who worked for Lord Shrewsbury. S. John's church, and the castle, can be seen in the background. (MJF 1997)

exists, but Pugin included a small sketch of it in his letter. S. John's churchyard contains many other memorials of the period which reveal unmistakably the hand of Pugin and the trouble he took to ensure that the Catholic families of Alton did not lack an appropriately-inscribed headstone in the "true" style **(62)**. On Christmas Day 1845 Louisa Orrell, daughter of Richard Orrell of the Shrewsbury Arms, died at the age of sixteen, and within a month her two elder brothers were dead too - presumably from some epidemic. Orrell was a respected tenant of Lord Shrewsbury who entrusted him with handling admissions to the gardens and engaged him to provide food and drink at the tenants' feasts and other special occasions. Pugin was commissioned to design a memorial for the Orrell children: a fine ledger-stone with a cross, and the three names carved in his characteristic Gothic lettering[20] **(63)**. A standard was set for memorials which continued well after Pugin's death in 1852. When the painter Thomas Kearns died in 1858 he was buried under a coped ledger-stone in similar style to that of the Orrells.

The work which Pugin carried for the earl in Alton village was as important to him as anything he did at the Towers. In some ways it was more so, for it was in the village that Pugin was able to give expression to the social and moral aspects of Gothic architecture. Lord Shrewsbury's great friend and Catholic landowner Ambrose Phillipps, of Grace Dieu in Leicestershire, had wanted him to build a monastery on his estates in imitation of his remote ancestor Bertram de Verdun who had built Croxden Abbey in the twelfth century. A monastery, and a Cistercian one at that, emerged from the Shrewsbury-Phillips-Pugin partnership, but it was built near the Phillips estate and was named Mount Saint Bernard. For Alton village Pugin and Shrewsbury had a much more practical idea.

To Pugin's mind, monastic ruins such as those at Croxden, and the parish churches despoiled by "the sacrilegious tyrant Henry VIII and his successors in church plunder", represented the ugly side of Protestantism as destructive of a noble heritage of art and architecture. Equally abhorrent to Pugin was the nineteenth-century workhouse in which those "convicted" of poverty were treated no better than criminals,[21] instead he proposed

63. The Orrell memorial, S. John's churchyard, designed by Pugin in 1846. (MJF 1998)

64. The Hospital of S. John, Alton: Birds-eye view of the buildings as Pugin planned them *(The Present State of Ecclesiastical Architecture, 1843).* The chapel and the warden's lodging (on the left) were built as shown, but the design of the other buildings was altered. (Photo: Graham Miller)

a revival in Alton of the medieval "hospital" in which the poor would be treated with dignity and respect. By 1842 some of the hospital buildings were complete, including the chapel, dedicated to S. John the Baptist **(64)**.

Adjacent to the hospital, and separated from it by a deep dry moat, were the ruins of Alton Castle, another tangible reminder of the Talbots' Verdun ancestors. For reasons that have never been firmly established, the sixteenth earl resolved to rebuild it, preserving parts of the ruins but clearing away others. Pugin was, of course, put in charge of the operation, with Denny as clerk-of-works. During the course of the clearing operations a twelfth century thurible was discovered, and one would love to know what became of it.[22] On the earl's instructions, the castle chapel was built directly above the crypt of its twelfth-century predecessor, and this remains one of the most exquisite of Pugin's creations, with its lofty stone-vaulted roof crowned with coloured tiles **(65)**. As the 1840s wore on, work at the hospital and the castle slowed down, partly because the energies of clerk and work-force were being siphoned increasingly into the building and adornment of S. Giles', Cheadle (1841-46). Lord Shrewsbury began to feel the strain, for his wealth was not limitless. In 1843 he proposed some curtailments at the hospital, including the scrapping of the lodging for retired priests. They could be accommodated at the castle instead. This very practical suggestion drove Pugin to despair, for in his eyes the design of a building should reflect its purpose, and retired priests do not live in castles;

> *"..I implore and entreat of your Lordship if you do not wish to see me sink with misery to withdraw that dreadful idea about the alteration to the hospital. I would sooner jump off the rocks than build a <u>castelated</u> residence for <u>priests</u>. I have*

been really ill since I read the letter. The hospital as designed would be a perfect building .... I can bear things as well as any one but would almost as soon cut my throat as to cut that hospital to pieces".[23]

In the end neither the hospital nor the castle were completely finished, but they constitute one of the most beautiful and tranquil compositions of buildings that Pugin ever designed, and in a superb location, with the castle perched on the edge of a precipice like some Rhineland *Schloss.* For Pugin and Shrewsbury, however, success was measured in spiritual rather than aesthetic terms. In 1841 Pugin wrote enthusiastically to the earl - who was in Italy at the time - about the combined effects upon the village of the new buildings and the new chaplain, Dr. Henry Winter:

> *" ..Nobody now dies a Protestant at Alton even if they do not live Catholics. He (Dr Winter) is certainly a most indefatigable man and does not spare himself at all in the good cause..... The face of the village is catholicising. I think that the hospital is in the most lovely situation possible. I hope when Cheadle is finished that it will then be completed. It will be the most perfect thing in England".*[24]

The Anglican vicar of S. Peter's, Alton, the Revd. John Pike-Jones was less enthusiastic about the growth of Catholicism in the village, and he accused Dr Winter of proselyting in the way his predecessor, Dr. Rock, was alleged to have done. It could of course be argued that for three hundred years the Pike-Joneses of this world had had things very much their own way, with the benefit - until very recently - of penal laws to punish nonconformity. The Catholic Emancipation Act had helped to create a more level playing-field, and not unnaturally the newly-liberated Church was rejoicing in its "Second Spring". Yet Lord Shrewsbury had to steer something of a middle course. Although a Catholic, he held the patronage of S. Peter's as part of the Manor of Alton, and in this capacity had appointed Pike-Jones to the living.

65. Alton Castle - the chapel.
(MJF 1998)

On his visits to Staffordshire Pugin was impressed with the strength of Catholicism in the area, and the number of old Catholic families who had held to their faith in difficult times. While staying at the Towers he found time to explore the district and to look at medieval remains. The south transept and west front of Croxden abbey, with their superbly tall lancet windows, were studied and used in Pugin's designs for the cathedral at Nottingham. A little further afield the Shrewsbury estates included properties in and around the village of Brewood on the Shropshire border, and Pugin encouraged the earl to build a church for his Catholic tenants there. On a visit to Brewood in 1843 Pugin went to see the nearby ruins of an Augustinian priory known as Whiteladies, and was clearly delighted with what he found:

> *" I went to see the cemetery at White Ladies where there are Catholic inscriptions*

from the 12th to the present century. English inscriptions "pray for the soul" etc., in the 16th, 17th and 18th centuries. No Protestant has ever polluted the consecrated ground, and this in England. Delightful. We said the De Profundis in the middle of the old ruined church."[25] Anxious for the future of Catholic families in the area, Pugin pleaded with Lord Shrewsbury that if he could do no more than "build enough of an aisle to hold these poor people it would be a right good service".

Pugin's arguments were sufficient to persuade the earl to contribute generously towards the provision of a complete church at Brewood, thereby adding yet another to the list of Pugin buildings financed partly or wholly by Lord Shrewsbury. These included S. Marie's, Derby; S. Alban's, Macclesfield; S. Mary's, Uttoxeter; the cathedrals of S. Chad's in Birmingham and S. Barnabas' Nottingham; and of course the buildings at Alton and Cheadle. Moreover, from 1838 Pugin held the post of Professor of Ecclesiastical Antiquities at Oscott College where he was concerned with the furnishing of the chapel and museum, and eventually with the completion of the college buildings themselves. Again Lord Shrewsbury was a principal benefactor.

Although he began working for Lord Shrewsbury in September 1837, it was not until 1839 that Pugin carried out any alterations and additions to Alton Towers. He had work to finish for Charles Barry whom he had helped with the winning designs for the New Palace of Westminster. He was also producing drawings and models of interiors for Taymouth Castle for the Scottish architect James Gillespie Graham, and altering and extending Scarisbrick Hall near Liverpool. Pugin's diaries[26] record only two visits to Alton in 1838, and a few meetings with Lord Shrewsbury elsewhere, but in the Summer of the following year this changed dramatically. In August 1839 Pugin was at the Towers for a total of eleven days. He was there for most of September, and in 1840 and 1842 he made extended visits of up to two weeks at a time, with shorter ones in between. All of this would seem to coincide with the first phase of Pugin's constructional and decorative work at the Towers which comprised the building of the Talbot Gallery and the Doria Rooms, the remodelling of the Octagon, alterations to the kitchens, and new furnishings for the chapel. The year 1839 does therefore appear to have been a turning-point, coinciding as it did with the arrival at Alton of John Denny as clerk-of-works and almost certainly therefore with the departure of Thomas Fradgley.

Pugin's responsibilities as architect to the earl were by no means confined to the extension and decoration of the house. He became involved with the gardens too, specifically with the design of new conservatories and other garden buildings (see below, pp136-140). In 1839 he was instrumental in the appointment of a new head gardener at Alton, Alexander Forsyth. His letter of introduction written to Dr Rock in the earl's absence abroad is currently kept in the Towers archive **(66)**. Described as "a very zealous Catholic and a convert", Forsyth had been recommended by Joseph Knight, a well-known horticulturalist who ran a nursery garden in the King's Road, Chelsea. Pugin, who was at this time also living in Chelsea, knew Mr Knight, and according to his diary dined at his house on January 1st 1839. Forsyth's appointment could well have been discussed then. Pugin's letter is dated April 5th.

Pugin's understanding of theatrical effect has already been noted. The Romantic interiors of Alton and the fabulous gardens afforded him opportunities to stage-manage spectacular events, sometimes in collaboration with Alexander Forsyth. In May 1839 his beloved wife Louisa was received into the Church in a glittering ceremony in the Towers chapel which was

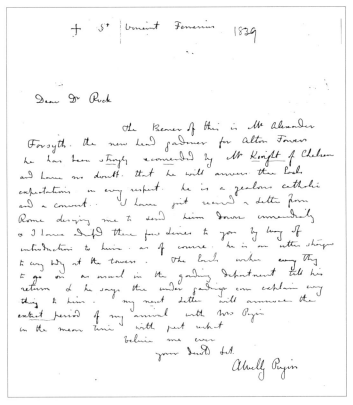

66. Letter from A.W.N. Pugin to Dr. Rock introducing the new head gardener at Alton Towers, 5th April 1839. (Alton towers Archive)

decked with garlands of flowers for the occasion, and with the liturgical arrangements directed by Pugin himself (see below, pp. 151-152). Then, in July, the earl's eldest daughter Mary arrived at Alton with her new husband, Prince Doria Pamphili. They had been married in Rome in April, and although their arrival at Alton on July 3rd is merely noted in Pugin's diary - as indeed most things are - it is sufficient to show that he was there. Other entries show that he had been there during the previous three days too, indicating that he was involved with the arrangements for the welcoming of the Prince and Princess. The *Orthodox Journal* fills out the details. Having been met at Uttoxeter by the earl and countess, Prince and Princess Doria were greeted at Quixhill Lodge by about a hundred of the tenantry, the Alton band, boys of Alton school, and girls with baskets of flowers and bouquets. The cavalcade then wound its way towards the house, and under a triumphal floral arch "the tastefulness and beauty of which reflects great credit on Mr. Forsyth, his lordship's head gardener". The family proceeded to the chapel, strewed with choice flowers, for a solemn *Te Deum* presided over by Dr Rock, and it is here no doubt that Pugin would have come into his own as Master of Ceremonies. "Such a day of grandeur and festivity has seldom been witnessed in the county of Stafford", wrote one observer, describing the great feast given for the tenants and estate workers. The dancing and merriment continued well into the night.[27]

The merrymaking over, Pugin was soon applying his mind to the designing of a new suite of rooms for the use of the Prince and Princess on future visits to the Towers. They were done in 1843, the year in which Pugin was heavily involved in preparations for one of the most spectacular events ever to have taken place at Alton Towers - the five~day visit of Henri de Chambord, the Legitimist Pretender to the French Throne **(67)**.

The story of the Comte de Chambord has several melodramatic twists that would have appealed to Pugin. After the fall of Napoleon the Bourbons returned to France in the shape of Kings Louis XVIII (1814-1824) and Charles X (1824-30); brothers of Louis XVI who had been executed during the Revolution. On February 13th 1820 Charles' only son and heir, the Duc de Berry, was assassinated, thus bringing to an end the senior line of the House of Bourbon - or so it was thought until his widow discovered she was pregnant. On September 29th she gave birth to a son, Henri de Chambord, known for obvious reasons as *L'enfant du miracle.* Ten years later Henri's grandfather, Charles X, was driven from the throne in yet another French Revolution, to be replaced by a distant cousin, Louis-Philippe, *Le Roi Citoyen.* In the eyes of true Royalists, however, the rightful king of France was the Comte de Chambord, whom they hailed as "Henri V". By the 1840s France was becoming bored with her citizen-king, and the Legitimist cause was flourishing. Such is the political background of Henri's visit to England in 1843.

It would appear that Henri - who also held the title of Duc de Bordeaux - had met the Earl and Countess of Shrewsbury in Rome - possibly at the Palazzo Doria Pamphili. They shared a common interest, namely the Catholic Revival which was taking place not only in England but also in France in the aftermath of the Revolutionary and Napoleonic Wars. Henri bestowed on the earl and countess the courtesy-title of *amis,* and the friendship

67. Henri de France, Duke of Bordeaux.
(Illustrated London News, 14th October 1843)

was sealed when the countess commissioned the sculptor Tenerani to carve a bust of the Duke to place in the Talbot Gallery at Alton.[28] A visit to England was planned, including a reception at Alton Towers, and no secret was made of it. Considerable embarrassment must have been felt in Government circles on both sides of the Channel, for Henri's visit happened precisely at a time when efforts were being made to improve the previously strained relationship between the Orleanist régime in France and the British Government.

Pugin had already met one set of royal pretenders. On a visit to Scotland in 1842 he dined with the two self-styled Stuart princes, John and Charles Edward Sobieski, who claimed descent from "Bonnie Prince Charlie". He wrote enthusiastically about them, and their appreciation of Gothic architecture, in a letter to Lord Shrewsbury: "...they are both edifying Catholics. There is a prophecy in the highlands that the Stewarts are yet to be restored. What a grand thing a Gothic king and a catholic would be; we should have grand restorations of art and churches .... I would fight for him".[29] The Sobieski Stuarts' claims were almost certainly spurious, and one wonders why Pugin seems to have taken them so seriously. On the other hand, Pugin was never too enamoured of the Hanoverian dynasty in England, and the hope of a Catholic Stuart Restoration may have been very real to him: a part of what Rosemary Hill calls "the romance of facts".[30] Given his own family's background in pre-Revolutionary France, the appearance in the following year of the Royalist Pretender to the French crown could well have stirred up in him the embers of that old Franco-Scottish alliance which had lasted into the reign of Mary, Queen of Scots, whose life had recently come to the fore again through the novels of Sir Walter Scott. There was certainly a Franco-Scottish dimension to Prince Henri's

93

visit to England in 1843, for it included a journey to Scotland where he saw – amongst other things - Melrose Abbey and Walter Scott's house at Abbotsford. In his entourage there would undoubtedly have been some who were present at the Marie Stuart Costume Ball which the Prince's mother had held in Paris in 1829, and at which she had appeared dressed as Mary, Queen of Scots.

Pugin's diary for 1843 is unfortunately missing, but letters sent by him to Lord Shrewsbury speak of his direct involvement with preparations for Henri's visit to Alton. In one of these - dated July 28th - he mentions that the Duke had visited William Wailes' stained-glass factory at Newcastle-on-Tyne and had been delighted with the glass which was being made for Pugin's churches at Southwark, Nottingham and Cheadle.[31] In the same letter Pugin gives a list of items he has purchased in London on the earl's behalf - fire-engines, canvas, lamps, sugar-basins and envelopes. Other letters written in the autumn of 1843 also refer to "fire engines" or "garden engines", the construction of wooden framework for an awning, the installation of "illumination lamps", the purchase of yards of material for the awning, cloth tassels, and figured cloth for *prie-dieux* (prayer-desks). Pugin was also trying frantically to obtain two more silver sugar-basins to match the first pair.[32] The fact that John Denny and carpenter Thomas Harris were involved makes it plain enough that all this was connected with some event at Alton Towers, but it remains a mystery until it is known from other sources that the event was the arrival of Henri de Chambord.

Two accounts of Chambord's visit to Alton are known to survive, one English and the other French. The English account appears in the *Staffordshire Advertiser,* November 11th 1843. The French version forms part of *Relation du voyage de Henri de France en Ecosse et en Angleterre* written by Joseph Alexis Walsh ("M. le Vicomte Walsh") and published in Paris in 1844.[33] From these accounts it becomes clear that Henri was to arrive at Alton on Saturday 4th November at around 5 p.m. It would be dark, so there was to be a torchlight procession. The "fire engines" referred to by Pugin were not fire-fighting machines but pyrotechnic devices for floodlighting the Towers, creating quite a spectacle on a winter's evening. Pugin was not so happy with the "illumination lamps" for the gardens. "They will look like a Vauxhall night", he wrote to the earl. "I think I can arrange something better".[34] The Prince was to enter the house via the steps up to the Grand Entrance, hence the need for an awning just in case it was raining when he alighted from his carriage. "I have made the awning 12 feet high..... If your Lordship thinks it too high it may be reduced, but it should not be too low to enter such lofty doors." Knowing only too well the earl's concern for economy, Pugin explained that he had designed the framing for the awning in such a way that it could be taken to pieces and stored for some future occasion.[35] The reference to *prie-dieux* relates to preparations for special services in the Towers chapel, while the search for matching silver sugar-bowls may relate to an intended gift.

The principal difference between the English and French accounts of Prince Henri's visit is that the *Staffordshire Advertiser* omits all reference to the Catholic ceremonies which formed a part of it, and makes no mention of Pugin who played such a key role in it all. Pugin was not unused to being snubbed by the Press. However, on the main elements of the visit the two accounts agree. Having been received at the Grand Entrance by the Earl and Countess and a distinguished party of English and French nobility and gentry, the Prince was conducted through the brilliantly-lit galleries, octagon, and house conservatory into the Drawing Room. After the house-guests had been presented to him, he retired to the State Rooms in the West Wing. Walsh adds that these rooms were known as the royal apartments because they had been built for the exclusive use of persons of royal blood. These were, of course, the rooms used by Queen Adelaide on her visit in 1840.

Shortly before eight o'clock the royal party descended the grand staircase into the dining-hall for a banquet, during the course of which an orchestra played alternately Scottish and French airs; a significant choice. From time to time the orchestra gave way to the earl's blind harper, Edward Jervis, who, as well as playing the harp sang a selection of Welsh folk-songs. "I am happy to sing for the Prince", he is reported to have said to the bystanders, "but you are more fortunate than I because you can see him". Pugin was among the 35 guests who sat down to dinner, as were Bishop Wiseman, Lord Littleton, and Captain and Mrs Washington Hibbert of Bilton Grange (the step-father and mother of the earl's cousin and heir, Bertram).

The following day being a Sunday, the Duke and his entourage accompanied the Earl and Countess to Mass in the Towers Chapel. Vicomte Walsh was enraptured by the chapel, the east end of which had recently been re-furnished and decorated by Pugin. The *prie-dieux* referred to in the correspondence with Lord Shrewsbury were placed on the tribune, that for the Prince being covered with a velvet cloth embroidered with *fleurs-de-lis*. The side-galleries were reserved for special guests. The earl's chaplain, Dr. Winter, was the celebrant, and Dr Wiseman gave a homily.

On the next day the mood changed. The 6th November being the anniversary of the death of Henri's grandfather, King Charles X (1836), the Prince had asked for a Requiem to be sung in the chapel. Vicomte Walsh records that Pugin was responsible for the reordering of the chapel for this event, including the provision of black drapes and a catafalque decorated with silver tear-drops and fleurs-de-lis. This helps to explain the quantities of fabric referred to in Pugin's earlier correspondence with Lord Shrewsbury.

The Prince and his entourage used the Towers as their base from which to make visits to the Duke of Devonshire at Chatsworth and the Duke of Sutherland at Trentham. A visit was also arranged - by Pugin no doubt - to Herbert Minton's tile-works in Stoke-on-Trent where the magnificent encaustic tiles were being produced for S. Giles', Cheadle, and other churches of the Pugin-Shrewsbury partnership. Before finally leaving Alton, the Prince planted five oak trees in the lawn in front of the Towers as a reminder, wrote Vicomte Walsh, "*aux générations qui suivront la notre que HENRI DE FRANCE avait séjourné dans ce lieu*". By way of a sequel it should be added that Henri de Chambord's intended visit to London had to be post-poned because of an official visit by the Duc de Nemours, a son of King Louis-Philippe, and also that his political career ended in circumstances almost as bizarre as those in which his life had begun. The Crown of France could have been his for the taking, but, ultra-royalist to the last, he forfeited it by refusing to accept the tricolore as the national flag.

Though the visit of the Duc de Bordeaux was probably one of the most spectacular events staged at Alton Towers in the mid-nineteenth century, one should not forget the celebrations which surrounded the dedication of S. Giles', which in many ways marked the pinnacle of Pugin's achievements as an ecclesiastical architect and designer. The story of the building of

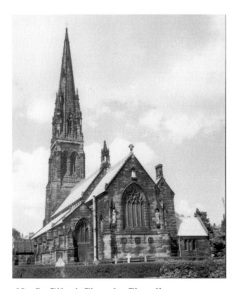

68. S. Giles' Church, Cheadle. (MJF 1994)

S. Giles is told elsewhere.[36] Suffice it to say here that it is the story of a project of initially modest proportions being steadily enlarged and enriched into something far bigger and far more splendid than Lord Shrewsbury had first intended **(68).** An original budget of £5,000 escalated to a final figure of £40,000. There were many differences of opinion along the way, but the fact that Pugin was able to carry the earl along with him is a tribute both to the infectious enthusiasm of Pugin for the causes he believed in, and to the earl's sincere admiration of Pugin's many talents. Though Pugin loved its every detail - and possibly because of that - S. Giles' took its toll on him for he was so anxious that it should be perfect in every way. In 1846, the year of the consecration of the church, Pugin had long spells of illness, and it was left to Lord Shrewsbury himself to make the arrangements for the transporting of guests, and the choir from S. Chad's cathedral, Birmingham.

The consecration of what became known as "Pugin's Gem" on August 31st was essentially a private affair, but on the next day crowds of spectators gathered in Cheadle to witness the arrival of guests for the first Solemn Mass. Eight carriages arrived from Alton Towers bearing the earl and countess and their guests, eleven bishops and two archbishops were in attendance. On the previous evening Lord Shrewsbury had entertained his principal guests - over fifty of them - at a banquet in the dining-hall at Alton. The Welsh harper was on duty again to play "favourite airs as the company descended the magnificent staircase of the mansion".[37] Pugin was among the company, as was the architect Charles Barry.

For Pugin gatherings such as these were of great importance professionally, bringing him into contact with prospective clients whom he would never have met but for the patronage of Lord Shrewsbury. The celebrations surrounding the consecration of S. Giles' provided the occasion for finalising Lord Shrewsbury's gift of Cotton Hall, close to Alton, to Frederick Faber and his Brothers of the Will of God.[38] Pugin was to design new buildings there, including the church of S. Wilfrid. Meanwhile Alton Towers itself was developing into a series of showrooms in which Pugin could display the combined talents of those who executed his designs: John Gregory Crace, John Hardman, Herbert Minton, and George Myers.

Addressing a Parliamentary Committee in 1841 Charles Barry had concurred with the view that Pugin's decorative work at the Towers would apply equally well to the New Palace of Westminster,[39] and it was not long before Pugin had the responsibility for all the interior fittings and decorations for that huge building, down to small details such as key-plates and door-handles.

The sheer volume of work which Pugin undertook was breathtaking. A glance at almost any page of his diary reveals a pattern of travel extraordinary even by today's standards. As if to convince Lord Shrewsbury that he really was busy - for of course he had other clients to deal with - he sent a copy of his week's schedule:

"My work is set out for every hour till Saturday

Monday	*Northampton and Nottingham*
Tuesday	*Sileby and on to Darlington*
Wednesday	*Newcastle on Tyne*
Thursday	*Newcastle and on to Lancaster*
Friday	*Kirkham and Liverpool*
Saturday	*Brewood, Stone and Alton* " [40]

When on another occasion Lord Shrewsbury dared to imply - and probably in jest - that he might not have enough to do, Pugin penned the following indignant response:..... *"Your lordship says I cannot have much to do; now this is too bad to a man who has hardly time to dine. I never had so much to do. I have had several plates to engrave, diverse articles to write, new churches at Newcastle, Birtley, London; finish buildings at Liverpool, London, Loughborough, Downside etc., all sorts of altars, stained windows, screens etc., I have not an instant to spare, __nothing to do!!!__"[41]*

Lord Shrewsbury was well aware of the pressures that Pugin found himself under, and on more than one occasion urged him to relax. In July 1841 Pugin was invited to spend a few days with the earl and countess at Spa in Belgium, which he duly did, but then, much to the disappointment of his hosts, he cut the visit short in order to get back to work. *"It is too bad of your Lordship to scold me for stopping so short a time at Spa"*, he wrote from Alton after his return. *"I was absent from England more than 13 days altogether and you can form no idea of the accumulation of letters and wants by the time I returned"[41]*

In another letter Pugin relates, how after taking leave of the earl and countess in Spa, he was robbed of 25 francs by *"a ferocious looking rascal in a conical hat, moustache and beard; a compound of both infidel and republican, not a soul came to help. The other passengers who saw the whole injustice of the business left me to this horrid ruffian."* [42]

Pugin seems to have had a fear of radicals and revolutionaries, particularly foreign ones. *"Whenever I see a man with a conical hat, a beard, and a pipe I shall avoid him most carefully"*. He longed to show Lord Shrewsbury St. Augustine's Grange, the new family home he was building in Ramsgate in the 1840s, a place where he really could relax and enjoy one of his few pleasures - sailing in his lugger, the *Caroline*. *"Cannot you take refuge from the London heat by moving down to S. Augustine's?"* he wrote to Lord Shrewsbury in 1848, *"The sea breeze constantly blowing is delicious, the garden is all roses and honeysuckles, a delightful perfume; brass bed with a mattress - every possible inducement there is a fast train on Saturdays direct to Ramsgate stopping nowhere which gets here by 3".[43]*

Lord Shrewsbury probably never saw S. Augustine's, although Prince and Princess Doria did. By the late 1840s the earl and countess were spending more time abroad. They had long since given up their London house in Stanhope Street, and stayed instead at Mivarts Hotel whenever they were in town.

The earl calculated that by staying away from Alton during the summer he would save at

69. The chapel tower, from which Pugin heard "the chimes at midnight". (MJF 1997)

least £2,000 a year which could be diverted into church-building. There were to be no more grand occasions like the visit of Henri de Chambord. *"Of course we must come sometimes but I hope not often"*, he wrote to Ambrose Phillipps.[44] Meanwhile Pugin continued to supervise the work which, in spite of the earl's decision to stay away from Alton as much as possible, carried on, both at the Towers and at the hospital and castle in Alton village. At the Towers there was the Great Dining Room, conceived as early as 1843 but not actually started until 1848, and the subject of prolonged controversy between the earl and his architect (see below pp.121-129); and the second phase of work on the chapel. It has to be remembered that Shrewsbury was building not just for himself but for those who would succeed him.

With the family away in Italy and the staff at the Towers reduced to a minimum, Pugin sometimes found the place almost deserted and quite eerie. On an October night in 1849 he was staying in a room in a remote part of the Towers, with a strong gale blowing outside. As if that were not enough, Pugin heard the sound of bells tolling every few minutes as though for a funeral. So strong was the wind as it blew through the openings in the chapel tower that it had set the bells tolling. *"You cannot imagine anything more desolate than this mansion house"*, wrote Pugin[45] **(69).** There were lighter moments too. In the same letter Pugin writes of merrymaking down at S. John's: *"...Balls in the Guild Hall, dancing till 2 in the morning, the Rev. Dr. (Winter) playing the French Horn!!"*

In between their sporadic visits to England the earl and countess relied on Pugin to keep them informed of progress at Alton, and also to keep an eye on the workforce. *"Keep a very sharp look out after Denny and his men and see that they do a deal of work"*, he wrote from Palermo in February 1851.[46] At the same time he asked Pugin to send him a sketch of the domestic apartments as viewed from Her Ladyship's garden to give some idea of the new rooms that were being built over the Drawing Room, and one of the north front too.

Lord and Lady Shrewsbury were clearly delighted when, after three unsuccessful courtships, Pugin met and married Jane Knill who thus became Mrs Pugin No. 3. *"I can assure you"*, the earl wrote shortly after the wedding in August 1848, *"that nothing has given us more pleasure for a long time past than the announcement of your sudden and happy marriage. Prudence has now rewarded you for all your past sufferings, and given you a happy home for the rest of your life".*[47]

No-one at the time could have realised how brief the rest of Pugin's life was to be. In 1848 he was at the height of his career, established as the foremost exponent of the Gothic Revival with several major publications to his credit, and solid achievements which all could see in buildings such as the churches at Cheadle, Birmingham and Nottingham, and notable domestic architecture such as his additions to Scarisbrick Hall, Bilton Grange, Alton Towers, and of course his new home at Ramsgate. Yet he was only thirty-six years old.

In 1851 Pugin had the opportunity to display his talents as an interior designer to a much wider public. Along with the manufacturers who worked to his designs -such as Minton, Hardman and Crace - he created one of the most spectacular features of the Great Exhibition, namely the Medieval Court. Though the Crystal Palace was a technological wonder, Pugin had a poor opinion of it, and when its designer, Joseph Paxton, asked him what he thought of it, he received the terse reply, *"Think? Why, that you had better keep to building greenhouses, and I will keep to my churches and cathedrals".*[48] Yet Pugin took endless pains to present as wide a range as possible of ecclesiastical and secular work, most of it executed from his own drawings. Items either borrowed from, or intended for, Alton Towers, were to be included: the huge brass-and-crystal chandelier, the sideboard, and the "Grand Talbot" window for the Dining Room; one of the tile-clad stoves for the Long Gallery, and *coronae* from the Talbot Gallery and small dining room. Lord Shrewsbury was in Italy at this time, and Pugin had to write and ask permission to borrow the enamelled brass *coronae* (chandeliers). Shrewsbury had no more confidence in Paxton's "greenhouse" than Pugin, but realised what a great opportunity the Medieval Court afforded to Pugin and Hardman, so he wrote from Palermo:

> *"....How is the glass palace getting on? I should have liked to have seen it filled with the works of the world. I hope you and Hardman will be ready and cut a good figure... You may have the coronas out of the Talbot Gallery - but I think*

70. The Medieval Court at the Great Exhibition. Several items from Alton Towers can be seen, including (left) the Great Stove, and (right) the sideboard for the dining hall. (Illustrated London News, 20th September 1851)

the smaller one out of the little dining room would answer your purpose much better...... You must be answerable for damage, for I fear the building will be blown down altogether".[49]

The Crystal Palace was not blown down, as the earl feared it would be, and the items from Alton Towers appeared in several published illustrations of the Medieval Court **(70)**. The Exhibition attracted an immense number of visitors. The population of Great Britain was then 21 million, of whom 6 million visited Hyde Park. The Medieval Court was one of the most popular parts of the exhibition, and from it literally millions of people took home ideas for the furnishing and decoration of houses as well as churches. Thus Pugin's "Gothic Passion" became widely and irresistibly infectious.

It was also the cause of his early death. Pugin's doctors told him that he had tried to pack a hundred years into a mere forty; an understatement because most of his major achievements date from the years 1836-1851. The exact nature of his final illness has been the subject of a good deal of controversy and discussion, but to say simply that Pugin died insane will not do.[50] Anxiety and overwork undeniably played their part. One of the most amazing things about this extraordinary man is that although the execution of his designs was entrusted to other people, the designs themselves, the ideas, the sketches, the drawings, the correspondence, all come from Pugin himself. He had no pupils apart from his eldest son Edward and his son-in-law John Hardman Powell, and employed no clerks to do the routine parts of his designs.

Having been ill throughout December 1851 and January 1852, Pugin made a sudden recovery, news of which clearly delighted Lord Shrewsbury who wrote to him from Palermo giving him the good news that he now wanted the hospital at Alton to be finished as a residence *before* the castle. The earl also invited Pugin to spend a few months at his summer residence, the Villa Belmonte, assuring him that all the things that he liked, such as the sea and ships, would be there to delight and refresh him, and in a climate far healthier than that of Ramsgate *"We have built a wooden Gallery, for shade and shelter, Grecian style! looking on the sea with the prospect of every ship that comes and goes, and every boat that hoists".[51]* Pugin was not convinced that Palermo was a healthy place in which to live; he wondered how Lord Shrewsbury could stand the summer heat in Palermo, and had been told that the gardens at Belmonte were full of huge snakes and lizards.[52] On a previous occasion, having heard that plague had broken out in Palermo, Pugin had expressed grave anxiety for the earl's health:

"I hope your Lordship will not go into any dangerous places. Pray be careful. There should be a law made, as for the Queen, that you should not go above a certain distance from your dominions. I assure your Lordship that I am always in a most anxious state when you go so far away".[53]

Pugin's recovery was only temporary and around the time of his fortieth birthday, March 1st 1852, he became seriously ill again. Having received news of his relapse from Mrs Ambrose Phillipps, Shrewsbury wrote to Jane Pugin insisting that he stop working immediately, and offering to accommodate him for up to a year in Palermo so that he could make a full recovery in a warmer climate:...... *"we most strongly advise him to take advantage of the fine climate. It has wonderful flowers for restoring a healthy circulation I know of no place where he could pass the Spring and Summer with such advantage and with such safety, and Winter too. I would recommend him not to lose a day"* (details of trains and steamers included).[54]

To the Right Honourable

The Earl of Shrewsbury, Waterford, and Wexford.

My very good Lord,

It would be most unnatural and ungrateful in me, when putting forth a Treatise relating to the Revival of Christian Architecture in England, were I not to dedicate the same in an especial manner to your Lordship, who has been the main support in the furtherance of that good work, and to whom I am so greatly bounden.

May God in his mercy grant, that as your Lordship's noble ancestor, the Talbot of famous memory, extended the temporal glory of England by deeds of arms, so may your Lordship continue to increase the spiritual welfare of these realms by reviving the ancient glories of the English Church, of whose faith your noble house has furnished so many witnesses.

That your Lordship may long be blessed with health and strength to carry out to a happy conclusion the many good designs you have in hand, is the constant prayer of

Your Lordship's devoted and faithful Bedesman,

✠   A. Welby Pugin.

71. The dedication page from Pugin's *Apology for the Revival of Christian Architecture in England,* 1843

It was too late. Earl and architect never saw each other again. In November 1852 Earl John returned to England in a coffin, having succumbed - as Pugin feared he might - to malaria, by which time Pugin himself had lain several weeks in his vault at Ramsgate, having died on September 14th - Holy Cross Day.

Thus ended a unique partnership of architect and patron which Pugin had sometimes symbolised by placing Lord Shrewsbury's coat-of-arms by the side of his own. Their respective mottoes, *Prest d'Accomplir* ("Ready to Accomplish") and *En Avant* ("Forward") were also in a way symbolic. *Prest d'Accomplir* though he may have been, in the best tradition of his forebears, it was Pugin's battle-cry of *En Avant!* which impelled the earl to accomplish far more than he sometimes considered desirable or affordable. Yet in spite of many disagreements - over Cheadle, over the hospital at Alton, over alterations at the Towers - Shrewsbury never lost faith in the abilities of architect. The extent and sincerity of his admiration is expressed in a letter to Ambrose Phillips:

> "....Pugin is decidedly the Catholic architect of the day, with more zeal, talent, Judgement and experience than perhaps any man so young has hitherto acquired in any profession whatever..... I look upon Pugin as the greatest acquisition for our body for an immense time past - a man more capable and willing to raise us up from a state of miserable insignificance in respect to our Places of Religious Worship to one of Pre-eminent merit and brilliancy than any one living. It is impossible for anyone to read any of his works without at once admitting this - they are so overflowing with zeal and talent and taste. <u>He</u> is the man to encourage".[55]

One of the "works" referred to by Lord Shrewsbury is *An Apology for the Revival of Christian Architecture in England* published by Pugin in 1843. It is one of the key works from which to understand Pugin's ideas on ecclesiastical and civil architecture, and it contains his own tribute to his patron **(71)**. This takes the form of an illuminated address in which the initial letter M is embellished with the kneeling figure of Pugin dressed in a medieval architect's robe presenting a book to Lord Shrewsbury who is attired in the robes of a medieval nobleman. Both the illustration and the text perfectly express that extraordinary partnership of *En Avant* and *Prest d'Accomplir,* the echoes of which still resound across the Churnet valley from where "Good Earl John" rests in his sanctuary, to the great house of which Pugin wrote, *"I am nowhere so happy".*

COLOUR PLATES

King Henry;
Welcome, brave captain and victorious lord!
When I was young, - as yet I am not old, -
I do remember how my father said
A stouter champion never handled sword.
Long since we were resolved of your truth,
Your faithful service, and your toil in war;
...Therefore, stand up; and for these good deserts
We here create you Earl of Shrewsbury;
And in our coronation take your place.
                    - Shakespeare, **Henry VI part I**

Henry VI presenting a sword to John Talbot Earl of Shrewsbury

"The Romance of Facts"

I The Grand Talbot.

Nineteenth-century print representing King Henry VI and John Talbot, first Earl of Shrewsbury. (Private Collection)

II Victorian medievalism:

Panel from the Bromsgrove altarpiece, formerly at Alton Towers, *c*.1840, showing John Talbot, 16th Earl of Shrewsbury, dressed after the fashion of the first Earl, with his patron saint, S. John the Baptist. The east end of the Towers chapel can be seen through the window.
(Photography: Graham Miller)

III The Altar and reredos from the Towers chapel. The gilt-bronze altar is older than the reredos which was designed by Pugin *c.*1840.
(Photography: Graham Miller)

IV Maria Teresa, Countess of Shrewsbury, with her patron saint, the Blessed Virgin Mary. The Flag Tower at Alton Towers is framed in the window. Detail from the Bromsgrove altarpiece.
(Photography: Graham Miller)

V & VI Aquatints published in 1819 by Thomas Fielding from drawings by the architect Thomas Allason showing the north-west and north-east prospects of Alton Abbey. (Trustees of the William Salt Library, Stafford)

Octagon
Alton Towers

VII The Octagon looking west towards the Talbot Gallery. The conservatory entrance is on the right. (Watercolour by an unknown artist, dated 1870: Private Collection)

VIII The house conservatory looking north towards the Drawing Room. (Watercolour by an unknown artist, dated 1870: Private Collection)

IX View from the North Library eastwards to the Music Room and Drawing Room.
(Watercolour by unknown artist, dated 1870: Private Collection)

X The Towers Chapel: Watercolour by Joseph Lynch, 1854. (Alton Towers)
(Photography: Guy Evans)

XI The Music Room, looking west towards the North Library. (Watercolour by unknown artist)

XII Maria Teresa, Countess of Shrewsbury (1797-1856). Portrait by John Julius Hamburger, 1832, formerly at Alton Towers and now at Ingestre Hall, Staffs.

XIII The oriel window in the dining hall. Heraldic glass designed by A.W.N. Pugin and executed by Hardman of Birmingham.

XIVPart of Pugin's all-or-nothing ultimatum to Lord Shrewsbury: the high open roof in the dining hall.

5

PUGIN at ALTON

'As regards the hall I have nailed my colours to the mast: a bay window, high open roof, lantern, 2 grand fireplaces, a great sideboard, screen, minstrel gallery, all or none' - A.W.N. Pugin

72. A Gothic bookcase from Pugin's *Gothic Furniture in the Style of the Fifteenth Century*, 1835.

Whatever may be the truth about the date of Lord Shrewsbury's first acquaintance with the work of Pugin, there is no doubt that Pugin produced furniture-designs for Edward Hull of Wardour Street, and that Shrewsbury was among Hull's customers. A volume of drawings of furniture by Pugin inscribed "Edward Hull" on the inside of the cover exists in the Victoria & Albert Museum; a kind of catalogue from which customers might choose designs.[1] Many are similar to the ones published in his book, *Gothic Furniture in the Style of the Fifteenth century (1835)* **(72)**. It is not unlikely therefore that furniture designs were among Pugin's earliest contributions to the interiors of Alton Towers, especially in the new West Wing.

By 1837 structural work on the West Wing was complete, but a description of them in Ebenezer Rhodes' *The Derbyshire Tourists Guide* published in May of that year states that they were not then completely finished or furnished. Gothic furniture known to have been in the West Wing state rooms at the time of the 1857 sale includes an oak wardrobe carved with figures of the Virgin and Child and saints, the state bedstead "of gothic design, painted and richly gilt", a superb state chest "of gothic design, painted in colours and gilt", and an oak cheval fire-screen carved with the Shrewsbury shield and crest. In the Arragon bedroom was "A very handsome gothic oak fourpost bed; St. George and the Dragon, and shields and trophies on the head, the footboard with an angel and linen-pattern panels". There was a matching set of carved bed-steps surmounted by figures bearing shields, and linenfold panels. The descriptions of some of these items accord with the kind of illustrations in Pugin's *Gothic Furniture* and in

73. The Gothic bed in the Arragon Room, *(Alton Towers Sale Catalogue, 1924)*

Edward Hull's collection. The bed and bed-steps in the Arragon room were unsold in 1857 and a photograph taken of them for the 1924 sale catalogue leaves no doubt as to the identity of the designer **(73)**.

The new libraries in the West Wing also needed furnishing. Several contemporary descriptions of these rooms make mention of the Gothic open bookcases, inscribed with texts such as "Truth will only dwell with those who love her", and "Wisdom strengtheneth the wise more than ten men". Writing in 1886 the Uttoxeter historian Francis Redfern attributes these to Fradgley, but then Redfern attributes almost everything at Alton to Fradgley and gives Pugin credit for absolutely nothing.[2] The 1857 Sale Catalogue is quite unequivocal however in attributing to Pugin seven out of the ten Gothic bookcases in the libraries.

By 1839 Pugin was moving on from furnishing to significant structural alterations and additions at the Towers. These are known to have comprised the new Talbot Gallery and the Talbot Passage to link the Gallery with the West Wing, the complete remodelling of the Octagon, the rebuilding of the Dining Hall, new servants' accommodation and alterations to the kitchens, the Doria Rooms, an eastward extension of the north terrace wall and the excavation of the fosse, or dry ditch, along the north front; the Barbican gateway, the new rooms over the Great Drawing Room, and the top-floor rooms west of the Long Gallery; the conservatories south of the Picture Gallery, and other garden buildings; the Station Lodge and alterations to Counslow Lodge. Pugin completely altered the internal appearance of the chapel, and redecorated the Great Drawing Room, Long Gallery, and several of the family rooms. The effect of the structural alterations and additions, especially on the north front, was profound **(74).**

THE TALBOT GALLERY

The Talbot Gallery was the last element to be added to the enfilade running westwards from the Entrance Tower, and at its west end it was connected to Fradgley's West Wing by means of a narrow corridor known as the Talbot Passage. As a terminal feature at the west end a tall square tower with a plain parapet was built to balance the Entrance Tower at the opposite extremity of the enfilade. The date of this work - and hence Pugin's execution of it - is certain enough. John Denny's accounts include several payments made to Peter and John Bailey in the summer of 1839 for "piecework on account of Gallery wall".[3] There is also the evidence of Pugin's Diary for 1839, the front end-papers of which include particulars of cast-iron ventilators and sky-lights for the Gallery to be ordered from the Britannia Foundry (Marshall, Barker and Wright) in Derby. This firm, which had supplied high-quality castings for the Towers over many years, seemed at this time to be experiencing some difficulties, for much to Pugin's distress they failed to honour their contract for the ironwork for the Gallery. Lord Shrewsbury wrote to Pugin from Rome in March 1840 urging him not to worry unduly: *"...the fault is not yours, and we must bear the disappointment as best we can, if it comes".*[4] In the same letter Shrewsbury expressed the hope that the Gallery would be ready for the furniture and paintings to be moved in during the family's summer visit that year, but urging him not to allow the walls to be papered until they had dried out thoroughly. He also referred to the heraldic glass being made by Thomas Willement for the windows in the west tower of the Gallery, and to the gilt-brass chandeliers, or *coronae lucis,* designed by Pugin and manufac-

74. Alton Towers - The North Front

(a) The north front of "Alton Abbey" as completed c.1820.
Sources: Aquatints by Thomas Allason, 1819; engravings by Hopwood and Radclyffe, 1820-23; Alton Towers Archive (for entrance window).

(b) The north front showing West Wing addition by Thomas Fradgley c.1835, and alterations and additions of upper floors and dining room by A.W.N. Pugin, 1843-51. The excavation of the fosse and the application of weatherings to the foundations were also done by Pugin.
Source: On-Centre Surveys Ltd., 1992. Missing features such as window tracery and glazing-bars drawn from *NMR* photographic survey, 1951.

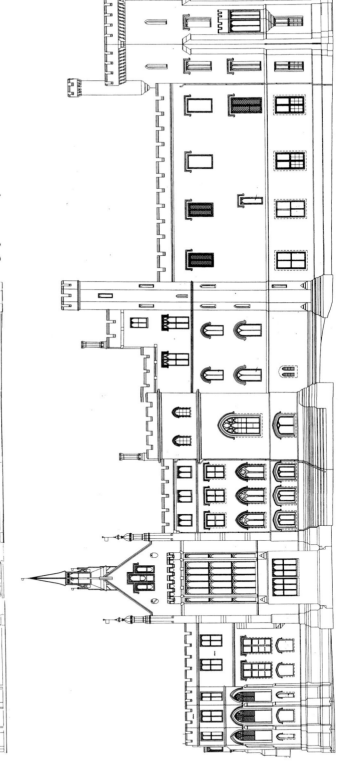

tured at Hardman's workshops in Birmingham. The Talbot Gallery may therefore be dated quite precisely: 1839-40.

The Talbot Gallery was, as the name implies, built to continue the theme of Lord Shrewsbury's illustrious ancestry as displayed in the Armoury, but on a much more lavish scale. The building itself was relatively modest - a long, low structure of similar proportions to the Picture Gallery east of the Octagon. Built directly on to an outcrop of sandstone, it required little in the way of foundations and footings for the most part, but at the north-western extremity the rocky outcrop fell away steeply. Foundations were therefore built up at the north-west corner of the building where the floor was carried on girders over the huge coal and slack vaults excavated under the tower and the west bay of the Gallery. Arches built out from the northern slope carried the Talbot Passage to connect with the Oak Corridor and the principal rooms of the West Wing.

The Talbot Gallery was buttressed down each side, and unlike the Picture Gallery it had no windows excepting those in the tower, the present square openings in the walls dating only from the 1940s. As was appropriate for a Gallery built to display works of art, illumination was

provided entirely from above, through skylights with delicate cast-iron tracery and panels of ground glass. These were set into the timber-framed roof supported by corbels in the form of Talbot hounds, although unlike the ones in the Picture Gallery these were made of cast-iron. Between the corbels ran brass picture-rails supported on gilt brackets. Illumination at night-time came from the eight *coronae* already referred to, each one carrying sixteen lights, and enamelled with the Talbot motto, *Prest d'Accomplir.*

75. Chimneypiece in the Talbot Gallery, *c.*1930
(The Lewis Family Collection)

Two magnificent stone chimney-pieces were set into the south wall of the Gallery. They are almost identical with the one designed by Pugin for the great hall at Scarisbrick on which he was working at the same time, and there can be little doubt that they were made in the Lambeth workshops of George Myers,[5] Pugin's principal builder and carver (75). In either one the fireplace was framed by a crocketed ogee arch with canopied niches either side containing Talbot hounds carrying banners. In the centre of the mantel the figures of two kneeling angels supported the Shrewsbury coat-of-arms, and these were flanked by figures in suits of armour - exactly as at Scarisbrick. The fireplace itself was lined with ceramic tiles embellished with the Shrewsbury "S" in yellow on red, and the Earl's initials I and T *(Iohannes Talbot)* in yellow on blue (76). These tiles were painted/printed rather than encaustic, and pre-date Pugin's association with ceramics manufacturer Herbert Minton which did not begin until 1842.

Above the picture rail a splendid frieze was applied. This consisted of a paper printed with diagonal bands containing the initials S and T alternating with ones carrying the motto *Prest d'Accomplir.* Superimposed on this paper were a hundred hand-painted shields showing the arms of Talbot ancestors and related families. The shields were the work of Thomas Willement, for Lord Shrewsbury sent some precise instructions for Willement regarding the heraldry for them.[6] As for the printed paper, although Pugin's formal association with J.G. Crace did not begin until 1844 it is not impossible that Crace was supplying papers for Lord Shrewsbury before this date, as indeed he was doing for Lord Breadalbane at Taymouth Castle for which Pugin was also producing interior designs. The frieze is very similar to the one in the Drawing Room at Knebworth House (Hertfordshire) which is known to have been done by Pugin and Crace in 1844.

Willement made the windows at the west end of the Talbot Gallery, containing the names, dates and armorial bearings of the 16th Earl and nine of his Talbot ancestors. The west end of the Gallery, i.e. the area under the tower, was delineated by a finely-moulded stone arch, and in this recess was placed the full-size statue of Raphael by Ceccarini, formerly in the Octagon Gallery.

76. Surviving printed tiles in fireplace, Talbot Gallery. (MJF 1998)

Towards the west end of the Gallery, in the north wall, a doorway opened into the Talbot Passage which gave access to the West Wing. This too was richly-decorated with heraldic devices. On the opposite side of the Gallery was another doorway giving access, via a bridge over the dry ditch, to a verandah and the terraces on the south side of the house.

Shorn of its furniture and great works of art at the time of the great sale in 1857, the Talbot Gallery was later turned into a billiard-room, and this is how it appears on a photograph taken in about 1890 **(77)**. As newly-completed, however, its impact on visitors was breathtaking:

"If the reader of these pages be, like ourselves, in the habit of making pilgrimages to the more celebrated palaces of our nobility, he must call to his recollection the most splendid hall, saloon or gallery, he has hitherto seen; he must charge his memory for the most brilliant spectacle of heraldic emblazonment and architectural decoration...... and his ideas will, we think, still fall short of the regal splendour of this, the last and noblest of the halls in Alton Towers". [7]

There is, alas, little noble about the Talbot gallery now: roofless and overgrown with saplings and brambles, the two splendid chimney-pieces badly eroded by rain and the ingression of weeds. Action to save them from total destruction is long overdue.

The addition of the Talbot Gallery and Talbot Passage put the finishing touches to the axial system of linked rooms and corridors which had been a part of the evolving scheme of the house right from the start. Though the building seems to have grown haphazardly, with bits added and altered at will, there was a plan and a logic to it. Nowhere is this seen more clearly than in the creation of the long enfilades which are so prominent a feature of the Alton plan **(78).** The building of the Oak Corridor created a new one of 174 feet in length, while the Talbot Gallery added another 140 feet to what was already the longest axis, making a total of 480 feet. Even though most of the furnishings and pictures had gone by the time the views down the

77. The Talbot Gallery looking west, c.1890. The fine furnishings and paintings of the 1840s have gone, and one of the Pugin-Hardman coronae has been adapted to illuminate a billiard table.
(Staffordshire County Museum, Shugborough Hall)

galleries were painted in 1870 *(**Col. Plate VII**)* it was still an amazing sight, the intervening open screens having a similar effect to the ones which Pugin regarded as a *sine qua non* in his churches: sufficient to give an impression of what lay beyond, but not to reveal all.

THE OCTAGON

The addition of the Talbot Gallery meant that considerable alterations had to be made to the Octagon immediately to the west of it. Prior to Pugin's arrival at the Towers, the Octagon acted as the terminal element of two enfilades; one running southwards from the Long Gallery and through the House Conservatory, and the other westwards from the Entrance Tower through the Armoury and Picture Gallery.

Unlike the Picture Gallery which is at a level intermediate between basement and *piano nobile,* the Talbot Gallery was to be built on the same level as the State Rooms and the new West Wing with which it was to be linked by means of the Talbot Passage. Standing on this higher level, the walls and roof of the new Gallery would rise above the Octagon parapet, so the Octagon had to be raised by several feet to accommodate them. The new upper section has tall narrow slits, two on each face of the outer walls. The battlements and square-sectioned

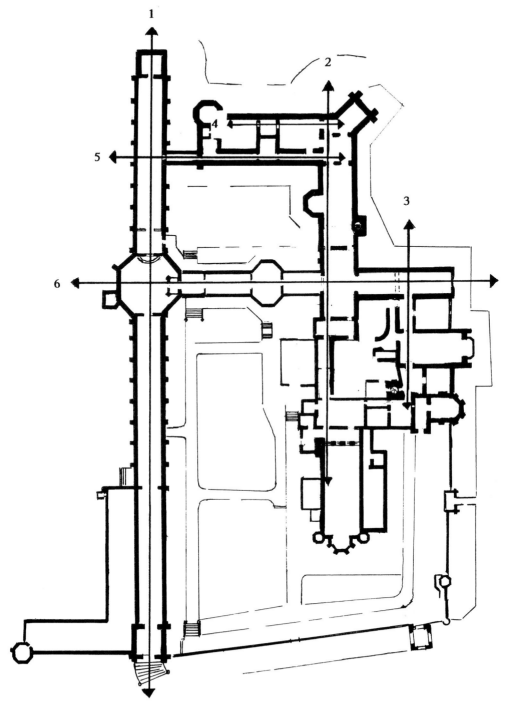

78. The grid-system of linked rooms, or *enfilades*, as finally developed at Alton. Almost invariably there was a focal point, such as a stained glass window, to terminate each vista.

1. Entrance Tower through Talbot Gallery (480 feet); 2. North Library to Chapel (265 feet); 3. Long Gallery to Octagon Lobby (108 feet); 4. West Wing State Rooms (100 feet); 5. North Library through Oak Corridor and Talbot Gallery (174 feet); 6. Long Gallery to Octagon (267 feet).

79. The Octagon looking west towards the Talbot Gallery. Note the replicas of the Talbot and Fitzherbert memorials on the left. (Illustrated London News, 8th August 1857)

pinnacles may represent a reinstatement of the original parapet. Finally a tower was built at the south-east angle.

There is no doubt that it was Pugin who was responsible for these alterations. The diaries, and letters preserved at the V&A Museum and in a private collection, give important information about much of what he did in the Octagon, and other features may safely be assigned to him on grounds of style. The work appears to have been done in stages between 1839 and 1842. In March 1841 Pugin wrote to Lord Shrewsbury, *"The ventilators are finished in the octagon hall and answer admirably. The centre pillar is not yet lowered but all is ready for it and it will be done on the first opportunity".[8]* This indicates that the external walls had been built up by this time, and that the circular ventilation windows had been put into the north and south walls just below ceiling level.

The reference to the "lowering" of the centre pillar is intriguing. It cannot mean a reduction in height because the overall height of the building was actually being increased. It must therefore indicate that the upper sections of the pillar removed during the alterations were then lowered back into position by some kind of crane, with additional sections inserted to give extra height. One has also to conclude that Pugin was obliged to sacrifice architectural honesty to sheer practicality over the reinstatement of the plaster ceiling with its sham rib-vaults **(79)**. Even with the help of the central pillar, the thinly-buttressed walls of the Octagon would not have supported the weight of a stone vault. It was almost certainly Pugin who added the stone shield-bearing beasts to the tops of the colonettes supporting the principal ribs. These ribs arched inwards to engage sockets cut in the top section of the central column, while lateral ribs springing from each of the colonettes arched upwards to meet at the centre of each of the eight walls. Ornamental shields, decorated with the arms of Talbot and related families, and painted by Thomas Willement, adorned the walls. In December 1841 Pugin wrote: *"I have got all the shields for the octagon, and the masons are now altering the pillar".* [9] The quality of the stonework inside the Octagon is exceptional. It is one of only two rooms in the Towers - the other being the Armoury - which had stone-faced interiors rather than lath-and-plaster, therefore the finish is smooth and finely-jointed.

A prominent feature of the Octagon is the "Bishops Window" in the South Wall **(80)**. The window is of five lights , and the lower panels contained portraits of Talbot Bishops including Richard, Archbishop of Dublin (d.1449). Willement made the glass to Pugin's design in 1840. The location of this window in the south wall created a glowing focal point at this end of the 260-foot enfilade running from the Long Gallery through the Drawing Room and Conservatory to the Octagon. The glass survived in its entirety until 1952 as the *NMR* photographs show, but a few heraldic fragments in the top are all that remain today. Pugin was not altogether

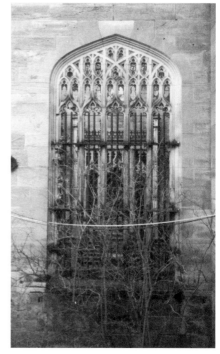

80. The Bishop's Window 1998. (MJF)

satisfied with the colours, and this window was a factor in his subsequent break with Willement whom he accused of over-charging for the windows at S. John's and of being interested only in making money: *"...A for agreements they are of no use with Willement. Did not your Lord-ship agree with him for the bishops window in the octagon & now he argues as a reason for what he now charges being dearer in comparison, that the octagon window is not rich & this latter glass* (i.e. at S. John's) *is rich. But the octagon window was <u>intended to be</u> rich & <u>with all I could</u> do he <u>could not make it</u> so. I never will work with Willement again".*[10]

There were of course other stained-glass artists to whom Pugin could turn, including London-based William Warrington (1796-1869) whom he had already used for work at Oscott and S. Chad's, Birmingham. Warrington was an authority on medieval stained glass, and a pioneer in its revival. He had the added advantage of being less expensive than Willement. Warrington's own handwritten list of works records the making of seven "lobby windows" and two quatre-foils for Alton, under the heading "Alton Towers Chapel". The chapel does not, however, have a "lobby", and the glass in the body of the building is known to be by Willement. It is therefore likely that the quatrefoils were for the two circular ventilation windows in the Octagon – one of which still survives, and that the "lobby windows" are in fact the windows of the Armoury, depicting key figures in the history of the Talbot and Verdun families.[11] If this is indeed the case, then the design of the Armoury windows may be attributable to Pugin. The Willement lists, which are far more detailed than Warrington's, make no reference to any work in the Armoury.

In the summer of 1841, while work on the Octagon was in progress, Pugin parted company with Warrington, specifically over the windows for S. John's hospital in the village. Pugin did not think that Warrington's heraldry was up to the mark – possibly because of his work on the Armoury windows – and he was also becoming expensive. Pugin expressed his disgust in a letter written to Lord Shrewsbury from Alton Towers at the end of August: *"...the Glass painters will shorten my days, they are the greatest plagues I have. The reason I did not give Warrington the windows at the hospital is this, he has become lately so conceited that he has got nearly as expensive as Willement......Warrington is a wretched herald".*[12]

Lighting in the Octagon would always have been subdued, and it seems that this was quite intentional, to provide a contrast with the top-lit Picture Gallery. The main source of natural light was through the conservatory entrance, and the effect of the sunlight flooding down the steps was not lost on contemporary observers. Being south-facing, the Bishops Window would have glowed with colour for much of the day, and together with the four smaller windows would have cast pools of coloured light across the stone floor. The glass for the small windows is not listed by either Warrington or Willement. They had diagonal bands containing the Talbot motto, *Prest d'accomplir.* Artificial lighting came from hanging lamps of Gothic design containing coloured glass, and from standards attached to the piers of the balustrade of the conservatory entrance. Stone benches ran along the walls, and Pugin added an octagonal stone bench around the central column.

The Pugin diaries make reference to the entrance that had to be constructed to give access from the Octagon into the new Talbot Gallery which was on a slightly higher level **(81)**. A flight of stone steps led up to a triple arch, the central section of which was flanked by slender compound piers decorated with crocketed pinnacles. On the top of these stood Talbot hounds

81. Renconstruction of entrance from Octagon to Talbot Gallery. (Pencil drawing by the author, 1998)

holding banners, while immediately over the arch was a crocketed ogee-moulding and six small metal shields emblazoned with the arms of the Talbots and associated families. The arches were filled with splendid oak screenwork. This may well have been made in the Lambeth workshops of George Myers, or possibly by Thomas Harris, a local carpenter who is known to have worked on other items for the Towers and also for S John's, Alton.[14] The screen is in the

Perpendicular style, each of the three sections having transoms with cresting in the form of strawberry leaves, and rich tracery in the heads **(82).** The screenwork and the doors in the central section were originally filled with glass. They are akin to those designed by Pugin for other great houses such as Scarisbrick Hall and Leighton Hall (Welshpool), and similar ones were made for the New Palace of Westminster.

82. Detail of the timber screen-work, Talbot entrance. (MJF 1998)

The raising of the Octagon and the creation of this splendid entrance into the new Talbot Gallery created an imbalance on the east side where another triple archway gave access into the Octagon from the Picture Gallery. These arches now appeared far too low in comparison with the ones opposite, with an expanse of unrelieved ashlar above. On the Picture Gallery side of the wall, however, these arches rose almost to ceiling level, so it was not possible to enlarge them upwards.

Pugin therefore adopted the expedient of paring back the walls on the Octagon side and continuing the mouldings upwards to create a triplet of blank arches over the existing doorways, rising to the same level as the entrance to the Talbot Gallery **(83).** Like the raising of the Octagon walls, it was a practical solution to problems created by the linking of buildings with differing floor- and roof-levels. The blank arches were filled with heraldic paintings on canvas done by Willement. The one over the central arch depicted a scroll with a verse inspired by the Talbot motto *Prest d'Accomplir-:*

"The redie minde regardeth never toyle,
But still is Prest t'accomplish heartes intent;
Abrode, at home, in every coste or soyle
The dede is done, that inwardly is mente,
Which makes me saye to every virtuous dede
I am still prest t'accomplish what's decreed.

But byd to goe I redie am to ronne,
But byd to ronne I redie am to ride,
To goe, ronne, ride, or what else to be done,
Speke but the worde, and soon it shall be tryde;
Tout prest je suis pour accomplir la chose
Par tout labeur qui vous peut faire repose.

Prest to accomplish what you shall commande,
Prest to accomplish what you shall desire,
Prest to accomplish your desires demands,
Prest to accomplish heaven for happy hire;
Thus do I ende and at your will I reste,
As you shall please in every action prest".[15]

83. The Octagon looking west into Picture Gallery during 1999 work, showing blank arches created by Pugin during his alterations of 1839-42 (MJF 1999)

The original (pre-Pugin) doors and traceried cast-iron panels in the side-openings were retained. These panels were identical in form to the ones applied to the doors of the Grand Entrance and those in the glazed doors of the Great Drawing Room.

It was not only the structure of the Octagon that was altered by Pugin; its contents and function changed too. Items such as neo-classical sculptures which accorded ill with the Gothic ambience of the hall were removed to other parts of the house, notably the Ceccarini *Raphael* which found a new location in the Talbot Gallery where it remained until the Great Sale of 1857. Its place in the Octagon was taken by replicas of the tombs of the first Earl of Shrewsbury and Sir Nicholas Fitzherbert, complete with recumbent effigies cast in plaster from the originals under Pugin's directions. In April 1841 he sent a plasterer named Samuel Firth to the church of S. Alkmund at Whitchurch to take a cast from the fifteenth-century effigy of the first Earl John. *"He has done the Fitzherbert's beautifully,"* Pugin remarked.[16] At Whitchurch only the effigy had

84. The effigy of John Talbot, first Earl of Shrewsbury: S. Alkmund's church, Whitchurch. (MJF 1998)

survived the rebuilding of the church in 1711, so Pugin had to design a completely new plinth for it, inscribed - in black-letter of course - with the appropriate epitaph recording the death in 1453 of the "Great Talbot" whose exploits in the French Wars had won him the title Earl of Shrewsbury **(84)**. The tomb of Nicholas Fitzherbert (d.1471) is in the chancel of Norbury church, about six miles from Alton, and just over the Derbyshire border. It is in many ways more splendid than the Talbot, complete with tomb-chest which has figures standing in canopied niches **(85)**. The Fitzherberts were related by marriage to the Talbots, and had also remained loyal Catholics after the Reformation. Though it may come as something of a surprise to know that the author of *The True Principles* was also the author of a pair of sham memorials, it has to be said in Pugin's defence that they never pretended to be anything other than replicas. In

85. The Fitzherbert monument at Norbury, copied by Samuel Firth for the Octagon. (MJF 1988)

the course of his travels on the Staffordshire/Shropshire border Pugin discovered another fine Talbot tomb about which he wrote enthusiastically to Lord Shrewsbury, suggesting that it was also worth casting, but nothing appears to have come of the idea .[17]

"The Octagon Job is done", wrote Pugin in March 1842, referring to the internal arrangements.[18] Some external features still awaited completion, for in November of the following year he wrote, "*... The last of the towers will never produce its proper effect till the last of the modern pinnacles round the octagon are worked up into ashlar".[19]* It has to be said that the truncated square pinnacles do not look very Puginian, although they do have Gothic panels carved on the front face. One wonders if

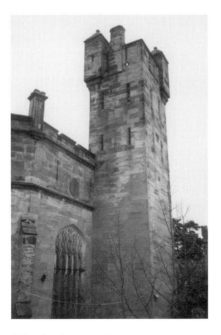

86. The Octagon Tower. (MJF 1998)

they were originally intended to have crocketed upper sections like those on the chapel tower, or gablets as on the octagon at Ilam church. The tower referred to in the letter must be the one which stands at the south-east angle of the Octagon. One would hesitate to assign this to Pugin on grounds of style, but the evidence of the letter is clear enough. The tower is quite obviously an addition **(86).** It relates rather awkwardly to the angle of the octagon against which it is built, and there is no bonding on the outside. It is clear that the tower never contained any habitable rooms, and one is drawn to the conclusion that it was there simply for effect, as Pugin hints in his letter, although this something which he would normally abhor as contrary to his "true principles". The square bartizans with their pyramid caps have more than a hint of the Scottish baronial about them. Pugin, it should be remembered, was thoroughly familiar with Scottish architecture, and in 1842 he paid three visits to Scotland, on one of which he met the Sobieski Stuart pretenders to the English throne *(see above, p.93).*

Externally there is much about the Octagon that is unsatisfactory, and Pugin cannot have been entirely pleased with it, but it needs to be said that the Octagon and its associated galleries were meant to be viewed from the inside, and they were not the only Pugin buildings in which the interior predominated, thus laying him open to the charge that he did not think in volume, and that he was basically a scene-painter who used his meagre walls simply as "flats" on which to apply masses of decorative work.[20] Certainly there were aspects of the Octagon and the Talbot Gallery which were theatrical and illusory, designed to re-create the medieval splendours of the Talbots which, though real enough in their time, had long since vanished. This was of course the age in which Sir Walter Scott's novels captured the public imagination with their vivid descriptions of baronial halls, banquets and tournaments, and in 1839 this spilled over into an actual medieval-style jousting tournament organised by the Earl of Eglinton along the lines of the one described in *Ivanhoe.* Held at the earl's Ayrshire castle, the "Eglinton Tournament" attracted many thousands of people including leading society figures who came dressed in medieval costume. Pugin was not there, although among the company was Lord Breadalbane for whom Pugin was carrying out improvements at Taymouth Castle.[21] It may be of some significance that in his library Lord Shrewsbury had a set of views of the Tournament published by J.H. Nixon in 1843.

THE GRAND TALBOT

Very much in the spirit of the Eglinton Tournament was Lord Shrewsbury's commissioning of a life-size equestrian statue of the first earl - "The Grand Talbot" - to occupy pride of place in the Armoury at Alton **(87)**. The idea seems to have been mooted in 1840 and its progress was raised in several letters which passed between Lord Shrewsbury and Pugin who was given the task of procuring a wooden horse and the correct armour and vesture for both horse and rider. Pugin saw a suitable horse in Edward Hull's shop in London and told Shrewsbury that he would not find better elsewhere,[22] but it was not until 1842 that any real progress was made. The fifteenth-century effigy on the Talbot's tomb at Whitchurch - a cast of which was already in the Octagon - was an important point of reference, and Pugin also went to the Tower of London to look at figures of armoured knights on horseback. Yet in spite of the trouble he took in making full-size drawings of everything, Edward Hull's French supplier of replica armour failed to live up to expectations:

87. "The Grand Talbot" - artist's impression based on contemporary descriptions and 1950s photograph

> *".......... the Frenchman is a complete humbug; he did not like the <u>trouble of making a proper suit</u> from the effigy & therefore sent some he had ready, but it is not even of the date but this is the way with all this generation, they think only of profit, and the vagabond thought he could make double by a set of common armour than by a really good one".[23]*

Some of the defects in the armour would be covered by a purple mantle, for Pugin insisted that the figure should be vested *"as a Knight of the Garter exactly as he is shown on the monument,".[24]* Since the earl was to be depicted as riding in state, Pugin argued, he should wear a coronet rather than a helmet:

> *" ...I have got every authority for the costume; if he is merely in armour it will look an every day thing and lose half its effect If your Lordship will trust to me I will not be at all extravagant but will make a glorious thing. If it is not well done I should not dare to meet Lady Shrewsbury for I know she expects it to be a truly good production,"[25]*

Standing on a Pugin-designed wooden plinth with coats-of arms set in panels around it, the Grand Talbot stood proudly in the Armoury until the 1857 sale, bearing a facsimile of the famous sword inscribed with the motto *Ego sum Talboti pro vincere inimicos meos* - "I am (the sword of) Talbot, for the vanquishing of my enemies". In more recent times the figure was identified and photographed in a Brighton antique shop, but its present whereabouts are not known.[26]

THE CHAPEL

Pugin's improvements to the chapel were carried out in two stages. The first of these (1839-40) included the installation of the reredos and the elaborate Gothic altar-screen, while the second stage (1849-51) comprised the decoration of the ceiling, the addition of a frieze and other decorative panels, and new picture-frames. Thus the sombre wainscot-lined chamber designed by Potter and Fradgley was transformed by Pugin into so gloriously rich a setting for the celebration of Catholic rites as to rival even the finest of his churches. Pugin's work at the Towers chapel is discussed in depth in chapter 6.

THE DORIA ROOMS

Following their marriage in Rome in 1839 and the grand reception at Alton, Lord Shrewsbury hoped that the Prince and Princess Doria would return to the Towers from time to time, and so commissioned a special suite of rooms for them. The "Doria" apartments, as they were called, were built over the Plate Glass Drawing-room (the former chapel) and the rooms immediately to the west. Another level was also added to the east entrance tower and this was crowned with a lantern which disappeared when the house was gutted, but it is visible on old photographs. Architecturally and historically this is one of the most interesting parts of the house, in which every stage of its development is represented **(88)**. The Doria suite consisted of four rooms: the Doria tower room, the boudoir, dressing-room and bedroom. Although the roofs and floors are now gone, three fine Pugin chimney-pieces survive in this area at the upper level **(89)**. One of these has a depressed ogee arch, unique amongst the surviving chimney-

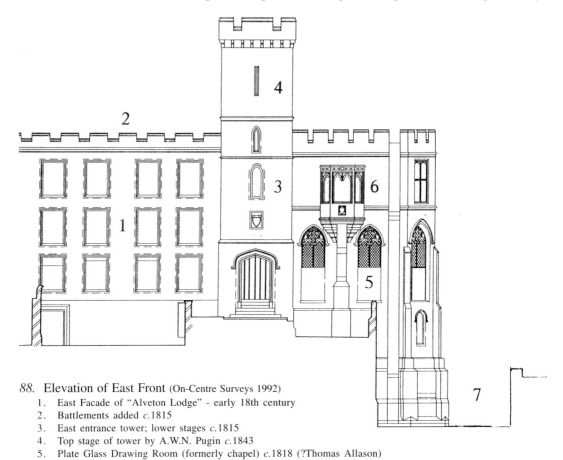

88. Elevation of East Front (On-Centre Surveys 1992)
   1. East Facade of "Alveton Lodge" - early 18th century
   2. Battlements added *c*.1815
   3. East entrance tower; lower stages *c*.1815
   4. Top stage of tower by A.W.N. Pugin *c*.1843
   5. Plate Glass Drawing Room (formerly chapel) *c*.1818 (?Thomas Allason)
   6. Doria Rooms (including oriel window and buttress) by Pugin *c*.1843
   7. Excavation of fosse and weatherings to footings of north front; Pugin *c*.1843

pieces at Alton, but similar to one at Taymouth Castle (Perthshire) where Pugin had been working with James Gillespie Graham on Gothic furnishings and decorations. Another fireplace has the letters "D" and "M", signifying Doria and Mary, in the spandrels of the arch. The "D" is in the backward-curving lower-case form which is so characteristic of Pugin.

89. Chimneypiece in the Doria apartments. (MJF 1998)

The Doria rooms appear to date from 1843. Pugin's diary for that year is, unfortunately, missing, but in a letter dated 17th October he expresses the hope that good progress is being made with the buttress for the Doria Room.[27] This refers to what is the finest external feature of these apartments, namely an cast-facing oriel window, corbelled-out and carried on a buttress built between two of the windows of the Plate Glass Drawing-Room. The front section is of two lights with cinquefoiled heads, and below are the impaled arms of Doria and Talbot. The cornice is carved with the Talbot arms, and lion-masks at the corners. At the base of the window, where the corbelling springs from the wall, there are tiny figures of a gryphon and a lion, again taken from the respective family arms. This window would have commanded spectacular views into the valley gardens, and it stands as one of the loveliest examples of Pugin's stonework to be seen at the Towers **(90).** To the great embarrassment of the architect, the Prince and Princess Doria arrived quite suddenly at Alton before the rooms were completely finished, and Pugin wrote most apologetically to Lord Shrewsbury, *".... I am very much mortified about it & I fear it will distress your Lordship".*[28] When completed, however, the rooms were furnished and decorated in a sumptuous manner. The curtains and other hangings were of figured velvet, and much of the furniture was in the style of Louis XIV.[29]

It is not known how frequently the Prince and Princess visited England - and Alton - in subsequent years, but in 1848 they were caught up in the wave of revolutions which swept across the Italian states, driving King Ferdinand from Naples and the Pope from Rome. Though the revolutions were short-lived and order eventually restored, Pugin wrote anxiously to Lord Shrewsbury:

".......... Prince and Princess Doria are home from Rome. They are very fortunate to get safe to England. I am afraid they will suffer serious lapses in their popularity at Rome. What has become of all their fine pictures? No place like England for security".[30]

90. The Doria window. (MJF 1998)

THE DEFENCE OF ALTON TOWERS

When Pugin wrote that there was "no place like England for security" he did so knowing that while revolution reigned in Italy, Germany and France in 1848, England remained free from any major civil unrest. Even the Chartist demonstration of that year - the last of its kind - was on the whole a peaceful affair. Pugin had not always been so confident in the triumph of order over violence, even in England, and Lord Shrewsbury shared his fear of popular uprisings during the period known as the "hungry forties". In 1842 Pugin fortified his own home against the possibility of attack by striking miners and in the same year extensive fortifications were constructed at Alton Towers. Alton was not very far away from the North Staffordshire coalfield which included not only Stoke-on-Trent but also parts of the rural areas close to Cheadle. In the summer of 1842 there was a considerable amount of unrest culminating in Chartist-led riots in Stoke during August. These convinced Shrewsbury and Pugin that measures were needed to protect the Towers against the possibility of an attack, for in spite of the multiplicity of towers, battlements and loops, the building was extremely vulnerable, and as Pugin had said only the year before, *"who would hammer against nailed portals when he could kick his way through the greenhouse?"*[31] The east side of the house was particularly exposed. The Armoury doors were strong enough, but almost anyone could go round the side, break into the House Conservatory and thus get into any part of the Towers. The whole of the north front was likewise unprotected, a carriageway running the length of the terrace and past the large windows of the basement storey. For an angry mob to assault and invade the Towers would therefore be no difficult task, and the prospect of it frightened both earl and architect.

91. The Barbican, by Pugin, 1842. (MJF 1998)

Pugin's solution was to fortify the most vulnerable areas. A barbican was built at the Northeast corner of the screen-wall to protect the approach to the Grand Entrance (**91**). Fitted-out with loops and machicolations, it was a serious piece of castellated architecture, and it bears the Shrewsbury arms and the date 1842 on the south side. Linked with this was the excavation of a deep ditch, or fosse, running the whole length of the north front. Standing on this side of the house today, one would be forgiven for thinking that this ditch was an original feature put in at the very beginning of the development of "Alton Abbey" in the early 1800s, but as we already know, the buildings were fronted at first by nothing more defensive than a terrace and flower-beds, with a large stained-glass window occupying the position of the original main doors.

The excavation of the fosse - alluded to somewhat cryptically by Pugin as "the undertaking" - is also mentioned in a contemporary French biography of the Shrewsburys' younger daughter, Gwendalyn.[32] It was a major "undertaking" involving the removal of many tons of soil and rock, and there is the possibility that it had the secondary objective of providing work for men who in these lean years might otherwise have had none. Some of the spoil was used in making the rampart and terrace walk east of the barbican. Even though the house had been built on solid rock, a certain amount of underpinning and shoring-up had to be done, and Pugin expressed concern for the safety of the building during the wet autumn of 1842: "...*The rains*

are incessant here, and if the pre-cautions are neglected I expect some serious accident will happen." [33]
On the north side the drop into the fosse is sheer, and it is fronted by a retaining wall; on the house side the bedrock was battered and weatherings were applied, thus creating the illusion that the fosse was a part of the original pre-1820s scheme of things. To allow access to the east entrance tower and the chapel a drawbridge was placed over the fosse, and the existing

92. The drawbridge over the fosse. (postcard of *c*.1930)

small gateway through the curtain-wall was modified accordingly, and a mechanism was installed so that the drawbridge could be raised if necessary **(92)**. Pugin could not afford to perpetrate the kind of architectural folly that had so recently received a sharp stab of his pen: *"...portcullises which will not lower down, and drawbridges which will not draw up!"* [34] As a finishing touch Pugin recommended that the fosse might be protected by stanchions and chains at the corners. *"The chain should be a good deal stronger than that used at the drawbridge and hang from stanchion to stanchion".* [35] Other precautions taken at this time may have included the placing of the sturdy iron grille on the outside of the Bishops' window in the Octagon. It was probably at this time too that the steps up to the Grand Entrance were improved by the addition of the stepped balustrade and shield-bearing Talbot hounds.

The fear of insurrection was always greater than the reality, and the fortifications proved unnecessary. Monsieur Zeloni attributed this to the veneration in which Earl John and his family were held by the people of the neighbourhood. Not for nothing was he known as "Good Earl John".

THE GREAT DINING ROOM

Catholic England, as Pugin was wont to remind his hearers and readers, was *"Merry England"*, where the nobility and gentry exercised their rights of hospitality to their fullest extent:

> *"........ They did not confine their guests, as at present, to a few fashionables who condescend to pass away a few days occasionally in a country house; but under the oaken rafters of their capacious halls the lords of the manor used to assemble all their friends and tenants at those successive periods when the church bids all her children rejoice..."* [37]

All of Pugin's designs for country houses had therefore, as an essential feature for such occasions, a great hall with an open timber roof, a dais at one end, and a minstrels' gallery at the other; a conscious revival of the medieval hall in which noble family, servants and tenantry would feast together. Among Pugin's executed designs were the halls at Scarisbrick (Lancashire) and Bilton Grange (Warwickshire), and he was determined that Alton Towers should have the grandest of them all, as would befit the residence of England's premier earl. Having been obliged to turn a blind eye to sham plaster-vaults in the Octagon, to spend untold amounts of time and energy tracking down fittings for a theatrical horse and rider, and to make the best he could of Fradgley's peculiar brand of Gothic in the chapel, Pugin at last had the opportunity to give his patron a taste of the "real thing", and one can well understand why he pushed his own ideas for the dining room to the very limit.

The bare bones, as it were, of the great dining hall were already in place when Pugin arrived at Alton: the former entrance hall which had already been turned into a dining room as shown as such in Samuel Rayner's pencil drawing of about 1840 **(14)**. Elegant though this room undoubtedly was, it suffered the great disadvantage of being on a lower level than that of the state rooms, guests on formal occasions having to descend into it by means of the original entrance-hall staircase. The sixteenth earl's original proposal for the alteration of the room may have involved little more than raising the floor level by about ten feet so as to match that of the other main apartments, and thus creating a new basement area below.

The scheme appears to have been discussed as early as 1842. Pugin's letter to Lord Shrewsbury about the excavation of the fosse contains an intriguing references to the foundations for a bay window:

> *"Denny writes me word that the underpinning is proceeding but the foundations of the bay window are omitted. This is a bad job for if the bare moulding is run across we shall lose the bond & it is likewise a great waste of work as the same weathering set further out with a rough backing would have done....."*[38]

Alton Towers has only two bay windows at ground level, i.e. ones with "foundations". One is the large bay in the Music Room on the south front which pre-dates Pugin, and the other is the great window of Pugin's dining hall of 1849-51. It seems therefore that as early as 1842 Pugin was thinking of the eventual construction of this bay to the dining room, and thought it prudent to set out the foundations and weatherings for it while work was going on in the fosse.

The north gable-end of the existing dining room had two Gothic windows, set one above the other. The large upper window dated from c1819 and was part of the original construction of the hall as the principal entrance to the house. The lower window had been put in around 1834 to replace the entrance doors when the hall was turned into a dining room. Aesthetically it was never a very satisfactory arrangement, the windows being of different styles **(93)**, and it would appear that Pugin was proposing at least to replace the lower one with a bay rising out of the fosse to illuminate the new basement level of the building. The upper window was however a different matter, and although Pugin may already have been thinking about replacing it with a great oriel, the earl and countess seemed determined to keep it:

> *".....Lady Shrewsbury has consented to retain the present large window in the dining room when that is to be done, so mind that is a settled point & you must not unsettle it on any account,"*[39]

The reconstruction of the dining room, and the controversies which accompanied it, are well-documented in the surviving Pugin/Shrewsbury correspondence. The earl seemed keen to retain many of the existing features, including the large window, and to begin with Pugin agreed, suggesting only that Eginton's glass - which Pugin described as "miserable" - be re-

93. The north front of Alton Towers *c.*1842 showing the two windows in the gable-end of the dining room before Pugin's remodelling. (Lithograph by G. Rowe for William Adam, *The Gem of the Peak*, 1843)

placed with something better. There were those who expressed disapproval of any alteration being made to such a fine room, and even Pugin agreed that to leave it as it was even with its plaster-vaulted ceiling - would be preferable to carrying out some half-measure that would simply ruin what was already there. He therefore insisted on a complete remodelling to include all of the features he considered necessary in the re-creation of a medieval hall, to the point of declaring that the earl must have everything or nothing:

> "...... *I intended to make a fine thing suitable to the purpose for which it is destined and not a common room fit only for an hotel .... If I am not allowed to exercise any judgement & make use of my knowledge & experience I am reduced to the condition of a mere drawing clerk to mark out what I am ordered & this I cannot bear..... I have nailed my colours to the mast: a bay window, high open roof, lantern, 2 grand fireplaces, a great sideboard, screen, minstrel gallery, all or none.*" [40]

Here is Pugin once more enunciating one of his basic principles that the whole design of a building must reflect the purpose for which it is intended. It was the earl rather than the architect who eventually gave way, but not without further misunderstandings and clashes of opinion. In the early 1840s Pugin carried out extensive alterations and additions to Bilton Grange, the Warwickshire home of Captain John Hubert Washington Hibbert who in 1839 had married the widowed mother of Lord Shrewsbury's cousin and heir, Bertram Talbot. Pugin's work at Bilton included a gabled dining hall with a high open roof, great fireplace, minstrels' gallery and large windows containing heraldic glass (**94**). Having seen this, and having con-

ceded Pugin's basic principles for his own new dining room, Shrewsbury evidently believed that a similar modestly-furnished hall would suffice at Alton. The very suggestion that what was suitable for a mere grange might also be adequate for the palatial residence of England's premier earl provoked another indignant response from Pugin:

> *"Your Lordship cannot seriously mean to have so plain a job as Bilton. The dining hall of such a mansion as Alton should be something superior to a grange. Everybody would condemn it and me too".[41]*

"Nailing his colours to the mast" involved the preparation of detailed drawings, and in 1848 Pugin produced a large picture of the proposed interior of the dining room for exhibition at the Royal Academy.[42] Though the present whereabouts of this picture are not known, the building itself and the pre-1952 photo-

94. The dining room at Bilton Grange. (MJF 1992)

graphs of it tell their own story **(95).** Instead of being left plain as at Bilton, the open timber roof at Alton was patterned in paint and gilt; the minstrels' gallery was enriched with pierced work; the wall-panelling was more intricately carved. Instead of a single fireplace there were two, made of white Banbury stone and deeply sculpted with the Talbot arms and motto. In magnificence as well as sheer size the hall at Alton far excelled what Pugin bad been able to achieve at Bilton, but it was a hard-won achievement which strained the relationship between architect and patron almost to breaking-point, Pugin pushing all the time for something far more splendid than Bilton Grange, and Shrewsbury urging against unnecessary extravagance. Pugin was even prepared to bring in Lady Shrewsbury as a kind of witness for his defence:

> *".......... when the dining room was decided to be done it was really my duty to design it in the best manner and to carry it out in such as way as would give your Lordship real satisfaction when compleat. The very last words her Ladyship admonished me at Alton were mind that the dining room is a fine thing, and how can this be if it is divested of all fine features..... It has proved already a most unfortunate business and I might almost say a fatal one to me if it leads to the result to which your Lordship alludes".[43]*

It is evident that Lord Shrewsbury seriously considered dismissing Pugin, who grieved to think that the patron whom he greatly admired should be prepared to dispense with him over this matter, and he wondered if there might be some ulterior motive. Having brooded to the extent of being unable to concentrate on his work, he took a trip to Flanders, and on his return to Ramsgate found a conciliatory letter from the earl waiting for him. In his reply Pugin expressed sorrow and regret for any misunderstanding, and his great relief that it had been resolved, but at the same time he defended the stance he had taken over the dining hall. There was still no room for compromise:

> *"all I now hope and trust is that your Lordship will give me credit for <u>better intentions</u> and again <u>I must earnestly</u> assure your Lordship that the letter was written merely to try and persuade you to make a good thing. I never intended*

95. Interior of the Great Dining Room *c.*1890. (Staffordshire County Museum, Shugborough Hall)

anything extravagant and really I cannot reproach myself with ever wasting any of the funds with which your Lordship has entrusted me".[44]

Another bone of contention was the large window in the north wall. For a time Pugin seemed content to keep it, so long as more suitable glass could be provided, but eventually he held out for a completely new oriel window as one of the conditions of his "all or none" ultimatum to the earl. While confessing that he had always been opposed in principle to the retention of the old window Pugin cleverly turned the argument back on Lord Shrewsbury, reminding him of precisely who had proposed its removal in the first place: *"...at one time your Lordship suggested it would do for the east window of a church to which I quite agreed, for it is a church window in design".*[45] Apart from eating his own words, what could the earl have done other than concur?

96. Drawing for north window of dining hall by J.H. Powell (John Hardman Studio, Lightwood Park, Birmingham). It shows a different arrangement of the heraldry from the window as finally executed (Col. Pl. XIII).

Pugin's preferred option would have been to place a window or windows in a side wall as he had done at Scarisbrick Hall and as he planned to do in his proposed rebuilding of Garendon Hall for Ambrose Phillipps. At Alton, however, the hall was set transversely in the north-facing range, so side-windows of any kind were out of the question. Nevertheless Pugin felt that it would be a pity to lose so fine a feature, especially as one of its functions would be to illuminate the proposed screen and great sideboard, so it was eventually agreed that a great oriel **(96)** should be built in the north gable-end **(97)**, towering above the dais where Pugin imagined the earl and countess would dine at high table on festive occasions. *"I am sure it would not be costly,"* Pugin assured the earl, *"as it would be all masons work".*[46]

In a medieval hall a screen at the opposite end to the dais was an indispensable feature, and many examples still existed, for example in the refectories of Oxford and Cambridge colleges as well as in castles and manor houses which had escaped re-modelling in post-medieval times. Its principal function was quite literally to screen off the servery area, and the access to the kitchens, from the main body of the hall. The screen normally had a doorway at either end, and usually a "screens passage" running along the back of it, and communicating with the kitchen doors. Pugin was determined to have such a screen at Alton, though far more splendid than the one he had installed for Captain Hibbert at Bilton Grange. This too became a bone of contention between himself and Lord Shrewsbury who wanted nothing too extravagant.[47] As eventually constructed the screen was a magnificent piece of furniture, complete with the minstrels' gallery which Pugin had always envisaged. The sideboard for the display of plate stood against the central section, while projecting sections on either side screened the doorways leading from the family rooms to the east and the state rooms to the west, and also those leading to the kitchen area behind the hall. The projecting sections had openwork panels with fine geometrical tracery.

The discussions and disagreements about the dining hall inevitably delayed the start of the build-

97. Elevation of dining room, north gable.

98. The Pugin-Hardman chandelier.
(Palace of Westminster)

ing programme, so that although the project may have been contemplated as early as 1843 building did not actually commence until 1849. *"I propose going soon after Easter to see the great work begun"*, Pugin wrote in February. *"I have just finished my drawing of the interior and it looks exceedingly well".*[48] The principal walls were of course already there: they needed to be built up by about ten feet to compensate for the raising of the floor level, and the wall on the east side had to be reinforced in order to accommodate the two great fireplaces which run back to a depth of 4' 6". Since the existing wall was little more than two feet thick it had to be backed by a brick reinforcing wall reaching up to the first-floor level in the rooms immediately adjoining it.

The north wall was remodelled to include a square bay-window at what was now the basement level. Above this rose the much-disputed great oriel, while in the south gable at gallery level Pugin set a five-light Gothic window with panel tracery in the head. The glass was designed by Pugin and manufactured at the Hardman workshops in Birmingham.[49] Pugin had by this time fallen out with the stained-glass manufacturers to whom he had entrusted his earlier designs - Warrington,

Willement and Wailes - and persuaded his friend and colleague John Hardman to add glassmaking to the comprehensive list of Gothic silverware, brasswork and ironwork which he was already producing. The large oriel was made up of twenty-seven lights blazoned with the arms of the Talbots and related families **(Col. Plate XIII)**. The glass in the south window was even more splendid, heraldic devices in the side panels flanking a representation of the Garter-robed Great Talbot in the centre light which was exhibited at the Great Exhibition of 1851. Most of this glass survives and was photographed *in situ,* but the Talbot was removed - and presumably sold - in 1952.

Supported on stone corbels ornamented with shield-bearing Talbots, the roof is similar in structure to those in other Pugin buildings such as Bilton, Scarisbrick and Lismore Castle (Ireland); i.e. it has wind-braces and a frieze **(Col. Plate XIV).** Unlike the one at Bilton it is richly-decorated with the appropriate heraldic emblems picked out in red, blue and gold. From the centre of the ridge there rises a lantern from which was suspended a great chandelier of gilt brass and crystal made by Hardman **(98)**. It is almost identical in design to one

99. Detail of panelling from dining room, now in S. Peter's Church, Alton. It would appear to have come from the front of the minstrel's gallery (see no.94). (MJF 1998)

made by Hardman for Eastnor Castle (Herefordshire), and the source for both is a medieval chandelier which Pugin saw in Nuremberg cathedral.

The lower parts of the walls were oak-panelled, and the carving of the upper panels, as well as that on the screen and minstrels' gallery, was particularly rich, as surviving fragments clearly show (99). Pugin was a great collector of medieval artefacts including examples of wood panelling. The patterns he used at Alton are recognisably derived from items in his collection and which are now kept at the Victoria and Albert Museum.[50] The upper parts of the walls were papered, no doubt with wallpaper designed by J.G. Crace. The woodwork of the dining room was almost certainly produced in the workshops of George Myers, and the same may be said of the two huge fireplaces (100). The encaustic hearth-tiles with the Shrewsbury/Talbot monograms in yellow and blue on a red ground were supplied by Herbert Minton. Thus the creation of the great hall drew together the combined

100. Chimneypiece in dining hall, *c.*1930. (The Lewis Family Collection)

talents of Crace, Hardman, Minton and Myers; the team to which Pugin could most confidently entrust the execution of his designs over a wide range of artistic media. A complete set of new metal-gilt plate was made by Hardman for display on the sideboard. This included an enormous dish measuring 30 inches in diameter, with the Shrewsbury shield in the centre, and a border of coronets and mottoes, and several smaller ones in similar Gothic style.[51] The sideboard, decked with several items of plate, was displayed in the Medieval Court at the Great Exhibition of 1851, as indeed was the great chandelier. A drawing published in the *Illustrated London News* (XIX, 1851) shows that the sideboard was elaborately carved and decorated (101). The very plain sideboard shown in the later-nineteenth-century photographs of the hall is clearly not the original.

101. The sideboard - detail from view of the Medieval Court. (Illustrated London News, 20th September 1851. The accompanying text states that the sideboard was made by Crace)

Sadly, neither the earl nor Pugin lived long enough to see the dining hall finished. Work was still in progress at the time of their deaths in the autumn of 1852. The Towers account books show that payments were being made to masons, carpenters, plasterers and painters for work on the hall as late as 1856, and documents in the Hardman archive tell of slow progress on the great oriel window.[52] Barely started at the time of Earl John's death, the glass was not fully completed and installed until 1856 **(96 & co. ppl. XIII)** The 1857 Sale Catalogue reveals that the pictures from the dining room, including the Barbarossa, were being stored in the Billiard Room at this time, as was the great chandelier, thereby indicating that interior fitting and decoration were still incomplete. Llewellyn Jewitt's account of the Towers after the sale also comments on its unfinished state:

"...... This hall, which was being remodelled and altered by Pugin at the time of the Earl's death, remains to this day in an unfinished state, but shows how truly grand in every way it would have been had it been completed. The sides of the room were intended to be panelled, as was also the minstrels gallery, with carved oak, and a part of this is already placed". [53]

There is evidence to show that Edward Welby Pugin took over his father's work at the Towers from 1852.[54] The death of the seventeenth earl in 1856, and the ensuing legal battle over the succession which was not settled until 1860, obviously caused further delays in the completion of the work, but photographs taken of the hall from about 1890 onwards show that it was eventually finished exactly as Pugin had envisaged it, with the exception of the label-stops of the south window which remain to this day as plain uncarved blocks.

THE "NEW ROOMS" and THE SOUTH FACADE

102. The south front of Alton Towers reveals a mixture of styles: the conservatory by Hopper, the lower floor of the main block by Allason, and the upper floors by Pugin. To the right is the south gable of Pugin's dining room. (MJF 1998)

While working on the dining room, Pugin carried out significant alterations and extensions to adjoining parts of the house. These included the addition of a fourth storey to the block immediately to the west of the dining room, the building of new rooms over the Drawing Room, and the raising of the octagon stair-turret on the north facade. The precise function of these rooms is not clear, and it seems strange that such large additions should have been planned when the family were spending a good deal of their time abroad. It may be that the principal suite was originally intended for the sixteenth earl's cousin and heir, Bertram, possibly to mark his coming-of-age in 1853. The death of the sixteenth earl - and of course that of Pugin too - brought about a temporary halt, but Bertram clearly wished the work to continue, and the Towers wages books for 1855 and 1856 list payments to masons, joiners and carpenters for work on the "New Rooms".

The form of the windows in these new rooms, together with details like strings and carved bosses, readily identify them as Pugin's, i.e. as the Gothic of *True Principles as* distinct from the archaeologically incorrect windows of Hopper and Allason on the lower levels **(102)**. On the south side the tower blocks at either end of the Drawing Room were built up by another two

103. Pugin's oriel windows (a) over the Drawing Room at Alton Towers, (b) at Alton Castle. (MJF 1998)

floors, and a new suite of rooms created over the Drawing Room itself, raising this block to the same level as the top storey of the Long Gallery. The principal features of this new south facade are two oriel windows, corbelled-out and supported, like the Doria window, by buttresses rising from basement level. These windows are identical to ones at Alton Castle which Pugin was building at the same time **(103)**. All of the windows on the upper level have stone mullions, cusped lights, and - a characteristic Pugin motif - small trefoils carved in relief in the spandrels. Above the windows and below the battlements is a cornice with bosses carved with lions' heads, Talbot hounds, family monograms and the *Agnus Dei* - the emblem of Earl John's patron saint, John the Baptist. Pugin also applied a new cornice, bosses and battlements to the large bay-window of the Music Room. One wonders why he did not at the same time remove the curious wooden tracery from this window and replace it with something better.

104. The "Pugin Rooms" above the Drawing Room, 1998. The oriels could be closed off by sliding shutters. (MJF 1998)

The two main rooms above the Drawing Room were equipped with

130

105. Illustration of a panelled room from Pugin's *True Principles* (1843). The "rew rooms" at the Towers appear to have been treated in similar fashion. Note the initials IT (?Ioannes Talbot) on some of the shields.

stone chimney-pieces of similar type to ones at Alton Castle, both lined with Minton tiles. Two doorways on the north side give access into the top floor of the Long Gallery, the former exterior windows having been adapted for this purpose. The rooms were part-panelled, and the windows were equipped with ingenious shutters which slid back into the wall-cavities at the sides **(104)** the "real thing" as distinct from the elaborate drapes and festoons which hung in front of the windows of the state rooms below. The appearance of these rooms would have been somewhat similar to the one illustrated by Pugin in *True Principles* **(105)** where he was attempting to show that domestic architecture in the "true" Gothic style need not be excessively costly if decoration consisted principally of "mere panelling more or less enriched by carving, with large spaces left for hangings and tapestry".[55] Some stone-carving was attempted in the spandrels of the oriel arches, but it is somewhat shallow and perhaps reflects the haste with which the rooms were eventually finished. They were clearly not in use by the time of the 1857 sale. An inventory taken in 1860 refers simply to "New Room at top of Pugin's circular oak staircase", "New Bed Room" and "Bedroom no. 2". They were at that time completely unfurnished, Bedroom no. 2 being little more than a repository for quantities of oak panelling, doors, and framing which were still waiting to be fixed in place.[56] The work was eventually completed, and the rooms were named the Pugin Bedroom, Pugin Dressing Room, and Pugin Landing. Known as the Pugin Stairs, the circular oak staircase referred to in the inventory was still *in situ* in 1952, and it was praised by architects for the way in which Pugin had skilfully used an awkward space.[57]

KITCHENS AND SERVANTS' QUARTERS

In March 1841 Pugin wrote to Lord Shrewsbury, *"The alterations in the kitchens and offices are completed and are certainly improvements".*[58] No particulars are given as to what precisely was done, but it is possible to discern the hand of Pugin in details such as pointed segmental arches and corbelling in the kitchen area behind the dining hall. Nineteenth-century architects and their patrons were aware of the

106. The large kitchen behind the dining hall. The principal cooking-range lay inside the arched recess. (MJF 1998)

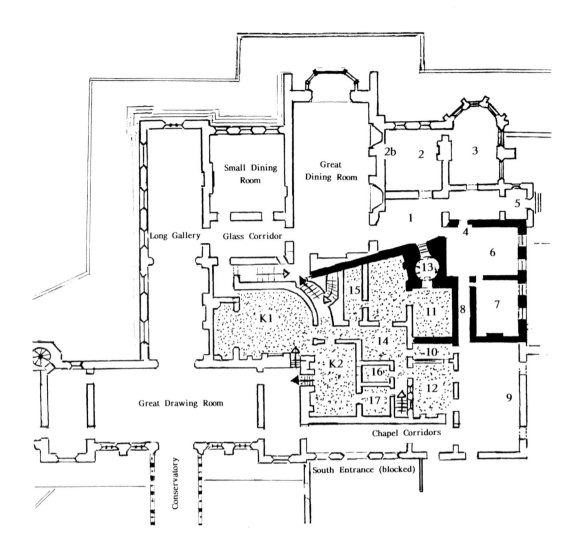

107. Plan of Family Rooms and "New Kitchens". (MJF & IF 1998)

Heavy shading denotes survival from "Alveton Lodge". Stippled areas indicate mezzanine between basement and principal floor levels, i.e. the former courtyard area (compare fig.55). Stairs from mezzanine to principal floor are marked with bold arrows, other stairs shown are up from basement level.

1	Site of octagon lobby	10	Passageway and staircase to upper
2	Family dining room		floor
2b	Wall reinforcement to accomodate	11/12	?Fleur-de-lis Rooms
	chimneypieces, Great Dining Room	13	The Old Round Tower
3	Plate Glass Drawing Room	14	Remaining part of open courtyard
4	North Wall of old Lodge	15	?Plate Closet
5	East entrance	16	?Privy
6	?The Earl's Sitting Room	17	Scullery
7	The former "Great Parlour"	K1	Kitchen no.1
8	Passageway	K2	Kitchen no.2
9	Area west of new chapel		

108. The Male Servants' accommodation built by Pugin alongside the north wall of the chapel. (MJF 1998)

need to keep kitchen smells out of the rest of the house in the days before there were such things as extractor fans. The new kitchens at Alton were almost immediately adjacent to the principal and family dining rooms **(107)**. Thus the large range in the main kitchen was set in an arched recess, and above it a commodious flue conducted the cooking smells skywards, aided by a strong up-draught **(106)** and there is evidence for direct access having been provided from this area to rooms on the upper level by means of staircases and exterior covered walkways. The new buildings in this area - which had formerly been an open courtyard fronted by the old south entrance - were single-storey ones with glazed conservatory-type roofs, some fragments of which survive in the rubble of this now-ruined area of the Towers buildings.

In 1846 Lord Shrewsbury proposed to provide additional accommodation for the servants, but it was not until 1849 that any real progress was made. Pugin wrote to say that he had the drawings ready, and he was obviously anxious to have the earl's approval to start work after Easter so as to tie it in with the rebuilding of the dining hall.[59] Built over an existing single-storey range of rooms adjoining the north wall of the chapel, the new block rose four storeys high, with a staircase tower at the north-west corner and two tall chimney-stacks. It has square-headed windows with foiled heads, and iron glazing-bars with lozenge-shaped ventilators **(108)**.

INTERIOR DECORATIONS, HEATING SYSTEMS, AND GLASS

As well as making structural additions and alterations, Pugin was called upon to design wallpaper, ceiling papers and other decorative items for existing rooms at the Towers, and also to supply furnishings and heating apparatus. It was after all as a furniture-designer that he allegedly first came into contact with Lord Shrewsbury in the 1830s. The actual production of Pugin's wallcoverings was done by John Gregory Crace, who from 1844 was entrusted with the execution of all of Pugin's designs in this medium. Among the Crace manuscripts at the Royal Institute of British Architects are some letters from Pugin concerning about wallpaper for the Towers,[60] but only one original design is known to exist.

The pattern consisted of Shrewsbury lions set in an octofoil bordered by coronets, linked by diagonal bars containing the motto *Prest d'Accomplir* **(109).** Later nineteenth-century photographs show that this paper was used to decorate the Great Drawing Room and Long Gallery, and we know from other sources that the paper was printed gold on crimson.[61]

Other correspondence about wallpaper includes an undated letter from Pugin to Lord Shrewsbury about the decoration of a dressing-room ceiling with a rose-patterned paper, and one of 1845 which refers to the papering of the ceilings in the earl's sitting-room and bedroom.[62] Photographs taken for the National Monuments Record in 1951 show two bedroom ceilings, both panelled and with round medallions at the intersections of the ribs. The panels were

133

decorated in the Pugin/Crace style, and in one of the rooms the round medallions contained the monogram BT signifying Bertram Talbot, suggesting that this was one of the rooms used by the sixteenth earl's cousin and heir, or even one of the "New Rooms" finished only after the deaths of Pugin and the sixteenth earl in 1852 (**111**).

Heating a sprawling complex of buildings such as Alton Towers must always have presented a problem. The account-books record large quantities of coal being brought by canal to the earl's wharf, and then hauled up the hill. Some warm-air systems were installed, for example in the (original) entrance hall, and in the Octagon and Talbot Gallery, but for the most part heating was by means of open fires. Many small fireplaces and register-grates survive, in addition to the large ornamented chimney-pieces such as those in the great hall and

109. Wallpaper design by Pugin for the Drawing Room and Long Gallery, 1844. (Worked-up by the author from partial drawing by Pugin, V & A Museum D.993-1908)

the Talbot Gallery, and a current member of the Towers staff has recently counted 189 chimneys and fireplaces. Fires would not of course have been lit in every fireplace every day, especially during the long periods in the late 1840s when the family were absent from England altogether, and the great state apartments in the western part of the house were for display rather than for living in. There was nevertheless a need to protect the building and its contents - including the art collections - from damage from frost and burst pipes in winter-time. In March 1841 Pugin wrote to Lord Shrewsbury that the frost had burst a great many pipes at the Towers, but fortunately there had been no serious damage in the Gallery where most of the valuable paintings were.[63]

110. The Great Stove - detail from illustration of the Medieval Court. (Illustrated London News, 20th September 1851)

One of Pugin's improvements to the heating system at the Towers was the introduction of a number of large, free-standing stoves, inspired no doubt by examples of tile-clad stoves he had seen on his travels in Europe. The largest of these (**110**) was exhibited at the Great Exhibition, and a chromolithograph of it was included in Matthew Digby Wyatt's *Industrial Arts of the XIX Century* (1853). The stove itself was clad in moulded and pierced majolica tiles made by Minton - a unique example of Pugin's use of coloured majolica glazes. His designs for these tiles are still kept at the Minton Museum in Stoke-on-Trent, and a few examples of the tiles themselves are held in a private collection and also at the Victoria & Albert Museum. At each corner of the stove was a Gothic brass column ter-

111. Ceiling of one of the "New Rooms": clearly a Pugin-Crace design, it incorporates the initial B signifying Bertram, the sixteenth earl's cousin and heir. (National Monuments Record). Copyright: © Crown Copyright. RCHME

minating in a coronet and Shrewsbury shield, and on the top there were four ornamental vanes emblazoned with the rampant lion. The entire stove was surrounded by a light wrought-iron screen: a dramatic example of the partnership of Hardman and Minton in executing Pugin's designs.

Although Pugin designs exist for at least four stoves on the scale of the so-called Great Stove, it was widely thought only one may ever have been produced, namely the one shown at the Great Exhibition. An Inventory of the furnishings and fittings of Alton Towers dating from 1860-69 however shows that this stove was one of a pair made for the Great Drawing Room. They are described as "Two massive Gothic stoves with solid brass Gothic towers".[64] Two similar stoves were listed in the Long Gallery. The Drawing Room and Gallery were linked to form the so-called "T-Room" - the largest open space in the Towers. Heated by only four modest-sized fireplaces, it would not have been especially warm, and much of the heat would have gone straight up the chimneys. The stoves on the other hand would have radiated heat directly into the room from four tiled surfaces, and convected heat from the top. They were both a practical and aesthetic improvement. They are not listed in the 1924 sale catalogue so one assumes that they had been removed from the Towers before then, and their present whereabouts are not known.

112. Contrasts: (a) Interior of house conservatory *c.*1870
(Photo: Courtesy Basil Jeuda). See also colour plate VIII.

(b) The same view *c.*1930.

Other decorative items designed by Pugin included stained glass. The glass for the Octagon and dining hall has already been discussed. Pugin also designed a large two-light window for the North Library depicting Gilbert Talbot (d.1419) and Lady Joan to provide a focal point at the west end of the enfilade running from the Library to the chapel tribune. Made by Hardman in 1848, this window was fortunately photographed by *NMR* before the room was gutted in 1952. Viewed from the chapel corridor end of the enfilade in the light of the setting sun, it would have glowed with rich colours. In his discussions with Lord Shrewsbury a few years earlier over the proposed west window for S. Giles' at Cheadle Pugin drew attention to the effect of the west-facing windows already in place at the Towers:

"....the most beautiful effect of stained glass is from the <u>setting sun</u>; is it not so in the state apartments at Alton. The reflection thrown from the west windows .... is glorious".[65]

GLASSHOUSES AND OTHER GARDEN BUILDINGS

Set at right-angles to the South Front was Thomas Hopper's conservatory of c1815 which formed a leafy corridor between the Drawing Room and the Octagon. Though the window frames were of iron, the glazed roof appears to have been made of timber which by 1846 had become rotten. In March of that year Pugin wrote to Lord Shrewsbury.

" I am very sorry to inform your Lordship that the <u>conservatory roof is in the most dangerous state</u> and past repair. It will be necessary to arrange for an entirely new roof as soon as your Lordship returns. Of course the glass will do again. It is a job I dislike exceedingly, but I fear there is no alternative".[66]

Pugin evidently did not feel that conservatories - especially those designed by other architects - were his *métier*, but the house conservatory at Alton was duly repaired, almost certainly on a like-for-like basis, existing wooden structures and ventilators being replaced with identical ones, and they appear on photographs taken between about 1880 and 1940. Some of these photographs also show a floor of patterned tiles. A significant section of this floor survives. The tiles are undoubtedly Minton, so it would seem that Pugin took the opportunity to re-pave the conservatory at the same time as he replaced the roof. The cornice of the conservatory itself was lettered with a quotation from S. Matthew's Gospel, chapter 6: *Consider the lilies of the field how they grow, they toil not neither do they spin, yet I say unto you, that not even Solomon in all his glory was not arrayed like unto one of these.* The cornice of the vestibule next to the Octagon proclaimed, *The speech of flowers exceeds all flowers of speech.*[67] (**112 & Col. Plate VIII**)

Pugin's repair and refurbishment of the house conservatory may have led some to assume that he was responsible for the design of the whole building, or they may pos-

113. Aerial view of Alton Towers *c.*1930 showing the glasshouses south of the gallery range. (The Lewis Family Collection)

114. The conservatory roof, Bilton Grange, Warwickshire. (MJF 1998)

sibly have confused this one with a conservatory in another part of the house which Pugin most certainly did build. Aerial photographs of the Towers taken in the 1930s show a timber-framed conservatory running out from the south side of the Picture Gallery close to its junction with the Armoury, and it is linked to two smaller glasshouses a little further to the east **(113).** These structures are marked on the Ordnance Survey maps of 1881-1922, with the older maps showing that there were in fact two parallel conservatories running southwards from the Gallery. Markings on the outside wall confirm this, the conservatories themselves having disappeared many years ago - one of them, it seems, before the Ordnance Surveys of 1900 and 1922.

The two principal conservatories - and probably the smaller glasshouses too - were designed by Pugin in 1848. They were almost identical to the one he had already built for Captain Hibbert at Bilton Grange, and this is fortunately still in existence. In November 1848 Pugin wrote to Lord Shrewsbury.

> *"I herewith send the working drawings for the conservatory which I trust you will approve. I have made a perspective view to give your Lordship an idea of the general internal effect. I think the arches are an improvement on the ones at Bilton & will look very handsome when the creepers are twining through the spandrels".[68]*

Just as he had done at Bilton Grange, Pugin designed an "honest" building of glass and timber, the main structural feature of which was an arch-braced roof with scissor-trusses and the open spandrils through which he envisaged creepers growing **(114).** He was determined that the conservatory should have the right kind of tiled floor. Dismissing an earlier suggestion by the earl that the tiles should have an heraldic pattern, Pugin argued typically that the design of the floor should reflect the purpose of the building which was, after all, a greenhouse. He therefore recommended a pattern consisting of white roses growing out of green-and-yellow tubs, and a border working into it. Knowing from experience that Lord Shrewsbury always had an eye to economy, Pugin argued that specially designed tiles need not be expensive: *"Minton is always ready to make new patterns from my designs when the ornament is one that can be* generally *used. In this case, he does not charge for making a pattern as it is a gain to him".[69]* Thus many of Pugin's tile patterns went into general production and found their way into

115. Her Ladyship's Oratory. (MJF 1998)

138

buildings with which Pugin himself had nothing to do.

On a visit to the Towers in 1851 William Adam described the new conservatory in its finished and planted state: *"Proceeding through the Octagon and Picture Gallery, we emerged suddenly by a side door into a splendid Gothic conservatory or flower gallery, 76 feet long by 16 wide, and here the sight was truly gorgeous: beautiful climbing plants in full flower covered the bosses and finials; the border was one mass of brilliant colour...... The enamelled vases, and encaustic tiles of which this floor is composed, were made at Mr. Minton's works, Stoke potters, and deserve to be generally known and introduced".*[70]

116. Pugin's "medieval pigeon", restored 1998. (MJF)

On the same visit to Alton, Adam noted another garden building designed by Pugin: a little Oratory in the corner of a walled garden not far from the Grand Entrance. Known as "Her Ladyship's Oratory", this delightful little building has a high-pitched roof with a floriated stone cross on the gable, a trefoiled doorway and a star window which at

117. The east terrace looking towards the Barbican. (Watercolour by unkown artist, 1870: Private Collection)

that time had a stained-glass window depicting the Virgin and Child: "A perfect gem", wrote Adam, "in Pugin's best style" **(115).**

Other garden buildings which exercised Pugin's fertile mind included the Pigeon House which was sited on an artificial mound close to the Oratory. He designed a weather-vane for it: *"I will get the weather-cock made with a medieval pigeon and send it ready for fixing".[71]* And so he did; and exactly 150 years later Pugin's "medieval pigeon" has been restored, re-gilded, and replaced on the pigeon-house roof **(116).**

The entire walled area east of the carriage-drive appears to have been laid out in the 1840s at the time of the excavation of the fosse on the north front. The huge quantities of rock and soil excavated at this time seem to have been used to construct the rampart east of the barbican. This enabled the terrace-walk to be extended, through the upper part of the barbican, along the top of a retaining wall some thirty feet above the carriage drive below **(117).** Spectacular views of the gardens can be had from this terrace. On the south side the rampart sloped downwards into what were the countess's private gardens where a rose-covered arcade led to the Oratory in the south-east corner of this walled area.[72]

THE RAILWAY, AND THE LODGES

In July 1846 a company was launched to build a branch of the North Staffordshire Railway along the Churnet Valley, thereby linking Alton, Cheadle and Uttoxeter with main-line stations. Pugin - a railway enthusiast - was excited at the prospect of the new line, not least because he thought it might provide him with the opportunity to design some stations for it. He believed that railway architecture could be cast in a Gothic mould, and had included some thoughts on this subject, and two drawings of Gothic railway bridges, in his *Apology for the Revival of Christian Architecture* (1843). On receiving news of the successful launch of the Churnet Valley Company, he wrote to Lord Shrewsbury, *"This looks well. I hope it will be carried through & then we may get some fine stations".[73]*

Pugin was particularly anxious that the railway buildings should harmonise, rather than clash, with those in the immediate vicinity, especially Alton Castle which he was rebuilding for the earl on the edge of the precipice overlooking the Churnet Valley, and in October 1847 he sent an urgent plea to Lord Shrewsbury on the subject of the proposed railway bridges, and some notes for him to submit to the Company:

> *"Included is a note which your Lordship can show respecting the architecture of the railway bridges. If you do not make this point a <u>sine qua non</u> the greatest horrors will be perpetrated under the very walls of the old castle & the whole place ruined. I entreat of your Lordship not to give up this point on any consideration. You might insist on a great deal more & nothing can be more reasonable than you should be secured against vile erections & designs on your Lordship's estate. No engineer ever was a decent architect & if they attempted Gothic it would be frightful".[74]*

Pugin then went on to prepare a full set of drawings for the proposed station at Alton for submission to the Company: *"I have supplied them with everything necessary as far as the exterior is concerned & I think it will make a picturesque building. I suppose it will be brick with stone dressings".[75]* At the same time Pugin admitted that he was somewhat out of his depth when it came to doing all the interior fixtures of the station, and it may have been for this reason that the Company finally decided not to use Pugin's designs. The station as eventually built - in the Company's own Italianate style - would not have pleased him. In the meantime a temporary station was provided ready for the opening of the line in July 1849, and in October Pugin wrote, *"I..... fully hope to reach Alton on Saturday for the 1st time by train".* [76]

118. Station Lodge. (MJF 1997)

Travellers alighting at Alton station would leave by means of a flight of steps up to the road, where they would find themselves facing one of the main entrances to the Towers estate: Jackson's Lodge; named, one assumes, after the gate-keeper who lived there. The coming of the railway appears to have been the principal reason for Lord Shrewsbury's decision to have a suitably grand entrance through which guests arriving by train could be conveyed by carriage up to the Towers. Though the old building was to be replaced, the earl proposed to keep the name "Jackson's Lodge", probably out of regard for an old retainer, but Pugin insisted quite vehemently that it should be called the Gate House: *"...Lodge is a modern word savouring of the Regent's Park, and Jackson is a plebeian name. All the entrances should be called gate, and gate houses, after the manner of the ancients".[77]*

So Gate House it was called, although Station Lodge is what it is most commonly called today **(118).** Pugin suggested iron gates to begin with as he thought wooden ones would be too heavy for frequent opening, but in the end wooden ones were agreed upon, with a wicket for pedestrians. Above the archway three shields were set in relief, and a large central panel with the full Shrewsbury arms. *"Without heraldry,"* wrote Pugin, *"it is impossible to make these buildings distinguishable from common erections".[78]*

119. Counslow Lodge. (MJF 1998)

Pugin also carried out alterations at Counslow Lodge, just off the main road from Alton to Cheadle, near the new quarry which he opened for the stone for S. Giles', Cheadle, and the building work at Alton.[79] Counslow Lodge stands at the entrance to the drive which leads to Dimmingsdale, constructed, so it is said, so that the earl could avoid paying the turnpike charges on the main road. Counslow Lodge **(119)** is a delight-

141

ful little stone building which, though it predates Pugin, has characteristic Pugin additions such as the stone shields and the standard-bearing Talbot on the gable. It is one of a number of existing buildings on and around the Shrewsbury estate which Pugin modified; there are others in Alton village.

Station Lodge was a completely new building, and there is nothing "common" about this fine piece of Gothic domestic architecture. Not long after its completion the coffin of the sixteenth earl - "Good Earl John" - was carried under its archway on the day of his burial in December 1852, following an elaborate funeral Mass in the Towers Chapel. Arguably one of the finest interiors created by the Shrewsbury-Pugin partnership, the chapel had been a continual focus of Pugin's attention almost from the moment he began work at the Towers until his death, also in the autumn of 1852. He was after all the country's foremost Catholic architect.

6
THE TOWERS CHAPEL

"Here have I built thee a lofty house,
A habitation for thee to occupy for ever' - I Kings 8, v. 13

In 1829 the Catholic Emancipation Act removed nearly all of the legal obstacles which for centuries had kept Catholics out of public life and deprived them of many civil rights. It was now possible for Catholic peers such as Lord Shrewsbury to take their seats in the house of Lords, and Catholics could contest for seats in the House of Commons. It may be that the grand new chapel at Alton Towers was conceived and built as an outward expression of what John Henry Newman described as the "Second Spring" of the Catholic Church in England. Like the old chapel on the north front of the house, it served not just the needs of the family and their servants, but also Catholics from Alton village who attended Mass there until Alton was given its own church in 1842.

Although the new chapel was structurally complete by 1833, its interior furnishing and decoration continued over many more years. The architects were Thomas Fradgley of Uttoxeter, and Joseph Potter of Lichfield, and there is evidence that the earl himself took a leading role in its design.[1] As a church historian of some note, Dr. Daniel Rock - the earl's chaplain from 1827 to 1840 - is also likely to have had some influence on the design and furnishing of the chapel. The author of several authoritative works on church history and liturgy, Dr Rock was an admirer of Pugin whose decorative work, carried out in stages between 1840 and 1851, completely altered the internal appearance of the Towers chapel.

Discounting the linked Galleries, the chapel is the largest single structure at the Towers, as doubtless it was intended to be: some 90ft long by 30ft wide and 60ft high. It was indeed "a lofty house". The overall style is Gothic: a curious blend of late-medieval styles of which the mature Pugin could hardly have approved, but of course it all pre-dates Pugin's "True Principles". Nor should one forget that some of Pugin's earliest essays in Gothic architecture were in those very late-medieval styles which he came to despise. Externally the Towers Chapel has features somewhat reminiscent of the college chapels at Eton and King's, Cambridge - namely an east gable flanked by a pair of turrets with ogee caps **(120),** but here the similarity ends. Instead of the huge expanses of glass that one would expect to see on the north and south sides of a "Perpendicular" chapel there is merely a matching pair of small circular windows towards the east end just below ceiling level, and two

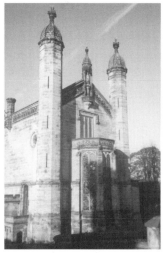

120. The Towers chapel - east gable and apse. (MJF 1998)

small pointed windows admit light at ground level on the south side. The tribune also has a pair of small circular windows in the west gable, and an iron-traceried Gothic window at both levels on the north side. Otherwise all is blank ashlar, and so the chapel must always have been starved of natural light. The principal windows are those at the east end: three of two lights each with a transom, arranged in a projecting apsidal bay, and is a straight-headed window of three lights in the gable above. These windows contained glass designed by Thomas Willement.[2] The central window in the apse had figures of the four evangelists, Matthew, Mark, Luke and John, standing under rich canopies, while those on either side of it portrayed the symbols of the evangelists, and the instruments of Christ's passion. The smaller window in the gable above has ornamented roundels with symbols of the persons of the Holy Trinity and of the Blessed Virgin Mary. Both windows were intact when the chapel was photographed by the National Monuments Record in 1951, but only the gable window is still (1999) in place. Some small fragments of original glass survive in the two lower side windows, and these also have some fine tracery.

Externally the principal ornament consists of richly-carved friezes: horizontal bands of cusped triangles and lozenge shapes with small castellated turrets at intervals along the parapets. These turrets contained the flues from the heating system. A similar frieze runs above the windows of the apse, and from the centre of the gable there rises an ogee-capped turret with a niche containing a statue of S. Peter to whom the chapel is dedicated - a conscious choice, one would imagine, since this was also the medieval dedication of the parish church of Alton.

On the south side of the chapel is the sacristy, and on the north side the servants' quarters added by Pugin in 1849. From the south-west angle there projects a three-storey tower block containing rooms known as the Lower and Upper Red Bedrooms, and the Green Room.[3] The ornamental frieze of the chapel parapet continues around this angle, stopping at its junction with the tallest and most spectacular of the towers which gave the mansion its new name (121). It consists of two stages separated by a projecting cornice. The lower stage, as the jointing shows, is of a piece with the chapel block. The south and west faces are both adorned with traceried panels. The upper stage is treated in a much more extravagant manner. Rich lozenge friezes run horizontally above the cornice, and vertically at the angles. They frame elaborate traceried panels which grow richer towards the top (69). The tall bell-openings, under floriated ogee arches, have transoms and Perpendicular tracery. All is crowned by a parapet of pierced stonework with pinnacles at the angles. The crocketed tops of the pinnacles are now missing. The names of the builders, P and J Bailey, are inscribed on the tower, and the date 1832.

The chapel is entered via a vestibule on the south side. This leads downwards into a narthex separated from the main body of the chapel by four stone arches with steps in between, again leading down. The chapel floor is thus on the same level as the basement storey of the house. Over the narthex is the tribune, on the same level as the principal floor of the house. This was for the private use of the Shrewsbury family who would have entered it by the corridors leading directly from their private apartments in the old part of the house, and the state rooms to the west. By contrast with the main body of the chapel, which was furnished with plain benches, the tribune was equipped with costly furniture, some supplied by Pugin.[5] The alignment of the new chapel with the family rooms and state rooms was a matter of some importance, and it involved building a corridor running westwards from the tribune. The west

121. Her Ladyship's Garden and the south side of the chapel photographed *c.*1880. Note the original form of the pinnacles which were lowered in the 1950s (see no.69) (by courtesy Basil Jeuda)

wall of the chapel quite clearly incorporates a former exterior wall of the house: this is indicated by blocked windows on two levels, all east-facing, and some with their hood-moulds still in place. The main entrance on to the tribune from the chapel corridor and state rooms was cut through this wall, partly utilising one of the former windows. As explained elsewhere, the entire plan of the Towers revolved around an axial system of linked rooms or *enfilades* with doors aligned to give vistas from one end of the house to the other. Thus it was possible to stand on the chapel tribune and look down the new corridor leading to the great Drawing Room, Music Room and Libraries, towards the window at the extreme west end of the house, a distance of some 270 feet. In the north-west corner of the tribune a pointed doorway gave access from the family rooms in the old part of the house.

The tribune is fronted by an elaborate arched screen made of cast iron, with some very intricate moulding in the upper parts, and clearly in the Georgian "gothick" tradition **(122 & 123).** The ceiling has ornamental cast-iron panels, and there is also a band of moulded iron set into the carved stone frieze immediately below the screen. The extensive use of architectural

122. Structural and ornamental ironwork on the chapel tribune. (MJF 1998)

123. The chapel interior from the tribune. (MJF 1998)

146

cast iron is a notable feature of the Towers generally, but the ironwork of the chapel is of exceptional quality and gracefulness. It was undoubtedly cast at the Britannia Foundry in Derby. Narrow extensions to the tribune ran eastwards for a short distance along the north and south walls of the chapel, with delicate iron railings matching those of the main galleries. The side galleries disappeared in the 1950s, but the rows of sockets on each wall still indicate their position. An upper gallery above the tribune was for choir and musicians, and it contained a pipe organ "of great size and power" installed by Parsons, a noted firm of organ builders based in Duke Street, London.[6] The base of a font, octagonal in section, stands in the lower gallery. The bowl is missing.

Cast iron was used extensively in the construction of the chapel ceiling, which is pitched several feet lower than the external slate-clad roof. Though originally painted dark brown to resemble wood, the angel-corbels supporting the trusses are in fact made of cast iron, likewise parts of the trusses themselves, while the cornice is composed of a series of cast-iron quatrefoiled panels surmounted by lengths of cast brattishing consisting of motifs from the coronet pertaining to an earl - strawberry leaves alternating with silver balls.

In 1834 - the year after its consecration - the Towers chapel was described in glowing terms:

> "....... as a domestic chapel (it) is not surpassed in beauty and richness, we believe, by any other in England; perhaps not in Europe.... The construction of the roof is particularly happy, and exhibits an admirable specimen of that beautiful feature in pointed architecture..... The altar is of gilt bronze, and is remarkable for its appropriate and elaborate ornaments, and is almost an exact copy of what is now denominated an altar-tomb".[7]

This description helps to establish what was in place before Pugin arrived on the scene in 1838. Structurally there could have been little about the building to excite this rising star of the Gothic Revival who came to Alton in the wake of the controversy aroused by the publication of his most influential book, *Contrasts* (1836). For Pugin the true Gothic style was not an option, but an historical, moral and religious necessity, particularly for English Catholics who claimed descent from the church of the Middle Ages,[8] and Alton Towers was soon to become a kind of summer-school for the education of leading clergy and laity in matters of good taste which, according to Pugin, had been in decline since the sixteenth century. It was important therefore that the domestic chapel of his most influential patron and client should be properly equipped and furnished. Later on, at Alton Castle, Pugin was able to demonstrate what the private chapel of a gentleman's country house ought really to look like when designed by the Master from scratch. At the Towers he had to make the best of what he found: basically a large stone box with a bay window at one end and at the other a tower which, though adjacent, seemed not to belong to it. Though it has been suggested that some external details were added by Pugin,[9] it was on the inside that he was able to carry out his most significant alterations and additions.

The focal point of the chapel was the altar, which stood in front of the east window. Made of gilt-bronze, with the front divided into eleven arched panels each containing a plain cross, with finials and crocketed gables above (**Col. plate III**) it was sufficiently Gothic in style for Pugin to want to retain it. To it he added a predella containing seven painted metal panels. The central one shows the Last Supper, while on the left are the Annunciation, the Nativity and the Presentation, and on the right the Descent from the Cross, the Resurrection and the Ascension. One would dearly like to know the identity of the artist; he was possibly one of the Nazarene School. The reredos consists of an elaborate frame of carved and gilded wood. The central niche contains the crucifix, and on either side are painted panels depicting the sixteenth Earl of Shrewsbury and Countess Maria Theresa in medieval costume and kneeling in the attitude of prayer. Earl John wears black plate armour and a tabard decorated with the Shrewsbury lions and other heraldic devices; i.e. after the manner of his fifteenth-century ancestor, the "Great Talbot" himself (**Col. plate II**). His patron saint - S. John the Baptist - stands behind him, and the east end of the Towers chapel can be seen through a window in the background. The countess is dressed in an ample gold-coloured gown trimmed with ermine, and she is watched over by the Blessed Virgin Mary, while through her window is a view of the Flag Tower as seen, not from within the grounds of the house, but from the opposite side of the valley (**Col. plate IV**). Both panels are flanked by colonettes carrying small figures of saints. Hinged side-panels carry painted figures of two of England's most celebrated saints, Thomas Becket and Augustine of Canterbury, both attired in copes and mitres. The reredos is of the same *genre* as the one installed by Pugin in the chapel of S. Mary's College, Oscott in 1837. This too has narrow side-panels depicting similarly-attired saints.

Pugin's treatment of the east wall of the chapel involved the removal of features of which he strongly disapproved, notably some cast-iron statuary, and on the wall just above the apse there is evidence of a large cast-iron feature of some kind having been broken away, leaving the fixing embedded in the wall. Later on Pugin was distressed and angry when he discovered that some of these discarded items had been relocated in a church he had built in Manchester:

"I was horrified on arriving at Manchester today to find that some pious persons had bought those horrid figures that came out of your Lordships chapel, <u>cast iron brackets and all,</u> and given them to be fixed in the church I have built at Manchester........ they pursue me like the flying Dutchman".[10]

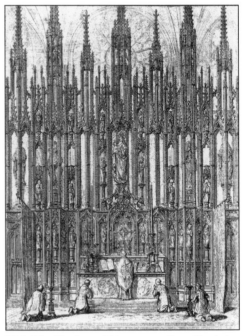

Pugin's *Contrasts* contains an illustration of an altar screen at Durham, as he imagined it to have been in the Middle Ages **(124).** This seems greatly to have influenced his treatment of the east wall of the Towers chapel. Around the sanctuary area ran a dado with brattishing along the top, and ornamental Gothic panels closely resembling those on the front of the altar. Some of this woodwork may have come from the chapel of Magdalen College, Oxford, which was undergoing considerable alterations at this time.[11] Pugin

124. The Durham Altar-screen from Pugin's Contrasts, 1836

was a collector of architectural antiques and other medieval artefacts which he liked to incorporate into his buildings to emphasise the point that "true" Gothic was but a continuation of the architecture of the Middle Ages. Above the dado Pugin constructed an elaborate timber screen of tabernacle work rising almost to ceiling level on either side of the altar-recess, and designed to complement the ornamental woodwork of the reredos *(frontispiece)*. Like the Durham screen, it had canopied niches containing statues of angels and saints. The larger ones continued the theme of the saints of England: S. Edward Confessor, S. Chad, S. Thomas of Canterbury, and S. George, all painted and gilded. A row of niches running over the top of the sanctuary archway contained figures of angels with scrolls on which were inscribed the words of the *Gloria in excelsis.* This work appears to have been completed in the summer/autumn of 1840, for in a letter to Lord Shrewsbury dated 17th June of that year, Pugin states his intention to come to Alton to supervise the fixing of the figures on the screen, and his diaries record periods of several days spent at the Towers between July and October.[12] The figures appear to have been made of plaster, but the screen itself was of finely-carved timber, gilded and painted, and produced almost certainly in the Lambeth workshop of George Myers. Though the screen was demolished in 1952, several portions of it have survived, still with their original gilding and colouring. It was one of the most elaborate pieces of carved and gilded woodwork ever produced by Pugin, and it was never repeated elsewhere.

Samuel Rayner's detailed drawing of the chapel interior, done in about 1842, **(125)** shows all of the features described so far, but it marks only the first phase of Pugin's work. The 1854 painting by Joseph Lynch **(Col. plate X)** reveals further additions and modifications for which plans and documents still exist. These include two pictures of saints in gilded frames either side of the gable window and other picture frames in the sanctuary, the decoration of the dado in the main body of the chapel with what appears to be a stencilled pattern, the addition of tall pinnacled panels to the north and south walls, the painting of the ceiling and the addition of a frieze.[13] The walls above dado level were already lined with oak wainscot, and hung with large pictures in gilt frames. Most of these were copies of religious themes by painters of the Renaissance and later, and thus rather out-of-place in a chapel which was becoming progressively more medieval in character, but of course they had to stay.

125. The chapel in *c.*1842 after the first phase of Pugin's alterations. (Pencil drawing by Samuel Rayner: Photography by Guy Evans; courtesy of Potteries Museum & Art Gallery, Hanley, Stoke-on-Trent)

The most important of Pugin's second phase of alterations concerned the ceiling. *The Gem of the Peak* describes it simply

126. The Chapel ceiling and frieze in 1951. (National Monuments Record) Copyright: © Crown copyright.
RCHME

as being "of oak, gabled and supported by bold ornamental arches, which rest on the kneeling figures of angels placed on wreathed corbels",[14] which is exactly as it is shown in the Rayner drawing, without any decoration, and without the deep painted frieze running between the angel corbels which appears in the painting of 1854. Like the roofs of the Armoury, Picture Gallery and Talbot Gallery it is a timber construction with some cast-iron details such as the cornice; a notable achievement in its own right, and very different from the sham "vaults" of the Octagon and "T" Drawing-room which were made of plaster. The decoration of the chapel ceiling consisted of painting the rafters, purlins and trusses in blue and red, with gilding applied to the bosses and other ornamental features **(126)**. The designs were by Pugin, and executed by J.G. Crace, perhaps in conjunction with Thomas Kearns, a local painter and decorator used by Pugin and Lord Shrewsbury.[15] The ceiling panels themselves were coloured deep blue and adorned with gold stars - a scheme very similar to Pugin's original treatment of the ceilings at S. Giles', Cheadle. Only the westernmost bay, above the organ gallery, was left untouched, and this still retains its original stained-oak appearance. The angel-corbels pre-date Pugin of course, but the colouring is his, and below each of the corbels he placed one of the tall and narrow panels already referred to, with pointed tops, crockets and finials to match those of the altar screen. There were ten of these in all, and they had the effect of dividing the chapel walls into regular rectangles corresponding with the principal divisions of the ceiling. Finally Pugin gave the ceiling a splendid frieze, running along each side between the angel-corbels, and carrying the words of Psalm 113 - in Latin, of course, and in impeccable black-letter. Painted on canvas, each panel had a sexfoiled circle containing the gilded letter M or some other symbol, and contrasting diagonal bands of floriated ornament on backgrounds of white and gold. Writing to Lord Shrewsbury from Alton in April 1850, Pugin comments on these alterations with a characteristic element of criticism of his own work:

> "...... It is very fortunate that I came to Alton as there are many things, particularly in the Chapel, which required attention. The general effect is very good. There is perhaps a little too much white but that is a fault on the right side. It will be a great improvement.." [16]

All appears to have been completed by May 1st when, on another visit to Alton, Pugin wrote home to his wife:

> "...... I arrived here this morning & I am very glad to tell you that both Lord and Lady Shrewsbury seemed delighted with what has been done. Certainly the chapel is a wonderful improvement and altogether the work gives great satisfaction... " [17]

Contemporary descriptions refer to the altar crucifix set with precious stones and surrounded by figures of saints and angels, a gilt reliquary containing the relics of many saints, and six tall candlesticks standing on the altar, and tall standard candlesticks in the sanctuary.[18] All of these appear in the Rayner drawing of c.1845 and the Lynch painting of 1854. One can reasonably assume that the Pugin/Shrewsbury partnership which in association with the Hardman workshop in Birmingham produced a fabulous array of ornaments for churches such as S. Giles', Cheadle, would also have seen to it that the Towers chapel was suitably equipped. According to one observer the interior of the chapel, with its decorations, furnishings and fittings as completed by Pugin, was equal in splendour to that of S. Giles'.[19]

The Towers chapel was the scene of some spectacular celebrations. One of these was the reception of Louisa Pugin - the second wife of the architect - into the Catholic Church. Pugin's first wife, Anne Garnet, had died in 1832 shortly after giving birth to their daughter. In the following year he married Louisa Burton, and although Pugin himself became a Catholic in 1835, it was not until 1839 that Louisa was herself received. By this time Pugin's career had advanced considerably because of the patronage of Lord Shrewsbury who took an interest in the architect's family. It was therefore appropriate that her reception into the Church should have taken place at the Towers. The brief entry in Pugin's diary for 8th May - "My dear Louisa received into the Church" - is amplified by a detailed description in the *Catholic Magazine*[20] of what was clearly a magnificent ceremony. Pugin had a keen sense of the dramatic and was known to have "stage-managed" the opening ceremonies of several of the churches which he and Lord Shrewsbury built. It is difficult to escape the conclusion that he was responsible for the arrangements on this occasion too. The chapel was lavishly decked with flowers, including an elaborate garland extending the full width of the building, the centre-piece of which was a floral crown suspended directly above Louisa's head.

> " .... At the appointed hour, as the full organ poured forth its majestic note, the Rev. Dr Rock, as priest, attended by the Rev. Messrs. Morgan and Fairfax

as deacon and subdeacon, walked in solemn procession from the sacristy to the sanctuary, preceded by the thurifers, acolytes and torchbearers. Their vestments were of the richest gold brocade. A grand High Mass was then sung, with all the usual inexpressibly affecting ceremonies of the Catholic Church. Immediately after the Gospel Dr Rock exchanged his superb chasuble for a splendid cope, robed with which he, at the foot of the altar, intoned the first words of the hymn to the Holy Ghost, **Veni Creator Spiritus** *in the old Salisbury chaunt which the choir continued with impressive effect".* [21]

Only Pugin himself could have designed the ceremonial candle which Dr Rock presented to Louisa during the course of the service, and which merited a detailed description in the Press:

"........ a large wax taper, ornamented in the style of the fifteenth century it arose out of a bouquet of rare exotic flowers. Around the lower part of this candle were rolled three labels, written in Gothic characters, with the following ejaculations: - **Jesu filii Dei, miserere me** *-* **O mater filii Dei, memento me** *-* **S. Michael, ora pro me.** *The higher part was ornamented with a wreath of flowers in brilliant colours, above which, attached by a golden string, was suspended a small Gothic label, upon the richly diapered ground of which was emblazoned, in the style of the fifteenth century, the Archangel Michael overcoming Satan."*

Perhaps it was this occasion which inspired P.F. Anson's frontispiece to Denis Gwynn's book, *Lord Shrewsbury, Pugin and the Catholic Revival* (1946) which depicts Pugin looking on as an impeccably-clad bishop and attendants line up in front of the house **(127)**.

A few months later the welcoming of the Prince and Princess Doria Pamphili at the Towers following their wedding in Rome (see above, p.92) included a glittering service of thanksgiving in the chapel, and in June 1840 there was a solemn act of thanksgiving for the thwarting of an attempt upon the lives of Queen Victoria and Prince Albert.[22]

Worship in the Towers chapel was conducted according to the revived medieval rites preferred by Pugin and Dr Rock to the more modern Italianate ones. Thus it drew in visitors, both Catholic and Anglican, who wished to see the Liturgy performed in a "proper" manner, much to Pugin's delight. The reference to the use of the Salisbury chant at the reception of Louisa Pugin is interesting. Pugin was keen to encourage the revival of medieval church

127. Frontispiece by P.F. Anson for Denis Gwynn, *Lord Shrewsbury, Pugin and the Catholic Revival*, 1946

128. The funeral of the sixteenth Earl of Shrewsbury, 14th December 1852. (Illustrated London News, 25th December 1852)

music, properly sung by male voices, in preference to the more "operatic" music of the Renaissance and Baroque periods. He even wrote a pamphlet on the subject, entitled *An Earnest Appeal for the Revival of the Ancient Plain Song (1850)*. The earl's chaplain, Dr. Rock, was also a noted ecclesiologist who carried out extensive research into the history of the Salisbury (Sarum) Rite.

Pugin was quite excited by the effect his work at the Towers chapel and at S. Giles' was having upon members of the Church of England: *"....... the number of Oxford men who come is quite surprising. They bow reverently to the altar in the chapel at Alton, speak in whispers, and Mr Winter has been asked by them before entering if the Blessed Sacrament was in the chapel, that they might pay their proper devotions. Cheadle also excites immense interest, so far from nobody seeing it hundreds come already".*[23]

The funeral of the sixteenth Earl of Shrewsbury gives a fascinating insight into the burial customs of a noble Catholic family in the mid-nineteenth century, based of course on medieval precedents researched by the Pugins. Earl John died in Naples in November 1852, and Edward Welby Pugin - fresh from superintending his father's obsequies at Ramsgate only seven weeks earlier - was called in to oversee the funeral arrangements at Alton. These included the design of the coffin, which was of Spanish mahogany covered with crimson velvet, and made by Hardman. There was a large floriated cross on the lid, and other metal-fittings including the famous Talbot hounds. While the chapel was re-ordered the earl's body lay in state in the Talbot Gallery where a temporary altar was set up for the daily offering of Requiem Mass.

An engraving made at the time shows how the chapel was rearranged for the funeral under the supervision of Thomas Kearns **(128).** The windows were covered with black drapery, likewise the most decorative parts of the walls and the greater part of the screenwork on the east wall. The sanctuary with its splendid altarpiece was screened off, and another altar, appropriately vested for a Requiem Mass, was set up in front of it. In complete contrast to these sombre surroundings, a most elaborate and richly-decorated herse was constructed over the catafalque where the coffin was to be placed. Supported on twelve pillars of carved and gilded wood, it consisted of a great gabled canopy ornamented with the emblems of the earldoms of Shrewsbury, Waterford and Wexford. On the tops of eight of the pillars there were Talbot hounds supporting branched candlesticks, and other branched candlesticks stood on the ground, making a total of between 300 and 400 candles.[25] Designed by E.W. Pugin, it bore a close resemblance to the medieval herse illustrated in his father's *Glossary of Ecclesiastical Ornament*, 1844 (p153).

The funeral Mass was celebrated by the Bishop of Birmingham, with the Bishops of Northampton, Shrewsbury and Clifton in attendance. Representatives of the various religious orders were present, along with 150 secular priests. At the end of the Mass Dr. Henry Weedall, who had been President of Oscott College in the 1830s, gave a eulogy which highlighted the earl's work for the Church, his generosity, and the fine example he had set to the Catholic laity. Afterwards the coffin was taken for burial on the north side of the altar of S. John's. So many people turned out to say their farewells to "Good Earl John" that, as the head of the procession reached the church doors, the coffin could be seen just emerging from the gatehouse nearly a mile away in the valley below. [26]

129. Memorial to Bertram Arthur, Seventeenth Earl of Shrewsbury, S. John's, Alton. (MJF 1999)

Soon after the earl's funeral the catafalque and other items of mourning were removed from the chapel, leaving it much as it is shown in Joseph Lynch's painting of 1854. As far as it is known there were no further additions or alterations until after the celebrated Shrewsbury Peerage dispute of 1856-60. In the meantime Earl John's widow died on June 4th 1856, and his successor, Bertram Arthur, seventeenth Earl of Shrewsbury, died on August 10th of the same year. The funeral of the countess took place in the Towers chapel amid solemn splendours similar to those of 1852, while Bertram, in accordance with his own wishes, had a more simple funeral in S. John's prior to burial on the south side of the altar. Memorial brasses - designed no doubt by E.W. Pugin and made by Hardman - mark the graves of the two earls, while the countess is commemorated by a simple inscription affixed to the wall **(129)**.

The eventual succession to the earldom and to the Alton estate of the Anglican Henry Chetwynd Talbot had a profound effect upon the Towers chapel and the way it was used. The sale catalogue of 1857 includes the furnishings of the tribune only, not those of the chapel itself. This suggests that the principal items may have been withheld by the executors of Earl Bertram's will who were responsible for the sale. What is known for certain is that in 1862 the gilt-bronze altar, with its splendid Pugin reredos and other ornaments, was installed in S. Peter's Catholic church in Bromsgrove, ironically in the same town as the Talbot tomb whose inscription had played a key part in resolving the peerage case.

From 1860 onwards any services at the Towers chapel would have been conducted according to the rites of the Church of England. A new altar - far less ornate than the Pugin one - was installed, but otherwise the remaining furnishings of the chapel were left intact. An annotated copy of the 1924 sale catalogue lists the contents as they were then. A pine altar with various cloths and frontals was sold for £1.10s; a large brass altar-cross with ruby glass mounts went for two guineas, a pair of brass candlesticks was sold for eleven guineas, and a set of Communion plate raised ten guineas. The rood screen in the parish church at Salt (Staffordshire), believed by some to have come from the Towers chapel, was in fact designed for Alton parish church in 1893. There never was a rood screen at the Towers chapel. [27]

Following the 1924 sale the chapel stood empty and largely unused except for the parade services held in it for the officer cadets during the Second World War. The photographic survey carried out by the National Monuments Record in 1951 show plainly

130. Part of the Pugin frieze in the chapel, restored 1997. (MJF 1998)

that all of the stained glass, the stencilled wall-panels and wainscot, the Pugin screenwork and frieze, were still intact at that time. Except for the Willement glass in the east gable window all of these items were removed over the next few months, and the walls of the building were stripped down to bare stonework. It is ironic that the centenary of Pugin's death in 1852 should have witnessed the ruthless and totally inexcusable destruction of one of the finest interiors produced by his "passion for Gothic". The painted ceiling was the sole survivor of the splendid decorations which had so enthralled visitors to the Towers even in the latter years before the Second World War. [28] This too was shortly to be obscured. In 1958 the chapel became the location of a new attraction for visitors - a huge model railway layout. A tent-like structure was erected over it, thus hiding from view all that remained of Pugin's decorations.

The fortunes of this fine building changed for the better following the acquisition of the Towers by the Tussauds Group. In 1993 the model railway was sold, and a decision was made to restore the ceiling to coincide with the Pugin Exhibition at the Victoria & Albert Museum in 1994. Missing windows were also replaced, those in the apse being designed by Claire Venables of the Leek School of Art. Though the composition is abstract, and no attempt was made to replicate the originals, these windows shed a carpet of coloured light across the stone floor on sunny mornings; a reminder of the vibrant colours which once enriched the entire building. More recently one of the painted panels from the frieze has been cleaned and restored, and put on display in the chapel, along with a modern copy **(130)**. In 1998 the surviving fragments of the Pugin's screenwork were re-discovered on the tribune and carefully examined **(131)**. The possibility of re-assembling these and replacing a significant section of the screen is being considered.

131. Fragments of Pugin's altar-screen, rediscovered in 1998. (MJF 1998)

7

CONCLUSION

'The house was no longer hers entirely, she sighed. It belonged to time now, to history, was past the touch and control of the living..... The great wings of silence beat up and down the empty house' - Virginia Woolf, *Orlando*

In June 1851 Pugin wrote to Ambrose Phillipps, *"You will be greatly pleased with the works at Alton which have improved the house amazingly".[1]* It is doubtful if what had been achieved by then marked the limit of Pugin's plans for the Towers, but it all came to an end following the death of Pugin in September 1852 and that of Lord Shrewsbury in November, aged sixty-one. Earl John's cousin, Bertram Arthur Talbot, aged nineteen, succeeded to the estates as the seventeenth Earl of Shrewsbury, while at the same time Pugin's eldest son Edward was attempting to fill the gap left by his father's death. At the end of November 1852 the new earl wrote to Edward:

"...I write these few lines to assure you of the deep interest I feel in your welfare and I shall feel myself happy in being to you what my dear Uncle Lord Shrewsbury would have been had God been pleased to leave him amongst us."[2]

Though he was in fact a cousin of the sixteenth earl, the relationship was, on account of their respective ages, more like one of uncle and nephew. Earl John assumed responsibility for his education and upbringing, grooming him for the role which he would one day inherit. Educated by private tutors, Bertram accompanied his uncle on visits to Italy. He did not enjoy the best of health, and this was one of the considerations which kept the family in Italy in 1851: *"Bertram is going on extremely well and it would be a pity to expose him to a colder climate for some time to come. All he wants is warmth to put his blood into good circulation".[3]*

Bertram shared the sixteenth earl's enthusiasm for church-building. One of the unfinished projects which he - and Edward Pugin - inherited was the provision of a Catholic cathedral in Shrewsbury, while work left unfinished at the Towers in 1852 included the great dining room and the "New Rooms" (see above, pp. 129-132). The association between new earl and new architect was a brief one, for Bertram died in August 1856. *"This is a most irreparable loss to me",* wrote Edward Pugin. *"....In Lord Shrewsbury we have lost a great as well as a good man. Under that diffident and somewhat nervous exterior lay hidden a most extraordinary and rare mind".[4]* Thus ended the senior line of the Talbot family, and all structural work at Alton Towers stopped, pending the outcome of the dispute which ensued over the inheritance. Entries in the various account-books ceased in 1856-7, one of the last being a record of payments to masons William and James Burton for *"making the Earl's grave".[5]*

Knowing that Bertram was unlikely either to live long or to marry and have children, Earl John had laid plans to keep the titles and estates in Catholic hands, and Bertram also made his

132. Luncheon in the Talbot Gallery to celebrate Henry Chetwynd Talbot's taking possession of the Towers, 13th April 1860. This picture is clearly the work of two artists: Joseph Lynch who drew the Gallery, and another who drew in the figures but could only guess the proportions of the room. Consequently the figures were drawn far too small in proportion to , for example, the chimneypiece which is only about six feet high. Compare no.77. (Illustrated London News, 28th April 1860)

will accordingly. In their eyes the legal heir to the titles was Lord Edmund Howard, the infant son of the fourteenth Duke of Norfolk, while certain lands and properties were willed to others including Ambrose Phillips. The succession was challenged by Henry Chetwynd Talbot of Ingestre Hall, and it also had to be decided which of the various properties were entailed and so inalienable from the title. In the end, after a long and costly legal battle, it was ruled that Henry was the rightful heir to the title, and that most of the landed property - including Alton Towers - was entailed. The new earl formally took possession of the Towers on April 13th 1860, but it was quite literally an empty victory for the buildings had been stripped of most of their contents three years previously, and the engraving of the eighteenth earl's celebration luncheon in the Talbot Gallery (132) shows the walls denuded of their pictures and the floor bereft of carpets and fine furniture. The settlement had serious consequences for the Catholic Church in North Staffordshire, for the benefactions it had enjoyed from the Talbots abruptly ceased, and institutions like S. John's Hospital had now to be self-supporting.

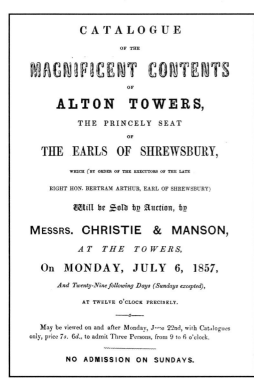

133. Alton Towers Sale Catalogue, 1857

Whatever the fate of the earldom and the entailed estates, there was no doubt about the legality of Earl Bertram's will as far as the moveables were concerned, so on the instructions of his executors the entire contents of the Towers were auctioned by Christie and Manson in an auction sale which began on 6th July 1857 and did not conclude until 8th August (133). Over 4,000 lots came under the hammer, including all the antique furniture amassed by the fifteenth and sixteenth earls, and fabulous art treasures including paintings by Bellini, Raphael and Van Dyck, to say nothing of 6,000 bottles of wines and spirits from the cellars. The contents of the Libraries were disposed of in separate sales at Sothebys in London. The Duchess of Sutherland purchased quite a number of items, for Trentham Hall no doubt. The great size of some of the works of art operated very much against their sale, but it was considered that the pictures brought their real value except on the first two days of the sale when some bargains were to be had. The huge canvas of Frederick Barbarossa from the dining room went for £33 - the frame alone had cost £255 - and J.L. David's *Belisarius* was sold for 120 guineas.[6]

It is one of those strange ironies of history that the structural work on Alton Towers was barely complete before the furnishings for which many of the rooms had been designed were removed. The 1857 sale catalogue lists various items of architectural metalwork and woodwork as being stored in the Billiard Room and the New Rooms, for example "fourteen coronets and lion crests, plated", "a set of panels of brass, for a staircase", "two large brass vanes, with the Shrewsbury cypher and motto". These were obviously awaiting installation in various parts of the building such as the dining room which was practically empty at the time of the sale. Some items remained unsold - for example the great chandelier made for the dining room, the Pugin/Hardman *coronae* in the Talbot Gallery, the state bed, and pieces which were too large to be readily saleable. These remained until the sale of 1924, and even then not everything was sold. In the meantime the eighteenth earl and his successors were faced with the problem of re-furnishing the Towers - no easy task in view of the size and number of rooms. Photographs of the interiors taken in the 1890s show an odd assortment of furniture, ornaments and carpets, and it is clear that the Towers was never again furnished on the lavish and elegant scale it had been in the days of the fifteenth and sixteenth earls. Nevertheless some attempts were made. In the Victoria & Albert Museum there is a coloured sketch by J.H. Pollen dated 1873 depicting Henry V preparing to lay siege to Harfleur.[7] It was one of a series of sketches intended to be worked up into wall-hangings for Alton Towers, and all on the theme of the Hundred Years' War and the Talbots' part in it. The Chetwynd-Talbots seem to have been no less proud of their medieval past than their predecessors had been, though they clearly lacked the means to express it so lavishly. It would appear that the wall-hangings were never actually made.

There is little record of structural work after 1860, apart from routine maintenance. The names of some of the rooms were changed. In the Inventory of 1869 the Green Dressing Room is also referred to as the Talbot Dressing Room, and the Red Bedroom has become the Talbot Bedroom. The Chetwynd Talbots' main residence was in any case Ingestre Hall, except for a brief period in the 1880s after a disastrous fire resulted in the virtual rebuilding of Ingestre. The greater glory of Alton Towers can be said to have departed with the death of Earl Bertram.

A set of fourteen water-colours painted in August 1870 confirm this impression. The artist is known only by initials which appear to be "LJT". He - or she - clearly knew the Chetwynd-Talbots, for Lady Shrewsbury and her three daughters appear in several of the pictures **(134 & Col. plate VII).** Together they make up a unique set of snapshots, as it were, of the Towers and grounds; a systematic tour beginning with a distant view from near the village of Farley, then progressing through the grounds to the east terrace. The interiors of the Octagon, House Conservatory, Music Room and Banqueting Hall are shown, with many empty spaces, but retaining of course all the rich decorations. A view from the North Library through the Music Room and into the "T-Room" recalls beautifully the internal vista along the southern side of the house towards the chapel corridor **(Col. plates VII, VIII, IX & XI).**[8]

134 East Entrance from terrace, 1870. (Watercolour by unknown artist. Private Collection)

It was the twentieth earl, Charles Henry (1877-1921) who began to develop the house and gardens seriously as a tourist attraction in the 1890s. "Monster Fetes", equestrian events, illuminations and firework displays attracted thousands of visitors. A programme for the Grand Fete of August 1892 included a performance by "Victorina, the strongest athlete on earth", whose feats included catching a cannon ball "fired from a real cannon with real gunpowder". Another attraction was Lieutenant Alberini, who mesmerised a lady in a den of four forest-bred lions. Later there was the ascent of "Monstre *(sic)* balloons representing the life-like figures of Her Majesty the Queen and the Prince and Princess of Wales".

On a visit to the Royal Castle in Nuremburg in 1892 Lord Shrewsbury saw a collection of instruments of torture, and, seeing the possibility of profit in exhibiting these, he bought them. As well as being displayed at the Towers, this gruesome collection was taken on tour to London, Manchester and Liverpool, and attracted a good deal of attention from the Press. Throughout these years the gardens at Alton were kept in immaculate condition by the Head Gardener, Mr. Rabone, and they were in themselves a great attraction.

The twentieth earl branched out into a number of business ventures. These included the design and marketing of horse-drawn cabs and coaches. During the summer of 1892 he ran a regular four-horse coach-service bringing in visitors to the Towers from the spa town of Buxton, some twenty miles away. Sometimes he drove the coach himself, and was proud of his achievements as a four-in-hand driver: *"The longest distance I ever drove four horses in one day was in 1887 when I covered the 121 miles from Llandudno to Alton Towers..... I started from Llandudno at 8-30 a.m. with a load of 8 passengers, and reached Alton Towers at 9-15 p.m., having stopped an hour on the way at Chester to see the Cup run for, and being considerably delayed in the last stage by unfortunately having no lamps, which necessitated a crawl for the last 5 miles".* [9]

In the early 1900s he branched out into the design and manufacture of "Talbot" motor cars, and in 1913 a Talbot car had the distinction of being the first automobile to cover 100 miles in an hour. At the time of the coronation of King Edward VII in 1902 suggestions were made that these business activities were incompatible with nobility, and that the earl might be disqualified from attending the coronation. He did in fact attend, and in 1907 he entertained the King at Ingestre and Alton.

The fortunes of the estate - and hence of the house too - suffered a reverse as a consequence of the separation of the earl and countess in 1896. The countess continued to live at Alton, but in reduced circumstances owing to the fact that the earl did not hand over the allowance that had been agreed. The general decline in the fortunes of landed estates in the early twentieth century also took its toll. In 1918 the bulk of the Alton estates were sold, and in 1924 the remaining properties including the Towers were sold to a group of local businessmen. So after some 700 years the Alton estate passed completely and finally out of the hands of the Talbot family.

Cleared of its furniture once again at an auction sale in 1924 the great house now stood empty; yet for a while it retained the fading splendours of its internal décor: the glazed doors, the panelling, grand staircases, fireplaces, ceilings and stained glass. The new owners consisted of a consortium including the three Cowlishaw brothers, Charles, Douglas and Vernon, whose aim it was to run the Towers as a tourist attraction, much as it had been before the War. A special siding was constructed at Alton station for special excursion trains, and the railway companies promoted these by means of posters and advertisments in carriages. The actual running of the enterprise was in the hands of Charles Henry Cowlishaw, who had bought some pieces of furniture in the 1924 sale, including the Pugin four-poster bed in

135. The Long Gallery in use as a refreshment room *c.*1930.

the Arragon Room[10]. There is evidence to show that some architectural woodwork, and even stone, was removed and sold at this time. In 1924 the Leek textile firm of Wardle and Davenport were building a palatial new office block at their Belle Vue Mill. Letters from the architects dated 31st July 1924 refer to the proposed purchase of oak panelling, doors and stone from the Towers to be used in the new offices. The letters refer to Mr Cowlishaw as having offered to sell the 250-foot run of panelling and five doors for £450. An unspecified quantity of stone was offered at four shillings per cubic foot.[11] Sadly this office-block was demolished in the 1970s so there is no means now of identifying the panelling and doors.

It was Charles Cowlishaw's declared intention to preserve as much as possible of the Towers, and to prevent it going the same way as so many country houses which suffered despoliation and demolition in the inter-war period. Uses had to be found for the state rooms, and some of them, such as the Dining Room, "T" Room and Music Room, were turned into cafés to serve the needs of the hordes of visitors who came to enjoy the gardens and the entertainments laid on by the Alton Towers company. Photographs and postcards of the 1920s and 1930s show these rooms full of tables and bentwood chairs (**135 & 136**). The Poet's Bay was stacked high with beer-crates, and a sign over the drawbridge entrance proclaimed Mary Z. Waddicor as licensee and café proprietress.

136. The Dining Room *c.* 1930.

Shortly after the outbreak of the Second World War, the house was requisitioned by the Army as the base for an Officer Cadet Training Unit. Even after the end of the war the Towers and gardens remained under requisition and it was not until 1951 that they were handed back to the Towers Company. The Army was blamed, unfairly, for causing considerable damage to the house.

True, they adapted the Talbot Gallery to their needs by cutting openings in the walls, and they may also have used the West Wing, but the other State Rooms appear simply to have been closed up for the duration of the war. The cadets had their own huts built on the lawns near the north front, and the only areas of the building in regular use at this time, apart from the ones already mentioned, appear to have been the kitchens, and the former family apartments in the eastern part of the house which were smaller and more practical than the vast state rooms. Some of the fireplaces in the eastern wing were partly bricked, and smaller iron grates inserted, as a wartime economy measure. The dining-hall fireplaces were also bricked up at this time, and cast-iron pillar-stoves placed in front.

The popular myth that it was the Army Cadets who wrecked Alton Towers is not borne out by the photographic survey made in 1951 - long after the army evacuated the buildings - by the National Monuments Record *(NMR)*. Though not every part of the Towers was photographed - notable exceptions being some of the former family rooms, the kitchen areas, and the West Wing - detailed studies were made of all the state rooms in the central area of the house. These show that the fine moulded plaster ceilings in the Music Room and the Libraries were still largely intact, likewise the groined ceilings of the Long Gallery and Drawing Room, and two of

the Pugin/Crace coffered ceilings in the family wing. The fine woodwork in the State Rooms, and the carved panelling in the Great Dining Room was still in place, and all of the beautiful stained glass in the Dining Hall, the Long Gallery, Drawing Room, Libraries, Octagon and Chapel was intact. Pugin-designed wallpaper still graced the walls of the "T" Room, and his magnificent screen and painted frieze survived in the chapel.

137. Destruction of the interiors, 1952, view from Music Room into North Library. Note the painting by Thomas Willement over the arches. (Alton Towers Archive)

Responsibility for the demolition of the interiors of the Towers lies with the new owners the buildings, the Bagshaws, of the Uttoxeter auctioneering firm of W.S. Bagshaw & Sons who had managed the 1924 sale of the contents of the Towers. It was Dennis Bagshaw and his two brothers who bought out the Cowlishaws and then recouped their money by stripping the lead from the roofs. The subsequent damage caused by rain-water penetration then gave them the excuse to strip out the whole of the interior, prior to which the photographic survey was carried out by the National Monuments record. Although the effects of water damage are visible in some areas, the majority of the pictures show how splendid a place Alton Towers still was after the war, giving the lie to the rumours that the damage had been done by the Army.

163

The sheer folly and short-sightedness of this asset-stripping exercise, and the great sadness and anger with which it was received locally, is well expressed in the reminiscences of one who lived through it:

"I can never forget the Sunday morning in 1951, when I was briefly at home in my parents' house in Alton and the telephone rang. A man who had been a boy when I was a boy, the son of one of the gardeners, said that he had all the keys and that he and I should go over the house for the last time. The stripping of the panelling and fittings began the next day. For a week my mother and I were distressed by the sound of hammers banging which drifted across the valley. But that Sunday the gardeners' son and I went through every single room of one of the greatest houses ever built in England; I can never think of this experience without tears coming into my eyes..."[12]

Within a few weeks the roofs, floors, staircases, stained glass - in short anything saleable - were ripped out and sold, the Potteries Demolition Company being called in to dispose of the residue (137). Residents still living in Alton can recall lorries piled high with timber and metals passing through the village day after day for weeks on end, and stacks of timber removed from the buildings being offered for sale on site (138). The destruction of the chapel was particularly distressing, for it had been rather better looked-after than other parts of the buildings and contained some of the most splendid furnishings and decorations. It was nothing short of sacrilege, and some onlookers were not afraid to say so, but to no effect.[13] Unwanted material accumulated in the eastern part of the house was set alight where it was, and this helps to account for the particularly derelict and unstable nature of this area which includes, of course, the remains of the original Alveton Lodge. Had Alton Towers survived but a few months longer - until the passing of the Historic Buildings and Ancient Monuments Act of 1953 - the story might have been very different.

Thus perished the glorious State Rooms of Alton Towers, and it was yet another accident of history that in the centenary year of Pugin's death his magnificent and unique screenwork was carelessly torn out of the Towers chapel, and other products of his creative genius were destroyed by people who were ignorant or careless of their historic value and importance. Yet not all was lost. The painted roofs of the chapel and dining hall remained, likewise the Hardman glass of great oriel window in the hall, and some portions of the south window too. The gilt-brass chandelier, also from the dining hall, was later discovered in pieces in a local second-hand shop, recognised for what it was, and rescued.[14] Having been lovingly restored to its former magnificence, it now graces the Pugin Room in the Palace of Westminster. Some panelling from the dining hall

138. Timber removed from the Towers stacked up for sale by the Grand Entrance, 1952. (Alton Towers Archive)

139. Restoration work in progress in the chapel, 1994. (Alton Towers Archive)

was re-worked into an organ case for S. Peter's church in Alton. The exquisite quality of the carving gives a clue as to the splendours which survived elsewhere in the house as late as the 1950s and it also raises questions as to where else one might find surviving fragments of the vast quantities of architectural woodwork and metalwork which were sold in that year. Some linenfold panelling from the Towers has recently been identified in the Masonic Lodge in Stafford, where it has been since 1952.[15]

The removal of complete floors from buildings which stood in some instances four storeys high posed the risk of eventual collapse of the exterior walls. This was especially true of the Long Gallery block which was particularly tall. The iron reinforcements which had been inserted in the walls at the time of their construction help to account for its survival. When surveyed for Pevsner's Staffordshire volume of *The Buildings of England* (1974) the buildings appear to have been abandoned except for the Armoury which was used as a Gift Shop, and the Chapel which housed the model railway. Pevsner commented on the sad state of the banqueting hall at that time: "totally given up and only reached along a tunnel and across rubble"[16]. Such buildings as remained in use were generally re-roofed in asphalt to replace the lead. Water-penetration gradually took its toll, and rot set into the structural timberwork.

The owners of the Towers from the mid-1970s onwards were more sympathetic to the conservation and restoration of the buildings, which were given Grade II* Listed Building status. New concrete and steel floors were constructed in the principal rooms so as to allow public access into these areas once again, and the fine timber roof of the dining hall was restored. In 1990 the Tussauds Group - then part of Pearson PLC - acquired Alton Towers. It was Pearson who sponsored the major exhibition on the life and work of A.W.N. Pugin at the Victoria & Albert Museum in 1994: *Pugin: A Gothic Passion,* and at the same time the Towers chapel was cleared and its magnificent Pugin ceiling restored **(139)**. Future restoration projects may include the reinstatement of the Pugin screenwork in the chapel. Repairs to the stonework of the beautiful Doria window were

140. Restoration in progress: stabilisation of the east front, 2003 (MJF)

carried out in 1999. At the same time the Octagon and Talbot Gallery were cleared of rubble and débris, and a section of the House Conservatory was restored, all in preparation for a new theme-park attraction which, although outside the historic buildings, is accessed via the Armoury, Picture Gallery and Octagon. Important survivals of stained glass in the Armoury and Music Room have been restored at the John Hardman Studio in Brimingham. The east front - a survival from the original Alveton Lodge - was restored and stabilised in 2003. The attractions which draw today's visitors to Alton Towers are principally those of the theme park, but at the heart of it all stands the great house: one of the most important buildings of the Gothic Revival, reflecting all the key stages of that movement, and the efforts of one of the nation's most notable families to re-create their past in an age of historical Romanticism.

141. Restoration in progess: glass by William Eginton from the Music Room under repair at the John Hardman Studio, Birmingham, 2003 (MJF). See above, pp. 66-67

NOTES

Abbreviations:

Belcher 1   M. Belcher, *The Collected Letters of A.W.N. Pugin*, Vol 1,
                   1830 to 1842 OUP 2001

Belcher 2   M. Belcher, *The Collected Letters of A.W.N. Pugin*, Vol 2,
                   1843 to 1845 OUP 2003

HLRO   House of Lords Record Office

SCRO   Staffordshire County Record Office

NMR   National Monuments Record: Royal Commission on the Historical
                   Monuments of England

1. ALTON LODGE

1.   Shrewsbury Papers, **SCRO** D240/E/F/9/9 (1815) and E/F/2/11 (1816)

2.   e.g. William Adam, *The Gem of the Peak,* 1851, p.242.

3.   **SCRO** D240/E/F/9/3

4.   Of the same family, one assumes, as the Bills of Farley Hall.

5. **SCRO** D240/A/2/16, Indenture dated 3rd October 1807. Lord Shrewsbury was to pay Charles Bill the sum of £157 per year.

6.   D240E/F/9/3

7.   The construction of the bridge was spread over several years and was separately accounted,
       e.g. D240/E/F/9/13

8.   D240/E/F/2/28, 29 & 30

9.   H.M. Colvin, *A Biographical Dictionary of British Architects,* 3rd edn. 1995, p.607. The date 1812 is given for alterations to the office-court at Locko Park, and 1814 for the interior of the library at Darley Abbey

10.   Alton Lodge Cash on Account Books D240/E/F/2/35 & 36; see also R. Speake (ed.), *A History of Alton and Farley,* Keele University 1996, pp. 302-305

2. ALTON ABBEY

1.   Shrewsbury Papers, **SCRO** D/240/E/F/2/18, pp 28-32. These chaplains also served the Cresswell and Painsley Missions which included the town of Cheadle.

2.   Hurriedly built on insecure foundations, and made to a large extent of wood and cement rather than stone and brick, the tower collapsed for the third time in December 1825, demolishing a large part of the house in the process. For descriptions of Fonthill see, for example, Clive Wainwright, *The Romantic Interior* (Yale 1989), ch.5, and Roy Strong, "The Fall of Fonthill", *Lost Treasures of Britain,* Viking, 1990).

3.   i.e. the buildings now referred to as the Ingestre Stables. The screen was completed in 1813-14. *Alton Abbey Cash Account,* **SCRO** D240/E/F/2/10 (1813), E/F/2/41 (1814).

4.   Memorandum from the Earl of Shrewsbury, 12th June 1818 on loose paper inside a volume of Alton Abbey accounts **SCRO** D240/E/F/9/19; also E/F/2/14

5.   *ibid.*

6.   D240/E/F/2/10 In September 1813 local haulier Daniel Warrington was paid expenses for going to the black marble quarries at Ashford with a waggon and four horses.

7.   D240/E/F/2/41

8.   *ibid.,* E/F/2/10. Alsop was paid £536 for bricks supplied in 1813.

9.   R. Speake (ed.), A *History of Alton and Farlev,* pp.227-8. The Abbey Accounts for 1820 record payments to John Farnell and John Bryan for "getting stone for wharf near the Gig" (E/F/2/21 p.61)

10.   **SCRO** D240/E/F/9/17

11.   *ibid.,* E/F/2/14, 16, 19 & 20.

12.   The Alton Abbey Stewards Cash accounts are particularly rewarding for the names of the various

mechanics" and what they did, e.g. D240/E/F/2/10-14 (1813-18); E/F/9/9 (Cash Book for 1815) contains the signatures of the artisans against the amounts that were paid to them. The painter Thomas Kearns later did work for Pugin at the Towers, at S. John's Church, Alton, and elsewhere.

13. **CRO** D240/E/F/2/10, 19 & 34. In August 1813 stonemason Thomas Bailey was working samples of mouldings ordered by Hopper. E/F/2/19 p.30 records a visit to Alton by Hopper in the summer of 1815

14. D240/E/F/2/13 & 20 p102 & 111-2; E/F/9/19 & 20. The design for the gable cross was amongst a collection of drawings formerly owned by descendants of stonemason Thomas Bailey and sold at Sothebys on 30th April 1987 *(Early English and Victorian Watercolours, Architectural Drawings and Watercolours,* Lots 514-518). Bought by Alton Towers, most of the drawings are currently in the Towers archive collection, with the exception of the drawing of the cross and several other items from Lot 518 which are not accounted for.

15. D240/E/F/2/14 & 20 (February and April/August 1818)

16. e.g. memoranda from both Thomas Allason and Lord Shrewsbury specifying work to be done at this time, D240/E/F/9/19, and the accounts of the Earl's Agent, Anthony Todd, for 1818-20, E/F/2/20 Allason's visits to Alton. and those of Mordaunt and Sinclair, are referred to in E/F/9/19 and 2/16

17. Alton Towers archive collection.

18. D240/E/F/2/18 & 19; E/F/9 & 10. Wright & Co were bankers to many Catholic families and were based in Henrietta Street, Covent Garden.

19. D/240/E/F/2/10

20. Payment to Hollins December 1817 D240/E/F/2/3. Allason was at Alton in June and November 1818 (E/F/2/16 & 19)

21. E/F/2/10 February/March 1813. Thomas Bailey was responsible for carving much of the ornamental stonework.

22. E/F/2/13 & E/F/2/20 (December 1817)

23. Memorandum of the Earl of Shrewsbury March 1818 D240/E/F/9/19

24. E/F/2/13 (July 1817) and E/F/2/21 (April 1821).

25. In February 1818 John Farnell was cutting the niches and also preparing the wall to receive the staircase E/F/2/14 p.6

26. E/F/9/19

27. E/F/2/14 p.82; E/F/2/16 p.30

28. E/F/2/21 p. 132.

29. E/F/2/10 (November 1813)

30. E/F/9/9 (1815); E/F/2/11 (June 1816). In February 1817 carpenter William Finney was setting brackets for the handrail to the staircase (E/F/2/13)

31. E/F/2/14, 16 & 20.

32. The Britannia Ironworks was eventually (1848) taken over by Andrew Handyside, and continued to make architectural and structural ironwork of superb quality. See for example "Andrew Handyside and his Workforce", *Derbyshire Miscellany,* vol. 12, part 4 (1990).

33. D240/E/F/2/10 & 13

34. E/F/9/9, June and October 1812

35. D240/E/F/2/16

36. D240/E/F/2/10 May 1813

37. E/F/2/41 September 1814

38. e.g. E/F/2/15: "...Thomas Bailey cutting away inside of stone walls to windows in west tower south front for frames" (January 1819)

39. e.g. E/F/2/13 p. 78 refers to the arch leading from the dining room to the conservatory. Obviously the house conservatory running southwards from the "T" Room is meant.

40. Memorandum and Orders from the Earl of Shrewsbury, June 1818, E/F/9/19; also E/F/2/16 p. 54

41. E/F/2/16 p.54

42. *ibid.*

43. *ibid.,* pp. 38, 54, 58 & 62; and E/F/2/17 pp. 50 & 56

44. Various publications of the period cite Muss as the artist responsible for this window, e.g. William Adam, *The Gem of the Peak,* 1843, p.256

45. e.g. Phoebe Stanton writes of the "claustrophobic density of the decoration" which, one must assume, she saw

at first-hand prior to its destruction in 1952: "Pugin: Principles of Design versus Revivalism", *Journal of the Society of Architectural Historians, xiii,* 3 (October 1954), p.24

46. e.g. Ross Williamson, "Staffordshire's Wonderland", *Architectural Review,* 87 (May 1940). Even Phoebe Stanton attributes to Pugin the "light Gothic conservatory to connect the octagon hall and the suite of state rooms" ("Some Comments on the Life and Work of A.W.N.Pugin", *Journal of the Royal Institute of British Architects,* December 1952, p.52.

47. See below, pp.136-140

48. D240/E/F/2/19 pp 40-43; ef also E/F/2/14 (1818) bricklayer John Farnell "laying and jointing flags, coal-house area south front".

49. E/F/2/13 p.78

50. E/F/9/19 p.19. In either case the order is given by Allason. cf payment to Bailey in July 1818 for altering the cill, E/F/2/20 p134

51. E/F/2/13, July 1817

52. E/F/2/14 p.28 (April 1818)

53. e.g. E/F/2/11 stone girder being built over octagon lobby (1817) E/F/2/16 "Thomas Bailey .... making a pedestal for urn to stand on in the octagon lobby" (1819); E/F/2/21 "John Dixon (plasterer) repairing in best staircase, Octagon Lobby (1821)

54. E/F/9/2 p. 90, Account of William Finney, carpenter, for 1823: "Addition to Abbey including Billiard Room"; cf. E/F/2/22 pp 16, 18 & 22, payments to Mellor and Beech for decorating Billiard Room, and to Finney for making a rack for cues. The significance of the billiard room as the nucleus of the "male domain" in the 19th-century country house is discussed by Mark Girouard in *The Victorian County House* (Yale 1979) pp. 34-38.

55. E/F/2/10 (August and September 1813)

56. Memorandum and orders from the Earl of Shrewsbury December 1817, E/F/9/19

57. Remains of later additions to this system were discovered in the summer of 1998 when new pipes were being laid to the fountain in Her Ladyship's garden. A duct was found, running from the south front towards the galleries and octagon, containing wires, rods and runners, all still in working order.

58. E/F/9/19 (March 1818). In November 1818 a Mr Howden was paid £95 for "fixing complete a Hot Air Dispenser at Alton Abbey" (E/F/2/20 p. 151) and in March 1820 Charles Rushton was paid for attending to the Hot Air Dispenser on Sundays between July 1819 and February 1820 when the family were in residence (E/F/2/17 p.10)

59. E/F/2/22 pp 19-28.

60. Snelston is illustrated in Burke's *Visitation of Seats and Arms,* 1854, p. 228. The original drawings are in the Derbyshire Record Office DIS7 M3030-30.

61. E/F/2/22 p.13 "Taylor & Brian, a day bill fitting in milestone plates April/May £1/11/31/2d"

62. E/F/2/21 p.146 "Bailey, Thomas, taking down entrance Gateway in gardens and unloading same at Quixhill" (July 1821); cf p.154 "Bailey preparing materials for gateway at Quixhill". The plans signed by Papworth are dated July 1822 and seem to represent an amendment to the original scheme and submitted to Papworth by Lord Shrewsbury's clerk-of-works, Mr Hobden. It is inscribed, "This is the way in which the work is prepared by the masons, and of which Mr Allason was not informed". A note in Papworth's handwriting reads, "These lodges are too small to suit the central archway"

3. "THE TOWERS"

1. Loudon's *Encyclopaedia of Cottage, Farm and Villa Architecture* (1833) gives the Gothic Temple as the location of the bust of the fifteenth earl and Campbell as the sculptor. In front of the Temple there is a circular stone platform which appears to have been made as the base for a piece of sculpture.

2. The Coalbrookdale Company provided estimates for the Pagoda in 1826 (D240/E/F/2/22 p. 85), but the fountain was not completed until the 1830s (Loudon).

3. E/F/9/19 p.17

4. E/F/9/2 p.59

5. E/F/2/22 pp.11, 20 & 70. The Britannia Foundry was at this time owned by Messrs. Weatherhead and Glover. Mr Glover came to Alton in person to supervise the construction of the models for the conservatory and temple domes, and in December 1825 the company was paid £325 "for castings including elliptical Domes of Conservatory, ornaments for ditto, cast iron pipes, etc."

6.   E/F/9/19 p.16. In 1823 Charles Manifold was paid £22 for gilding the windows of the Temple (E/F/2/23).

7.   Allason's drawing for the Gothic bridge was one of several drawings relating to Alton Towers sold at Sotheby's in April 1987 (see note 14 to Chapter 2), but it was not among those bought by the Towers Company.

8.   E/F/9/19 p.17

9.   Description of the colonnade in *The History and Topography of Ashbourne .... and Adjacent Villages,* 1839. See also E/F/2/10 for construction of colonnade.

10.   Adam, *Gem of the Peak, p.234*

11.   Loudon, *op. cit.,* quoted in *The History and Topography of Ashbourne, etc.,* 1839

12.   E/F/9/19

13.   J.M. Crook, Introduction to 1971 reprint of Eastlake, A *History of the Gothic Revival,* p 54

14.   It seems also to have started a trend: e.g. Horsley Towers, Surrey (1847-60); Mentmore Towers, Buckinghamshire (1850), Glenbegh Towers, County Kerry (1867-70), and Carlton Towers, Yorkshire (1873).

15.   D/240/E/F/9/2 p. 101 The Arundel Castle MSS include five estate plans by Fradgley relating to Alton, 1817-1838

16.   D240/E/F/2/20 p.205; E/F/2/21 p.40. I am grateful to Mr Peter Nixon of the Uttoxeter Heritage Centre for valuable information about Thomas Fradgley.

17.   E/F/2/24. As stated above, the Earl's bankers were Messrs. Wright & Co., Henrietta Street, London, Thomas Hart of this firm being Lord Shrewsbury's personal banker.

18.   e.g. a detailed description of the house after the 1857 sale *(Staffordshire Advertiser,* 22nd August 1857, p.7), also Francis Redfern, *History and Antiquities of the Town and Neighbourhood of Uttoxeter, 2nd* edition 1886 p.45lff. Though full of praise for Fradgley, Redfern makes not a single reference to Pugin's work at the Towers.

19.   See for example the article on Alton Towers in *The Tatler,* May 13th 1908: "... at one time carriages drove into the house for 100 yards, turning round a pillar at the end by the gallery door to come out again". It was perhaps the sight of these galleries, empty and forlorn after the 1857 Sale, which gave rise to this notion.

20.   D/240/E/F/2/22 pp. 33 & 35

21.   Shaw's drawings for the llam Octagon are in the Lichfield Joint Record Office, and are dated 1819. Pevsner gives the date incorrectly as 1831, probably from a misreading of the date on the memorial to David Pike Watts which was erected in 1826, i.e. MDCCCXXVI was read as MDCCCXXXI.

22.   Ebenezer Rhodes, *Derbyshire Tourists' Guide,* c.1834, quoted in *The History & Topography of Ashbourne,* 1839.

23.   Work surveyed in 1829-30 lists carpenters' work as follows: "The Drive and Coach-houses (afterwards turned into Armoury and billiard room etc) £123/12/81/2d". "Entrance Tower, and the drives, afterwards Armoury & Gallery £53/14/10d". D240/E/F/9/2 p. 107.

24.   D/240/E/F/9/2 p.107, Cash received on account of piece-work by Thomas Harris and Jonas Hartley, and see above n.23.

25.   William Adam, *The Gem of the Peak,* p.246.

26.   For a description of Bayons Manor (demolished in 1964) see Mark Girouard, *The Victorian Country House* (Yale 1979), pp. 103-109

27.   William Adam, *The Gem of the Peak,* p. 256. Rhodes *Derbyshire Tourists' Guide* of c.1836 refers to the dining-room as newly-completed

28.   The Willement papers at the British Library include his own chronological list of his principal works from 1812 to 1865 (Add. MSS 52413), and eight large portfolios of his drawings. Some drawings for AltonTowers are in 34871 and 34873. There is in addition to the items mentioned here a reference in the list to "a horizontal window of badges and ornaments for the ceiling of the ante-room", but it is difficult to say where this ante-room was.

29.   British Library Add. MSS 34873, f.96.

30.   i.e. the rooms which were converted into bars in the 1960s, and the present Costume Stores. The identification of these rooms as the Chaplain's Apartments is fairly clear from a survey and inventory carried out in 1869 (D240/G/4/1).

31.   *History and Antiquities ... of Uttoxeter,* 1886, p.451

32.   The Baptism Registers of S. John's, Alton, contain records of Baptisms which took place elsewhere in the parish before the church was opened in 1842. They were copied up by Dr. Daniel Rock, the Earl of Shrewsbury's domestic chaplain.

33. Some pieces of plaster cornice found amongst the rubble in this area are completely un-gothic in style, and include dentils, pellets, *guttae,* and other Classical forms.

34. e.g. William Adam, *op.cit.,* p. 258

35. D/240/E/F/2/24 p.14. A Mr Potter is referred to elsewhere in the Abbey/Towers accounts as measuring off construction work in the house and gardens for masons, carpenters and others between 1818 and 1827, e.g. E/F/2/22 p.5 & p.35 where payments to Potter totalling £379 are recorded "for sundry Drawings at the Abbey, making sketches & drawings & measuring off mechanics work during the years 1818, 1819, 1820, 1821, 22 and 23". cf. E/F/9/2 p.45. He may of course not be one and the same person as Joseph Potter of Lichfield; a quantity surveyor for example.

36. William Adam, *op. cit.,* p.261

37. E/F/9/2 p. 107 "Carpenters work to the whole of the west wing addition and joiners work to the mezzanine storey in the ditto - £515/6/0"; "continuation of lower part of new west wing £167/8/61/2d"

38. E/F/2/24 (William Bick's Cash Account with the Earl of Shrewsbury. Bick is described in *White's Directory of Staffordshire,* 1834, as a Land Agent, resident in Farley).

39. Alton Towers Sale Catalogue, 1857, lot 2184.

40. William Adam, *op. cit.,* p.263

41. See above, n.18

42. Redfern, *History and Antiquities..... of Uttoxeter*

43. *History and Topography of Ashbourne,* 1839, again quoting Rhodes' *Derbyshire Tourists' Guide*

44. Alton Towers Sale Catalogue, 1857

45. The accounts for 1824 include payments to stonemason Thomas Bailey for "underpinning the ruins at the old Castle to prevent their falling" D240/E/F/2/22

46. *Staffordshire Advertiser,* 22nd August 1857, p7

47. G. Waagen, *Art and Artists in England,* 1838, vol 3 p. 249

48. D240/E/F/2/13 & E/F/9/19

49. Clive Wainwright, *The Romantic Interior,* 1989, p. 61.

50. W. Adam, *op. cit.,* p. 246. Adam states that the screen between the Armoury and the Picture Gallery was designed by Lady Shrewsbury

51. In April 1997 a set of six coloured wax busts by Percy were shown on the BBC Television *Antiques Roadshow.* They were about half-size, and in frames, and included Elizabeth 1, Charles 1, and Sir Walter Raleigh. The set was valued at £12,000.

52. William Adam, *op. cit.,* p. 261

53. The books were sold separately from the other contents of the house. They were auctioned at Sothebys over twelve days, beginning on June 22nd 1857 (3,804 lots). Another and much smaller sale (43 lots) took place on May 18th 1858. Some lots consisted of single titles, others were multi-volume works, and there were also some bundles of books. The total number of individual volumes could therefore have been considerably greater than 4,000.

54. *SCRO* D240 EIF/2/14 p. 90 (Alton Abbey Accounts 1818) "By Allason, Mr. for Memoirs of Las Cassas (sic) purchased by him for the Earl, nine shillings".

55. ibid.,E/F/2/16 Stonemason Thomas Bailey working at Napoleon's arch, 1819

56. William Adam, *op. cit.,* p. 258

57. Letter in Alton Towers Archive.

58. An account of the royal visit - and a description of Alton Towers - appeared in *The Orthodox Journal,* vol. XI, no. 268, 15th August 1840.

59. William Adam, *op. cit.* p. 225 & 268-9.

60. Letter from Pugin to Lord Shrewsbury, *HLRO* 339/38, March 1842.

61. Letter from Pugin to Lord Shrewsbury, V&A Museum, L.525.1965, Wedgwood Catalogue nos. 18 & 19

4 EARL AND ARCHITECT

1. Letter from Lord Shrewsbury to Ambrose Phillipps, *HLRO* 339/10

2. Letter from Pugin to Lord Shrewsbury 1845, *HLRO* 339/47, Belcher 2, p. 362

3. So Pugin referred to Elizabeth in *Contrasts,* 1841, p. 65.

4. ***HLRO*** 339/3

5. ***HLRO*** 339/2

6. Bernard Ward, *Sequel to Catholic Emancipation,* 1915, vol. 1, p. 103.

7. Letter from Lord Shrewsbury to Pugin, 1850, ***HLRO*** 339/106.

8. Denis Gwynn, *Lord Shrewsbury, Pugin and the Catholic Revival,* 1946, p. xxxv. For a biography of Lord Shrewsbury see M.J. Fisher, *Pugin-Land*, 2002.

9. Bernard Ward, *op. cit., 1,* p. 34.

10. Benjamin Ferrey, *Recollections of A.W.N. Pugin,* 1861, p. 117.

11. Dr. Rock's letter to Pugin, dated 19th August 1836, is given in full by Ferrey, *op. cit.,* pp. 122-124.

12. *The True Principles of Pointed or Christian Architecture,* 1841, p. 49.

13. *ibid.*

14. Letter from Pugin to Lord Shrewsbury transcribed by Phoebe Stanton, *A.W.Pugin and the Gothic Revival,* University of London unpublished Ph.D. thesis, 1950, Appendix VIII, p. 17.

15. Letter from Pugin to William Osmond, January 1834, printed in Ferrey, *op. cit.,* pp. 85-86.

16. The summary account book (D240/E/F/9/2) contains a page headed "Alton Towers Cash Book. J.B. Denny in account with the Earl of Shrewsbury, but covering only July and August 1839, i.e. shortly after Denny's arrival at Alton. The first mention of Denny in the Pugin Diaries is under 1st July 1839: "At Uttoxeter. Denny arrived".

17. D240/E/F/2/24, p. 110.

18. ***HLRO*** 339/47.

19. Letter from Pugin to Lord Shrewsbury, 24th December 1841. Belcher 1, p. 306.

20. HLRO 339/96

21. A.W.N. Pugin, *The Present State of Ecclesiastical Architecture,* 1843, p. 95.

22. *ibid.*

23. ***HLRO*** 339/31 24th June 1843. Belcher 2, p. 83.

24. ***HLRO*** 339/17 Belcher 1, p.306, and for the detailed history of the Hospital & Castle see M.J. Fisher *Pugin-Land,* 2002.

25. ***HLRO*** 339/26. Pugin to Lord Shrewsbury, 20th April 1843, Belcher 2, pp. 43-44

26. Pugin's diaries are in the Victoria and Albert Museum. They have been edited and published by Alexandra Wedgwood in A. *W. Pugin and the Pugin Family (Catalogues of Architectural Drawings in the Victoria & Albert Museum),* 1985. They run from 1835 to 1851; 1843 and 1846 are missing.

27. *The Orthodox Journal, 1839,* 11, pp. 75-6.

28. M. le Vicomte Walsh, *Relation du voyage de Henri de France..,* (see below, n. 33) p. 199, and Alton Towers Sale Catalogue, 1857, lot 1145.

29. ***HLRO*** 339/87

30. Rosemary Hill, "Pugin in Scotland", *Caledonia Gothica: Architectural Heritage VIII,* 1997, Journal of the Architectural Heritage Society of Scotland, Edinburgh University Press, pp.10-21.

31. ***HLRO*** 339/83. Belcher 1, pp. 372-373

32. ***HLRO*** 339/28 & 72; see also Phoebe Stanton, *op. cit.,* Appendix VIII, pp. 13-15. Belcher 1, pp. 124-126.

33. M. le Vicomte Walsh, *Relation du voyage de Henri de France en Ecosse at en Angleterre,* Paris 1844. The Walsh family were Irish but settled in France in the 18th century and acquired noble status. I am most grateful to Clive Wainwright for drawing my attention to this fascinating document which provides the key to some otherwise enigmatic statements in Pugin's correspondence, and offers a rare glimpse of one of the grand functions at Alton. The *Illustrated London News,* 14th October 1843 and 6th January 1844 contain accounts of the Duke's travels in Europe, and a description of Alton Towers, but no details of his visit to Alton.

34. ***HLRO*** 339/72. Belcher 1, p. 123.

35. Phoebe Stanton, *op. cit.,* Appendix VIII p. 13. Belcher 1, p. 120.

36. There is a detailed account of the opening ceremonies and of the church itself in the *Staffordshire Advertiser,* 5th September 1846; see also M.J. Fisher, *Pugin-Land,* 2002 and *Perfect Cheadle,* 2004.

37. David Higham and Penelope Carson, *Pugin's Churches of the Second Spring,* 1997, p. 31.

38. Denis Gwynn, *op. cit.,* pp. 107-8.

39. *Report from the Select Committee on Fine Arts in connection with Rebuilding the Houses of Parliament,* 18th June 1841, p. 7. I am grateful to Lady Wedgwood for providing me with a copy.

40. *HLRO* 339/68. 8th July 1843, Belcher 1, p. 90.

41. *HLRO* 339/71. 9th March 1842. Belcher 1, p. 329

42. *HLRO* 339/18. Pugin had accidentally trapped this man's pipe behind a tip-up seat in the carriage and broken it, whereupon the "horrid ruffian" demanded 25 francs compensation and produced a knife. Pugin describes the incident in great detail, and even gives a sketch of the carriage seat!. Belcher 1, pp. 261-262

43. *HLRO* 339/4; undated but Pugin refers to the church at Ramsgate as though it were complete, so 1848-9 is likely.

44. Denis Gwynn, *op. cit.,* p. 68, quoting E.S. Purcell, *Life and Letters of Ambrose Phillipps.*

45. Letter to Jane Pugin, *HLRO* 339/274.

46. *HLRO* 339/100.

47 *HLRO* 339/109. Pugin's first wife Anne Garnet died in 1832 a week after the birth of their daughter Anne. In 1833 he married Louisa Burton who died in 1844.

48 Benjamin Ferrey, *op. cit.,* p. 258.

49. *HLRO* 339/100.

50. See David Meara, "The Death of A.W.N. Pugin", *True Principles* (The Journal of the Pugin Society), Vol. I no. 3, Winter 1997.

51. *HLRO* 339/113.

52. *HLRO* 339/291

53. *HLRO* 339/84 (1845).

54. *HLRO* 339/111

55. *HLRO* 339/104 (undated).

5 PUGIN AT ALTON

1. Volume of 13 drawings, with a label inside the cover *Edw. Hull,* and dated 1834. E.2588-2600-1910 (Wedgwood Catalogue 115). These might well have been the ones which Lord Shrewsbury saw at Hull's shop, in which case Ferrey's date of 1832 is clearly wrong.

2. Redfern, *History and Antiquites of Uttoxeter,* p. 451.

3. *CRO* D240/E/F/9, p. 109.

4. *HLRO* 339/101.

5. A detailed account of the life and work of George Myers has been written by Patricia Spencer-Silver under the title of *Pugin's Builder,* The University of Hull Press, 1993.

6. Letter from Lord Shrewsbury to Pugin, March 1840, *HLRO* 339/101. Shrewsbury was particularly anxious that Willement should get the correct references for the Doria Pamphili and Borghese arms. Willement's work in the Talbot Gallery is documented in British Library Add. MSS 52413 pp. 13 and 23.

7. W. Adam, *The Gem of the* Peak, 1843, p.266.

8. Letter from Pugin to Lord Shrewsbury dated 31st March 1841, given in Stanton, A. *Welby Pugin and the Gothic Revival,* unpublished University of London Ph.D. thesis, 1950, Appendix VIII, p.4, Belcher 2001 p.227

9. *HLRO* 339/17. Belcher 1, p.307

10. Letter from Pugin to Lord Shrewsbury dated 13th February 1842, V&A Museum, L.525 1965 Wedgwood Catalogue no. 24. Belcher 1, p.321

11. Warrington's list is in the V&A Museum, MS86 BB27

12. *HLRO* 339/71. 28th August 1841, Belcher 1, p.269

13. Letter from Pugin to Lord Shrewsbury, 1st October 1841, transcribed in Stanton, *op.cit.,* Appendix VIII, p.5.

14. e.g. the front end-papers of Pugin's diary for 1839 refer to a pattern for Harris to work from.

15. William Adam, *op. cit.,* p. 252. The paintings were still there is 1951 and appear on the *NMR* photographs. Willement says he was responsible for all the painted decorations in all the principal apartments, *British Library Add. MSS 52413, P.* 13.

16. Letter from Pugin to Lord Shrewsbury, see above note 8; also *HLRO* 339/71, Belcher 1, p.269, in which he comments on the fine quality of Firth's casting of the Talbot. Both of these replicas survive, though

somewhat mutilated, in one of the cellars at the Towers, and could well be restored at some future date.

17.	**HLRO** 339/30. Belcher 2, p. 43. The tomb at Albrighton is that of Sir John Talbot (d.1555).

18.	**HLRO** 339/38. Belcher 1, p.329.

19.	**HLRO.**, 339/32. 30th November 1843. Belcher 2, p. 141

20.	See for example Kenneth Clark, *The Gothic Revival,* 3rd edn. 1962, p. 139.

21.	The Tournament was cut short because of torrential rain. The great pavilion designed by L.N. Cottingham to seat 2,000 people at a lavish medieval-style banquet collapsed, so the banquet was cancelled. By an odd coincidence Theresa Cockerell, a step-daughter of the Earl of Eglinton born the year before the Tournament, was later to marry the 19th Earl of Shrewsbury. Two rooms at Alton Towers were consequently re-named "Eglinton Bedroom" and "Eglinton Dressing-room".

22.	V&A Museum L.525-1965 (Wedgwood Catalogue no. 18)

23.	Letter to from Pugin Lord Shrewsbury, July 1842 **HLRO** 339/91, Belcher 1, p.360.

24	Letter from Pugin to Lord Shrewsbury March 9th 1842 **HLRO** 339/38, Belcher 1, p.329.

25.	*ibid.*

26.	It was identified in the 1950's in "Armoury Antiques", The Lanes, Brighton, by Claude Blair of the Metal-work Department at the V & A Museum. The shop no longer exists. I am indebted to Lady Wedgwood for providing me with a copy of a photograph upon which my sketch has been based.

27.	**HLRO** 339/60 and 83. Belcher 2, p. 119

28.	**HLRO** 339/8. 5th July 1844. Belcher 2, p. 213.

29.	W. Adam, *The Gem of the Peak,* p.258; also the 1857 Sale Catalogue which lists the contents of the rooms.

30.	**HLRO** 339/12 dated June 28th 1848

31.	A.W.N.Pugin, *True Principles,* 1841, p.49

32.	Letter from Pugin to Lord Shrewsbury dated 16th November 1842 (previously thought to have been 1843), V&A Museum L525 1965 (Wedgwood Catalogue no. 34). A Zeloni, *Vie de la Princesse Borghese,* Paris 1843, p.32. Lady Gwendalyn - who had married the Prince Borghese died in 1840 at the age of 23. Her likeness was included in the painting of the last judgement over the chancel arch at S. Giles', Cheadle, where she is pictured amongst the blessed.

33.	Letter from Pugin to Lord Shrewsbury, see n.32 above.

34.	A.W.N. Pugin, *True Principles, p.48*

35.	**HLRO** 339/32. 30th November 1834. Belcher 2, p. 141.

36.	Zeloni, *op. cit.,* p. 32ff

37	A.W.N. Pugin, *True Principles, p.51*

38.	Letters from Pugin to Lord Shrewsbury; Stanton, *op. cit.,* Appendix VIII pp. 17 & 21; *see also n.32 above*

39.	**HLRO** 339/102, not dated, but references to other work, and to Mary Amherst, would put it at about 1845

40.	Letter from Pugin to Lord Shrewsbury, 30th July 1847; V&A Museum L525-1965 (Wedgwood Catalogue no. 52)

41.	Letter from Pugin to Lord Shrewsbury, 1847; Stanton, *op. cit.,* Appendix VIII p. 19

42.	**HLRO** 339/50. December 1848.

43.	Stanton, *op. cit.,* Appendix VIII pp 19 & 20

44.	Letter from Pugin to Lord Shrewsbury, Stanton. *op. cit.,* Appendix VIII, pp. 20 & 21

45.	See above, n. 43

46.	Letters from Pugin to Lord Shrewsbury; Stanton, *op. cit.,* Appendix VIII, p.25.

47.	*e.g.* **HLRO** 339/29 & 57

48.	Stanton, *op. cit.,* Appendix VIII, p. 27

49.	Letter from Pugin to Lord Shrewsbury dated 3rd June 1849: "I am preparing a scheme of all the armorial bearings for the window", V&A Museum L525-1965 (Wedgwood Catalogue no. 64). There was some considerable delay in finalising these windows. John Hardman Powell, Pugin's son-in-law and only pupil, was entrusted with some of the work, and at one point he lost the scheme for the Talbot window (Letter from Pugin to John Hardman **HLRO** 304/197). A coloured drawing by Powell for the large north window survives at the John Hardman Studio, Lightwoods Park, Birmingham, with a rather different arrangement of the coats-of-arms than in the window as eventually executed. Pugin wrote despairingly to Hardman, "Even what I designed right is spoiled by others. My great window of dining hall which would have been a grand thing is now totally ruined by recent alterations." (**HLRO** 304/956).

50.	See Atterbury & Wainwright, *Pugin,* 1994, p. 102

51. 1857 Sale Catalogue pp 109-10 lists fourteen sideboard dishes. The 30" diameter dish is described as quite new". The others vary between 16" and 25" diameter, some silvered and some gilt. Drawings for some of them are in a private collection at the City Museum, Birmingham.

52. *SCRO* D240/E/F/9/25 & 26. A cost sheet in the Hardman stained glass archive dated 6th February 1856 charges £311.19.6d to the executors of the 16th Earl for the completion of the oriel window. Information from Mr Stanley Shepherd.

53. This description was later printed in *Blacks Picturesque Guide to Alton Towers and the Surrounding District, 1870*

54. E.W.Pugin superintended the arrangements for Lord Shrewsbury's funeral in 1852. In a letter dated 28th November 1852 Earl Bertram writes, "I shall feel myself happy in being to you what my dear Uncle Lord Shrewsbury would have been had God been pleased to leave him amongst us" *HLRO* 339/114.

55. A.W.N. Pugin, *True Principles*, p. 34 and plate VIII

56. D240/9/4/1. The inventory is dated 1869, but the date 1860 also appears, and it may well have been drawn up in 1860 as a catalogue of the furnishings, fixtures and fittings remaining in the Towers after the 1857 sale and the conclusion of the Peerage Case.

57. Ross Williamson, "Staffordshire's Wonderland", *Architectural Review*, no. 87 (May 1940) p. 162. The "Pugin Rooms" are thus listed in the 1924 Sale Catalogue.

58. Stanton, *op. cit.*, Appendix VIII p. 4, Belcher 1, p.227

59. *HLRO* 339/56 & 69

60. Royal Institute of British Architects Library, *Crace MSS*, Pug/1/2, 4 & 5

61. The drawing is at the V&A Museum D.993-1908, and is dated 1844. The paper is described by William Adam, *The Gem of the Peak*, 1843 etc., p. 254.

62. *HLRO* 339/41 & 47. In the interests of economy Pugin used the same pattern of wallpaper to decorate two ceilings, but Lord Shrewsbury was not altogether satisfied with the result. *"I will never make any two things alike again"*, wrote Pugin. See also Belcher 2, pp. 181, 195, 209, 362.

63. Stanton, *op. cit.*, Appendix VIII p. 4. Belcher 1, p.227

64. *SCRO* D240/G/4/1, see above note 56. Designs for these, and two other stoves are in the City Museum, Birmingham.

65. *HLRO* 339/71. The documentation for the window in the North Library is in the Hardman Archive, Birmingham Central Library (Glass Day Sales Book 1845-54); also **NMR** AA52 7048.

66. *HLRO* 339/96

67. *Black's Picturesque Guide*, 1870, pp. 31-2

68. *HLRO* 339/52 (25th October 1848)

69. *HLRO* 339/39, and Stanton *op. cit.*, Appendix VIII, p.24

70. Adam, *The Gem of the Peak*, 1851, p. 237

71. Letter from Pugin to Lord Shrewsbury, 12th November 1848, *HLRO* 339/40

72. Adam, *The Gem of the Peak*, pp, 236-7

73. V&A Museum L.525-1965 (Wedgwood Catalogue no.51)

74. *HLRO* 339/89

75. V&A Museum L.525-1965 (Catalogue no. 65)

76. *ibid.,* Cat. 66

77. *HLRO* 339/53

78. *HLRO* 339/45; Stanton, *op. cit.*, Appendix VIII pp. 23 & 24

79. Pugin was particularly proud of the Counslow Quarry: *"The Counslow quarry is capital... I think there is as good a masons shed as any in England, they can work in it during the severest frost as it all shuts up and the blocks of stone run into it on a sort of railway from the crane, 2 labourers sleep there to protect the tools and the men have a capital refectory..."* (Letter from Pugin to Lord Shrewsbury : *HLRO 339/17*). Remains of the buildings are still to be seen, also "Beggar's Well" which supplied water for the quarrymen and masons.

6. THE TOWERS CHAPEL

1. For Joseph Potter see above, p.63 White's *Directory of Staffordshire*, 1834, refers to the Towers chapel having been finished in 1833 under the architectural directions of the present earl" (p. 725)

2. *Willement Papers: British Library Add. MSS 52413*, p. 12

3. They are thus described in the Alton Towers Sale Catalogue of 1857

4. Yet the tower is shown in T. Fradgley's drawing of c1830, reproduced in West's *Picturesque Views ... in Staffordshire and Shropshire,* which therefore probably shows Alton Towers as Fradgley finally envisaged it, rather than as it actually was in 1829-30

5. In a letter to Lord Shrewsbury dated 17th June 1840 Pugin refers to his impending visit to Alton to supervise the completion of the chapel screen, and then adds, "I am sure your Lordship will be exceedingly pleased wᵢ the chairs which are in the true style". V&A Museum L.525-1965 (Wedgwood Catalogue no. 17)

6. R. Speake, *op. cit.,* pp 79-80, citing T. Richardson, *The Stranger's Guide or Description of Alton Towers,* 1852, and an undated article in the *Transactions of the Staffordshire Catholic History Society*

7. *Catholic Magazine,* V, 1834, pp. 662-37.

8. Roderick O'Donnell, "Pugin as a Church Architect", in Atterbury & Wainwright (ed.), *Pugin: A Gothic Passion,* 1994, p.64

9. Phoebe Stanton, *Pugin,* 1971, p. 172

10. Letter from Pugin to Lord Shrewsbury,. November 1847 **HLRO** 339/79

11. A description of the Towers chapel in the *Orthodox Journal* vol XI, 1840, p.112 states, "Around the sanctuary are arranged the panels formerly belonging to Magdalene College, Oxford". Pugin was a friend of the Revd. J.R.Bloxam of Magdalen College, but the architect responsible for the restoration of the college chapel (1829-34) was Lewis Nockalls Cottingham.

12. Letter: V&A Museum L525-1965 (Wedgwood catalogue no. 17).

13. The V & A Museum has Pugin's drawings for a number of gilded frames for the chapel, and for the tall panels with pinnacles (Wedgwood Catalogue, 1985, nos. 179-184).

14. William Adam, *op. cit.,* p. 259.

15. Kearns lived in Alton village, and his name appears several times in the Pugin diaries as doing work for the architect, e.g. at S. Barnabas' Cathedral, Nottingham, which was financed largely by Lord Shrewsbury. The *Post Office Directory* for 1850 lists him among the residents of Alton as a plumber, glazier and ornamental painter. He died in 1858 and is buried in S. John's churchyard. His son, also named Thomas, was working with him at the Towers in the 1850s.

16. V & A Museum L525-1965 (Wedgwood Catalogue no. 67) dated 9 April 1850

17. *ibid.,* & Wedgwood Catalogue no. 83. He also includes instructions to Jane as to how the May Devotions should be conducted at Ramsgate in his absence.

18. W. Adam, *op. cit.,* p. 259. The Lynch painting shows a large crucifix under a canopy fixed to the north wall, just to the west of the altar rail. The dorsal and canopy for the cucifix were designed by Pugin and are mentioned in a letter to Lord Shrewsbury as "filling up the space beyond the communion rail in a very satisfactory manner" Phoebe Stanton, *op. cit.,* Appendix VIII, pp. 6-7 (December 1841)

19. *Illustrated London News,* Dec. 25th 1852, p. 563. A list of metalwork items for the chapel is given in Belcher 2001, p.337.

20. *Catholic Magazine, III,* 1839, pp 498-9. May 8th was at this time a feast of S. Michael, Archangel.

21. *ibid.* The correspondent acknowledges the *Staffordshire Examiner* as his source.

22. *Orthodox Journal,* XI, 1840, p. 412.

23. Letter from Pugin to Lord Shrewsbury, 28th August 1841, Phoebe Stanton, *op. cit.,* Appendix VIII, Belcher 2001 p.270

24. For a detailed account of the preperations for the funeral, see R. O'Donnell, "'No Maimed Rites' - the funeral obsequities of the 16th Earl of Shrewsbury", *True Principles - The Voice of the Pugin Society,* Vol 2, no.4 (2002)

25 Description and engraving of the chapel at the time of the funeral in *Illustrated London* News, December 25th 1852

26 Fr. S.J.Gosling, parish priest of S. John's, Alton 1923-1950, evidently knew people in the village who had actually witnessed this great procession. D. Gwynn, *Lord Shrewsbury, Pugin, and the Catholic Revival,* 1946, p. xxvi.

27 Even Phoebe Stanton states that the screen came from the Towers chapel *(Pugin,* 1972, p.209). The confusion may have arisen out of the common dedication of both buildings to S. Peter. The *Guide* to Alton Parish church refers to a dispute between the twentieth Earl of Shrewsbury and the Vicar of Alton as a consequence of which the screen was removed to Salt church in 1908; cf. Robert Speake, *op. cit.,* p. 141.

28 Arthur Mee's *Staffordshire,* 1937, p. 24 refers to "the charming east window with figures of the Four Evangelists, and painted reredos (he obviously means the Pugin screen) with statues of four Englishmen, Augustine and Becket, the Confessor and St Chad, with delightful figures of angels appearing here and there".

7. CONCLUSION

1. **HLRO** 339/119. Phillipps, who lived at Grace Dieu in Leicestershire, was a mutual friend of Pugin and Lord Shrewsbury, and was much involved with their church-building schemes and the promotion of the Catholic Faith.

2. **HLRO** 339/114

3. **HLRO** 339/100

4. Diary of E.W.Pugin in a private collection; copy in **HLRO**

5. **SCRO** D240/E/F/9/26. The Monumental Brasses Index in the Hardman Archive shows that the brass for Earl Bertram was not done until 1873.

6. *Staffordshire Advertiser,* 11th July 1857

7. V & A Prints and Drawings Collection D10-1906

8. The watercolours were sold by auction at Sotheby's on 19th March 2003, and bought by the Earl of Shrewsbury. *The British Sale: British Paintings 1500-1850, British Drawings and Watercolours, Victorian Pictures,* p. 129. The significance of the pictures is discussed by M.J. Fisher, "Alton Towers", *Country Life,* 5th July 2001.

9. *The Road,* Christmas number, 1891

10. He paid £52 for the bed according to an annotated copy of the Sale Catalogue in the possession of Mrs. D. Brereton of Alton.

11. **SCRO** 1262/A/6/1

12. Mr. P.W. Avery O.B.E., King's College Cambridge; Letter to the author dated 26th August 2002.

13. Information given by Mr. S. Walker.

14. Information given by Clive Wainwright

15. Information and picture given by Mr. K. Rider.

16. N. Pevsner, *Staffordshire,* 1974, p.5

SELECT BIBLIOGRAPHY

Archival material

Alton Towers, Staffordshire: *Alton Towers Archive.* A large collection of material, mainly post-1924 (i.e. relating to the pleasure-park), but with a few earlier documents and pictures.

Arundel Castle, West Sussex: *Arundel Castle Archives,* Contains some estate maps of Alton village and lands surrounding Alton Lodge/Abbey.

Birmingham Central Library: Hardman Archives

House of Lords Record Office: *Pugin Family MSS in a Private Collection,* Historical Collection 339

Staffordshire County Record Office. *The Shrewsbury Papers.* Over 100 volumes of Alton Lodge/Abbey/Towers ledgers, cash-books etc., c.1797-1870 catalogued under D240

Victoria & Albert Museum, London: Pugin diaries, letters, correspondence between Pugin and Lord Shrewsbury; some drawings of items for Alton Towers chapel etc., Crace Archive.

The British Library, London: *The Willement Papers,* Add. MSS 52413; 34866-34873, documenting stained glass and other decorative work done by Thomas Willement, with some drawings.

Unpublished Research

Stanton, Phoebe, *Welby Pugin and the Gothic Revival,* University of London Ph.D. thesis, 1950

Printed Sources

Adam, William, *The Gem of the Peak,* London, J. & C. Mozley, various editions, 1838-1857. The 1838 edition makes only a passing reference to Alton Abbey. Adam visited for the first time in 1839, and subsequent editions contain detailed descriptions. The 5th edition (1851) is the one most frequently referred to in this book.

Aldrich, Megan, *Gothic Revival,* London, Phaidon Press, 1994

Atterbury, Paul, and Clive Wainwright (ed.), *Pugin: A Gothic Passion.* New Haven and London: Yale University Press, 1994

The Bard Graduate Centre for Studies in the Decorative Arts, New York, *A.W.N. Pugin, Master of Gothic Revival,* New Haven and London: Yale University Press, 1995

Belcher, Margaret, *The Collected Letters of A.W.N. Pugin*, Vol I, 1830-1842, Oxford, OUP, 2001.

Belcher, Margaret, *The Collected Letters of A.W.N. Pugin*, Vol II 1843-1845, Oxford, OUP, 2003.

Caledonia Gothica: Pugin and the Gothic Revival in Scotland: Architectural Heritage VIII (Journal of the Architectural Heritage Society of Scotland), Edinburgh, University Press, 1997

Clark, Kenneth, *The Gothic Revival: An Essay in the History of Taste,* 3rd edn., London: John Murray, 1962

Colvin, Howard, A *Biographical Dictionary of British Architects 1600-1840,* 3rd edn., London: John Murray, 1995

Curl, James S., *Encyclopaedia of Architectural Terms,* Shaftesbury: Donhead Publishing, 1992

Eastlake, Charles, A *History of the Gothic Revival,* 1872. Reprint; Foreword by J.M. Crook, Leicester: Leicester University Press, 1971.

Ferrey, Benjamin, *Recollections of A. W. N. Pugin and his father Augustus Pugin, 1861;* Reprint; Introduction and index by Clive and Jane Wainwright, London: Scholar Press, 1978

Fisher, Michael J., A *Vision of Splendour: Gothic Revival in Staffordshire, 1995*

Fisher, Michael J., *Pugin-Land*, Stafford, 2002

Girouard, Mark, *The Victorian Country House,* New Haven and London, Yale University Press, 1979

Gunnis, Rupert, *Dictionary of British Sculptors, 1660-1851,* London: Abbey Library, 1968

Gwynn, Denis, *Lord Shrewsbury, Pugin, and the Catholic Revival,* London: Hollis & Carter 1946

Hussey, Christopher, "Alton Towers", *Country Life,* 2nd & 9th June, 1960

Jewitt, Llewellyn, *Black's Picturesque Guide to Alton Towers and the Surrounding District,* 1870

Pevsner, Nikolaus, *The Buildings of England: Staffordshire,* Harmondsworth, Penguin Books Ltd., 1974

Pugin, Augustus Welby Northmore, *An Apology for the Revival of Christian Architecture in England,* London, 1843

    „   *Contrasts, or a Parallel between the Noble Edifices of the Middle Ages and Corresponding Buildings Showing the Present Decay of Taste,* 2nd edition, London: Dolman, 1841

    „   *Gothic Furniture in the Style of the 15th Century,* London: Ackerman, 1835

    „   *The True Principles of Pointed or Christian Architecture,* 1841. Reprint, Oxford: St. Barnabas Press, 1969.

    „   *The Present State of Ecclesiastical Architecture in England,* London: Dolman, 1843

Redfern, Francis, *History and Antiquities of the Town and Neighbourhood of Uttoxeter,* 2nd edn., 1886

Rhodes, Ebenezer, *The Derbyshire Tourists Guide, 1837*

Speake, Robert, (ed.), A *History of Alton and Farley,* Keele: Centre for Adult Education, Keele University, 1996

Spencer-Silver, Patricia, *Pugin's Builder: The Life and Work of George Myers,* Hull: Hull University Press, 1993

Stanton, Phoebe, *Pugin,* London: Thames & Hudson, 1971

    „   "Some Comments on the Life and Work of A.W.N. Pugin", *RIBA Journal, 3rd* Series, 60 (December 1952)

The Stranger's Guide or Description of Alton Towers, Staffordshire, London: T. Richardson, 1852.

Strong, Roy, M. Binney & J. Harris, *The Destruction of the Country House,* London: Thames & Hudson, 1974

Trappes-Lomax, Michael, *Pugin: A Medieval Victorian,* London: Sheed & Ward, 1932

Wainwright, Clive, *The Romantic Interior: The British Collector at Home, 1750-1850* New Haven and London: Yale University Press, 1989

Walsh, M. le Vicomte, *Relation du voyage de Henri de France en Ecosse et en Angleterre,* Paris, 1844

Ward, Bernard, *The Sequel to Catholic Emancipation,* London & New York: Longmans, Green & Co., 1915

Wedgwood, Alexandra, *Catalogue of the Architectural Drawings in the Victoria & Albert Museum: A. W. N. Pugin and the Pugin Family,* London: Victoria & Albert Museum, 1985.

Williamson, R.P. Ross, "Staffordshire's Wonderland", *Architectural Review,* 87, May 1940.

Zeloni, A., *Vie de la Princesse Borghese,* Paris, 1843

Index

(Numbers of illustrations given in bold italics)

Abraham, Robert, 10, 12, 20, 50, 51, 52, 55-57

Adam, William, 53, 139, 149-150

Adelaide, Queen, 9, 77, 95

Allason, Thomas, 10, 20, 27, 30, 46, 51, 65, 86, 129;
Colour Plates V & VI

Alsop, William (brickmaker), 26, 87

Alton Abbey (later Alton Towers), Ch. 2, *9, 11, 13, 14, 15*

Alton Castle 72, 89-90, 130, 140, 147, *1, 65*

Alton - Railway Station, 140-141

Alton, S. John's Hospital and church, 12, 35, 78, 88-9, 98, *102,* 112, 113, 159, *62, 63, 64*

Alton, S. Peter's Church 88, 90

Alton Towers -
- Armoury, 57, 58, 59-60, 74, *47*
- Arragon Bedroom 103, *73*
- Billiard Room 45~46, 62, 159
- "Black Prince" Window 40, 62, 72, *25*
- Boudoirs 77
- Cellars 18, 29, 48, 159, *11*
- Chapel 33, 34, 62-3, 98, 117-8, Ch. 6, 143-156, *18, 19, 48, 49, 121-128, Col. Plates III & X,* Frontispiece
- Chapel Corridors 55, 75
- Conservatory (house) 41-45, 48, *29-31, 112, 135, Colour Plate VIII*
- Conservatories (garden) 48, 50-51, 136-139, *37, 113-4*
- Demolition of interiors 1952, 11-12, 164, 166; *137, 138, 139*
- Dining Room (small) 82, 99,
- Dining Room (principal) 121-129; *94-101, 136, Colour Plates XIII & XIV*
- Doria Rooms 118-9, *88, 89, 90*
- Drawbridge Entrance 63, 121, *92*
- Drawing Room 35-41, 43, 44, *20, 26, 27*
- East Front *88*
- Entrance Hall 29-33, 61, *14, 14, 15*
- Entrance Tower 57, 59, 121, *46*
- Farm buildings 24, *7*
- Flag Tower 20, 50, *25, 36*
- Fortifications 120-121, *91, 92*
- Gardens 50-54, *37-41*
- Glass Corridor 61, 62, 72
- Great Stove 134-5, *110*

- Kitchens 131-133, *106, 107*
- Loggia, 53, *40*
- Long Gallery 35-41, *20, 21, 22*
- Libraries 75-77
- Music Room 65, 67, 68, *51, 52, 53*
- "New" Rooms 129-131, 134, 157, 159, *103, 104, 105, 111*
- North Front 22, *5, 13, 33, 74, 93*
- Oak Corridor 55, 68, 106, 107, *54*
- Octagon 57-9, 108-116, *44, 44, 45*
- Orangery 51
- Oratory ("Her Ladyship's"), 138, *115*
- Paintings Collection 73, 159
- Pigeon House 140, *116*
- Plate Glass Drawing Room 63, 72, 77, 118, 119, *48, 138*
- Poet's Bay 65, 67, 68
- Restoration work 156, 165-6, *140, 141*
- Sale (1857) 11, 72, 103, 104, 115, 129
- Sale (1924) 161-162
- Servants' Hall 25, 44, *11*
- Servants' Quarters 131-133, *108*
- Smoking Rooms 62, 72, 75
- South Entrance 45, *32*
- South Front 130, *23, 30, 102-3*
- Station Lodge, 104, 141~142, *118*
- "T" Room 35, 41, 45, 72, *20, 27*
- Talbot Gallery 57, 104-7, 114, *75, 76, 77, 132, 157*
- Talbot Passage 104, 107, 108
- Wartime occupation 162, 164
- West Wing 64-70, 93, *49, 50*
- "Alton Towers Triptych" 78, *57*

Alveton Lodge (later Alton Towers) Ch. 1; 72, *1, 2, 3, 8*

Amherst, Mary, 82

Arundel Castle, Sussex, 57

Ashbourne, Derbyshire, 9, 30

Ashford, Derbyshire (marble quarries), 26

Askey, John (lathcleaver) 26

Austen, Jane, 23

Bailey, John (stonemason) 87, 104, 144

Bailey, Peter (stonemason) 87-8, 104, 144

Bailey, Thomas (stonemason) 26, 33, 40, 44, 51, 52

Barry, Charles, 91, 96

Bassetts, ironfounders, 26

Batalha Abbey, Portugal, 57

Bayons Manor, Lincs., 61

Beckford, William, 10, 23, 59, 75

Berry, Duc de, 92

Bick, Michael, 27

Bick, William (Land Agent), 65

Bill, Charles, 18, 20

Bilton Grange, Warwickshire, 98, 122, 123, 124, 127, 138, *94, 114*

Birmingham -
- S. Chad's cathedral, 91, 96, 98, 112

Bonaparte, Laetitia, 73

Bonaparte, Napoleon, 65, 76, 92

Bordeaux, Duke of - see Chambord

Brewood, Staffs., 23, 90-91

Britannia Ironworks, Derby (Weatherhead & Glover/Marshall, Barker & Wright), 35, 41, 51, 52, 104, 147

Bromsgrove, Worcs.
- S. Peter's church 155

Bunbury Hill 15, 24, 27

Burton, John, 18, 20, 23, 24, 29

Burton, W & J., masons, 157

Campbell, Thomas (sculptor) 54, 59

Carlton House, London, 43

Catholic Emancipation Act, 23, 55, 62, 85, 90, 143

Chambord, Prince Henri de, 92-95, *67*

Charles X, King of France, 92, 93, 95

Chartists 120

Cheadle, Staffs., 80
- S. Giles' Church 78, 80, 82, 87, 89, 95, 98, 102, 149, 154, *68*

Chetwynd-Talbot, Henry (18th Earl of Shrewsbury), 155, 158, 159

Chetwynd-Talbot, Charles Henry (20th Earl of Shrewsbury), 161

Choragic Monument 54, *41*

Churnet, River, 9, 20, 26

Churnet Valley Railway 139-140

Clay & Udale, Messrs., 37

Clewes, John (stonemason), 26, 33

Coalbrookdale Iron Co., 50

Cottingham, L.N., 48, 68

Cotton Hall, Staffs. 96

Cotton - S. Wilfrid's Church, 96

Counslow Lodge, nr. Cheadle, 104, 141-2, *119*

Counslow Quarry, 141

Crace J.G., 50, 96, 99, 107, 128, 150

Croxden Abbey, Staffs., 15, 75, 88, 90

Crystal Palace, 99, 100

Davis, J.P. (artist) 61

Denstone, Staffs., 10

Denny, J.B., 87, 91, 94, 104, 122

Devonshire, Duke of, 26, 77, 95

Disraeli, Benjamin, 9, 53

Dixon, John (plasterer), 26, 30, 33, 40

Doria Pamphili, Prince, 92, 97, 118-19

Doria Pamphili, Princess - see Talbot, Mary

Durham Minster 148, 149, *124*

Eagle Foundry, Birmingham (Smith & Dearman) 32

Eastnor Castle, Herefordshire, 128

Edward VII, King, 9, 161

Eginton, Francis, 33, 40

Eginton, William Raphael, 33, 122

Eglinton Tournament 116

Evans, John (bricklayer) 26

Faber, Frederick, 96

Farley, Staffs., 11, 21, 35, 78

Farnell, John (bricklayer) 26

Ferrey, Benjamin, 85

Finney, William (carpenter), 26, 33, 40, 87

Firth, Samuel (plasterer), 87, 115

Fitzherbert, Nicholas (*d*.1471) - effigy of, 115

Forsyth, Alexander (Head Gardener), 91-92

Fone, Mr. (clerk-of-works) 29, 30, 33

Fonthill Abbey, Wiltshire, 10, 23, 30, 33, 54, 59, 61, 75, *6, 42*

Ford, Peter (stonemason), 26, 29

Fower, Thomas & Henry (stonemasons) 26, 35, 52

Fradgley, Thomas, 10, 41, 55, 62, 63, 65, 68, 86, 87, 91, 104, 118, 122, 143

Garendon Hall, Leics., 126

Garnet, Anne - see Pugin, Anne Garnet

Grafton Manor, Worcs., 84

Graham, James Gillespie, 91, 119

Great Exhibition, 1851, 80, 99, 128, *70, 101*

Green, John (stonemason) 26

Gwynn, Denis, 152

Hardman, John, 78, 80, 96, 99, 127, 128, 137, 151, 155

Harris, Thomas (carpenter), 87, 94, 113

Heythrop, Oxon., 15, 54, 73

Hibbert, John Washington, 95, 123, 126, 138

Hobden, Henry (clerk-of-works) 29

Hollington, Staffs. - stone quarries, 26

Hollins, Peter, 10, 27, 32, 53, 54

Hollins, William, 10, 26, 27, 30, 46, 52

Hopper, Thomas, 10, 26, 29, 30, 41-43 65, 86, 129, 137

Hopton Wood limestone, 26, 32

Howard, Lord Edmund, 159

Hull, Edward, 74, 85, 104, 117

Ilam, Staffs.

   - church 58, *43*

   - hall 48, 58

Ireland, Joseph, 10, 27

Kearns, Thomas (painter & glazier), 26, 35, 87, 88, 150, 154

Keates, Richard (bricklayer), 44

Knight, Joseph, 91-92

Knill, Jane - see Pugin, Jane.

Knebworth House, Herts., 107

Leadbitter, Matthew, 27

Leek, Staffs.

   - Ball Haye Hall, 73

   - Messrs. Wardle & Davenport 162

Lees, William (architect), 10, 20

Leighton Hall, Powys, 114

Littleton, Lord, 95

Loudon, John Claudius, 10, 12, 20, 50, 53

Louis XVI, King of France, 92

Louis XVIII, King of France, 92

Louis-Philippe, King of the French, 93, 95

Lynch, J.A. (artist) 149, 151, *60, 132, Col Plate X*

Macclesfield, Cheshire

   - S. Alban's church 91

Martin, John (stained glass artist) 41

Mary, Queen of Scots, 75, 76, 93, 94

Mary 1, Queen, 75

Mellor, William (plumber) 26

Minton, Herbert, 80, 95, 96, 99, 106, 128, 134, 135, 138

Mivarts Hotel, London, 97

Mordant, Mr. (clerk), 27

More, Thomas 78

- Thomas More Triptych *56*

Morris, William, 9

Mount Saint Bernard Abbey, Leics., 88

Muss, Charles (artist), 40

Myers, George, 96, 106, 113, 128, 149

Nemours, Duke of, 95

Norbury, Derbyshire, 115

Nottingham

   - S. Barnabas' cathedral 90, 94, 98

Nuremburg cathedral 128

Orrell, Louisa, 88

Orrell, Richard, 78, 88

Oscott

   - S. Mary's College, 63, 91, 148, 154

Oxford, Magdalen College, 148

Padbury, George (estate surveyor) 18, 21, 27

Palermo 98, 100

Papworth, John Buonarotti, 10, 49, 52

Parsons (organ builder) 147

Paxton, Joseph, 99

Percy, Samuel (waxwork artist) 37, 65, 74-5

Phillipps, Ambrose, 88, 98, 102, 126, 157, 159

   - Mrs. 100

Pike-Jones, The Revd. J., 90

Pitt, W., *History of Staffordshire,* 23

Plot, Robert, 15

Potter, Joseph, 62, 76, 87, 118

Powell, John Hardman, 100

Pratt, Samuel (broker), 74, 78

Pugin, Anne (*née* Garnet) 151

Pugin, Augustus Charles, 82-83

Pugin, A.W.N., 9, 10, 11, 13, 15, 22, 25, 37, 41, 43, 55, 57, 59, 61, 63, 68, 70, 78, 78

   - portrait *58*

   - as a collector 78

   - and Lord Shrewsbury 80-102

   - *An earnest appeal for the revival of plain song,* 154

   - *Apology,* 102, *71*

   - *Contrasts* 86

   - *Designs for Gold & Silversmiths* 85

   - *Glossary of Ecclesiastical Ornament* 154

   - *True Principles* 86, 131, *49b, 105*

   - work in Alton village 88-90

   - *Gothic Furniture* 103, *72*

   - habits of work, 97

   - at Alton Towers 103-142; 147-154

- illness and death 98-102
Pugin, Jane (*née* Knill), 98, 100
Pugin, Louisa (*née* Burton) 82, 151, 154
Pugin, Edward Welby, 100, 154, 157

Quixhill Bridge 20, *4*
Quixhill Lodge 9, 27, 49, 52, 59, 78, 92, *35*

Rabone, Mr. (Head Gardener) 161
Railway, North Staffordshire, 140-141
Ramsgate
   - S. Augustine's 97, 102, 124, 154
Rayner, Samuel (artist), 32, 61, 122, 149, 150, 151, *14, 28, 52, 124*
Redfern, Francis, 104
Rhodes, Ebenezer, 103
Rock, Dr. Daniel, 85, 90, 91, 92, 143, 152, 154
"Romantic Interiors" 65-70

St. Helens, Lancs., 26
Scarisbrick Hall, Lancs., 91, 98, 106, 114, 121, 126, 127
Scott, George Gilbert, 48
Scott, Sir Walter, 15, 75, 93, 94, 116
Shaw & Co., Lead founders, 26
Shaw, John (architect) 48, 58
Shrewsbury Arms, Farley, 78, 90
Shrewsbury, Earls of - see Talbot, and Chetwynd-Talbot
Sinclair, Mr. (clerk), 27
Snelston Hall, Derbys., 48, 68, *34*
Sobieski Stuart, 93, 116
Southwark, S. George's church, 94
Stoke-on-Trent 26, 120
   - Minton Museum, 134
Sutherland, Duke of, 95
Sutherland, Duchess of, 159

Talbot, Bertram Arthur, 17th Earl of Shrewsbury, 123, 130, 134, 135, 155, 157, 159, *129*
Talbot, John, first Earl of Shrewsbury ("The Grand Talbot", *d*.1453), 127, *87, col. Plate I*
   - effigy of 115
   - equestrian statue of, 115-117
Talbot, Charles, 15th Earl of Shrewsbury, 9, 10, 18, 25, 26, 27, 32, 37, 50, 52, 71-72
Talbot, Lady Gwendalyn, Princess Borghese, 82, 120
Talbot, John, 16th Earl of Shrewsbury *60, Col Plate II*
   - re-names Alton Abbey 54, 74
   - as a collector 74-78
   - ancestry & education 82

   - character 85
   - benefactor of churches 91-96
   - patronage of Pugin 80-102
   - extensions at Alton Towers 104-142
   - death 102
   - funeral 142, 154, *128*
Talbot, Maria Theresa, Countess of Shrewsbury, 59, 84, 117, 122, 124, *col. Plates IV & XII*
Talbot, Lady Mary, Princess Doria Pamphili 84, 92, 118, 152
Talbot, William, 84
Taymouth Castle, Perthshire, 91, 107, 116, 119
Todd, Anthony (agent), 27
Trentham Hall, Staffs., 95, 159
Trubshaw, T. (architect), 27

Uttoxeter, Staffs., 26, 80, 92
   - S. Marie's church 91

Verdun, Bertram, 15, 88
Verdun - family, 15, 60, 89, 112, *47*
Victoria, Princess 77
Victoria, Queen, 9
Victoria & Albert Museum 103, 128, 156, 160, 166

Waagen, Gustav, 73
Wailes, William, 94, 127
Walsh, Vicomte, 94, 95
Watts-Russell, Jesse, 48, 58
Warrington, William, 60, 112, 127
Waxworks, 37, 75
Weedall, Dr. Henry, 154
Westminster, Palace of, 26, 57, 90, 96, 165
Whitchurch, Shropshire
   - S. Alkmund's church 115
William IV, King, 74
Willement, Thomas, 61-62, 63, 68, 104, 106, 107, 111, 112, 114, 127, 156
Windsor Castle 84
Winter, Dr. Henry, 90, 95, 98
Wiseman, Bishop, 95
Woodhead Colliery 46
Wright & Co. (bankers) 29
Wyatt, James, 12, 23, 30, 87